The Inner Game
of Management

The Inner Game of Management

How to Make the Transition to a Managerial Role

Eric G. Flamholtz
and
Yvonne Randle

amacom
American Management Association

This book is available at a special
discount when ordered in bulk quantities.
For information, contact Special Sales Department,
AMACOM, a division of American Management Association,
135 West 50th Street, New York, NY 10020.

Library of Congress Cataloging-in-Publication Data

Flamholtz, Eric.
    The inner game of management.

    Bibliography: p.
    Includes index.
    1. Management.   I. Randle, Yvonne.   II. Title.
HD31.F538   1987   658.4'09   87-47705
ISBN 0-8144-5867-X

Printing number

10 9 8 7 6 5 4 3 2 1

To
P. F. and ***B. R.***
We couldn't have done it without you!
Standard toast.

Preface

During the past few years, there has been a growing recognition that the United States is at the precipice of a major economic crisis. Some of our historically most important industries, including steel, automobiles, and consumer electronics, have gone into sharp decline. Moreover, there is widespread evidence that the decline of corporations is not limited to a few locations. Once great and powerful companies, such as General Motors, Bank of America, and International Harvester (now Navistar), as well as scores of others, such as Disney, Wickes, Pan Am, Kodak, Control Data, Arco, LTV, and many, many others, are all troubled, if not endangered.

Many explanations have been offered for this phenomenon. One explanation is that the U.S. economy is in the transition from an industrial, smokestack economy to a service economy and, accordingly, that the decline is inevitable. We have also been told that myopic managers are managing our way to economic decline with a focus on short-term profitability, rather than planning for and investing in the future. A third explanation is that the Japanese have superior (and copiable) management styles that have made them world-class competitors.

Like the proverbial story of the man who is searching for his car keys under a street lamp, not because he lost them there, but because the light is better there, these explanations leave a great deal to be desired. They obscure as much as they illuminate, for they distract us from what we believe is the most fundamental reason for this phenomenon of widespread organizational failure.

In brief, it is our hypothesis that the major reason for this epidemic of organizational turmoil is the failure of the managers of these enterprises to *manage themselves* effectively. We believe that, perhaps quite unconsciously, a great many American managers are victims of their inability to manage their own psychological needs, and that this leads them to behaviors that not only damage their careers but also contribute greatly to widespread organizational failure and the perceived impending economic decline.

We have labeled the processes through which managers must deal with their own psychological needs the "Inner Game of Management." As explained in Chapter 1, the Inner Game of Management takes place in the mind of the manager. This game is one in which the managers must deal with their own self-esteem, the need for control, and the need to be liked, in such a way that they will be effective in a managerial role. Although the metaphor of a game is used, it is certainly not a trivial game—often, it has a deadly serious quality.

Although individual managers are the primary focus of this book and are the ultimate cause of their own and their employers' failure, they do not bear the responsibility by themselves. Organizations that do not provide the opportunity for people to participate in management development programs dealing with the Inner Game of Management are setting their managers up for failure. Moreover, educational institutions also bear a great deal of responsibility.

The Inner Game of Management is not even recognized, let alone taught well, at the leading business schools. These are content to turn out technologically sophisticated students who are oblivious of the need to master the Inner Game of Management. Institutions such as The Harvard Business School, Stanford, Wharton, The University of Chicago, Columbia, and our own institution, UCLA, have a plethora of courses dealing with the psychology of managing *other people*, but few, if any, dealing with the critical issues of an individual managing his or her own inner needs. Perhaps this omission is because the subject is taboo, or perhaps it has simply been missed because of the bias toward quantifiability and rationality that characterizes Western thought.

Whatever the reason for the omission of this subject from academic curricula and scholarly inquiry, it is a serious deficiency. Our research and consulting experience with managers for more than a decade have indicated that the primary reason for their career difficulties or failures is not the lack of technical management skills such as planning, organizing, and decision making but their inability to master the principles of what we have called the Inner Game of Management.

This book is intended to introduce, explain, and illustrate the nature of the Inner Game of Management as well as the symptoms or syndromes it produces when it is not mastered. The book is also intended as a challenge to individual managers whose careers are at stake, to corporate CEOs whose companies are at risk, and to corporate Vice Presidents of Human Resources whose responsibilities include management development. Finally, it is aimed at the faculty of the leading business schools, inviting them to rethink the true nature of the problem facing modern management. For, to paraphrase Hamlet, "The fault, dear manager, is not in the stars, but in ourselves."

Acknowledgments

The publication of a book is never the result of its authors' work alone. It is the product of the efforts of a number of individuals who contribute in a variety of ways. We would like to take this opportunity to thank these individuals for their efforts.

This book is the outgrowth of a number of years of research by Eric Flamholtz, who studied the reasons why people are successful or unsuccessful in making the transition to a management role. This research came to the attention of Denise Marcil, a literary agent, who suggested the possibility of converting this research into a book. Denise provided guidance in preparing the book proposal and was instrumental in bringing the proposal to the attention of Ron Mallis at AMACOM. We would like to thank her for her support, encouragement, and guidance throughout the entire process of converting an idea into a completed book. Similarly, we would like to thank Ron Mallis for his enthusiastic support of the project, his guidance in developing the manuscript, his detailed constructive criticism in all aspects of the manuscript, and his overall support of our efforts in the development of this book. Without the efforts of these two individuals, this book would not have become a reality.

We would also like to thank the managers who contributed to this book by giving us permission to cite their life stories. Specifically, we are grateful to Betsy Wood Knapp, President and CEO of Wood, Knapp & Company and Director of Knapp Communications Corporation; Terry Donahue, Head Football Coach at UCLA; and Dan Sandel, Founder and President of Devon Industries. Each of these individuals took the time to meet with us, discuss their development as managers, and provide feedback on our efforts to write about their experiences. Most importantly, we appreciate their willingness to allow us to share their experiences with our readers. These individuals are all outstanding managers and we hope that studying their managerial histories will provide valuable insights to our readers.

With the exception of the three individuals named above, case studies presented in this book are all hypothetical. These hypothetical case studies are intended to illustrate "generic" Inner Game issues and problems rather than provide a description of any one individual's actual experiences. Accordingly, the names, backgrounds, companies, and experiences of the characters included in this book are the creations of the authors and any similarity to real individuals and companies is purely coincidental. It should be noted, however, that all of the cases created by the authors illustrate real aspects of the behavior of people who confront Inner Game issues and problems.

There are also a number of people behind the scenes who made this work possible. Various individuals read parts of the manuscript and provided feedback on it. We would especially like to thank the senior author's wife, Diana Troik Flamholtz, for her constructive feedback on Chapter 1 as well as on various other aspects of the text. Her support of the entire project is gratefully acknowledged.

The word processing and preparation of the manuscript were done by the operation support staff of Management Systems Consulting Corporation, especially Karen Nitao under the direction of Robbie Amodio, Operations Coordinator. This was no easy task, at times, because the handwritten revisions were often so illegible that the authors themselves had difficulty reading them. Special acknowledgment is also made to Sigal Goland and Robin Baker, research assistants, in the Center for Human Resource Management, Institute of Industrial Relations, UCLA, for preparing the annotated bibliography for the book. Ms. Goland also prepared the case study on Gina Lacommare, included in Chapter 11.

Although we acknowledge with gratitude the contribution of all those cited above, we remain responsible for the book and its imperfections.

Contents

Part One

Understanding the Inner Game of Management

Chapter 1

The Nature of the Inner Game of Management

This book deals with an aspect of management that is critical to the success of individuals as well as the organizations that employ them. This dimension is rarely recognized and even more rarely discussed. It is not taught even in the most prestigious MBA programs.

This book deals with the need for managers to manage their own psychology and mindset in order to be effective in their roles. It focuses on the way people who are managers think about themselves and their roles and the ways in which they manage (and sometimes mismanage) their own psychology. It examines how these mindsets and psychological issues, in turn, influence their performance and effectiveness as managers. We call this the Inner Game of Management.

In examining the nature of the Inner Game of Management and the difficulties individuals experience when they fail to play it effectively, we draw on the experiences of managers in real organizations. Their experiences were used to create the case histories that appear throughout this book. Three individuals (Betsy Wood Knapp, President and CEO of Wood, Knapp & Company and Director of Knapp Communications Corporation; Terry Donahue, Head Football Coach of UCLA; and Dan Sandel, Founder and President of Devon Industries) provided us with detailed accounts of their experiences

3

as managers and allowed us to identify them by name. With the exception of these three individuals, case studies presented in this book are all hypothetical. These hypothetical case studies are intended to illustrate "generic" Inner Game issues and problems rather than provide a description of any one individual's actual experiences. Accordingly, the names, backgrounds, companies, and experiences of the characters included in this book are the creations of the authors and any similarity to real individuals and companies is purely coincidental. It should be noted, however, that all the cases created by the authors illustrate real aspects of the behavior of people who confront Inner Game issues and problems.

We begin this chapter with an examination of the case history of an individual who experienced difficulties in a management position. We shall see how the person's mindset and psychological needs adversely affected his performance as a manager.

The case is that of Gunther Schmidt, an Executive Chef. The problems experienced by Gunther were attributable to his failure to master the Inner Game of Management.

Gunther the Chef

Gunther Schmidt began his career as a butcher for one of the major international hotel chains. Although our image of a butcher is stereotypically of someone who wields a meat cleaver, the modern butcher in a hotel kitchen uses a meat slicing machine. Butchering meat is a technical skill that not everyone can do well.

As the hotel chain grew, its need for personnel grew correspondingly. Because Gunther was a good employee and a good butcher, he was promoted first to Sous Chef, which is an under chef, and finally to Executive Chef at one of the chain's hotels in a major city in the United States.

Unfortunately, Gunther had problems with his responsibilities as an Executive Chef. Although things were fine when the hotel was not very busy, problems arose whenever the hotel had an unusually large number of guests, such as during conventions and special holidays.

Whenever the hotel became especially busy, Gunther would retreat to a corner of the kitchen and begin to slice meat. The other staff members were left to do whatever they felt was necessary. When one of the more assertive employees approached Gunther and said: "Gunther, the kitchen is very busy. Why are you slicing meat? Why don't you tell us what you want us to do?" Gunther replied: "There are lots of people in this hotel, and a great many of them will want meat. I slice meat better than anyone on this staff. So, I will slice the meat, and you should do whatever you think is appropriate."

What Was Gunther Doing?

Whenever Gunther could not cope with the pressure of being an Executive Chef, he retreated to the thing he did best: he recreated his old job as a butcher, even though he was supposed to be a manager. He was not comfortable with his new job, its responsibilities, or the skills required, even though he held the title of an Executive Chef. Gunther was still a technical specialist and was unable to think and act like a manager.

The Doer Syndrome

Whenever a group of managers, regardless of their industry or level, hears the story of Gunther the Chef, there is nervous laughter. On the one hand, the story is humorous in and of itself, for it seems that Gunther is behaving in a somewhat ridiculous manner for someone who is supposed to be an Executive Chef. There is also an element of tragedy, for it is clear that poor Gunther will ultimately fail as a manager and perhaps return to what he does best and is most comfortable doing: being a butcher. However, the nervous laughter is more than mere empathy for Gunther; there is a touch of self-recognition as well.

Many of us see something of ourselves in poor Gunther. We recognize that we, too, often recreate our old jobs and retreat to what we do best rather than learn the new responsibilities and, more important, psychologically accept them as our new role. We also fear that Gunther's probable fate will become ours as well.

If the situation faced by Gunther the Chef were an isolated case, it would not be of much interest or significance. It would just be the personal problem of one individual. However, the example of Gunther is, in reality, an illustration of a widespread phenomenon—the Doer Syndrome.

The Doer Syndrome refers to the phenomenon in which people who have been promoted to managerial roles continue to think and act like technicians, functional specialists, or "doers" rather than true managers. The mindset they had in their old role remains unchanged in the new, managerial role, even though the nature of the role has changed, with corresponding changes in title and responsibilities. The victims of the Doer Syndrome are unable to make the transition to the new role, because they have not been able to *manage* certain underlying psychological issues that relate to their self-esteem and need for control.

The Doer Syndrome is only one form of the problems that arise when people fail to play the Inner Game of Management effectively. On the basis of our research, we have identified ten common syndromes that result when people fail to master the Inner Game of Management. Each of these syndromes, including the Doer Syndrome, will be examined in Part II of this book.

In order to help people like Gunther Schmidt make the successful transition to management roles, it is essential to understand more about the nature and dynamics of the Inner Game of Management. To do this, we shall look first at management as a game and then at the Inner Game of Management per se.

At the outset, it ought to be noted that although we are using the term *game* in our discussion of management, we are talking about something that is quite serious. The game metaphor is being used because of its analytical power in helping to understand and deal with the complex social and psychological processes that are the focus of this book.[1] At times, the games with which we are dealing have a devastating impact on the manager, his or her subordinates, and the organization. Thus, although we are talking in terms of games, the games are not mere child's play.

Management As a Game

Management is typically defined as the process of using resources to achieve organizational objectives. This concept of management is based on the view that management is a set of activities or functions (such as planning, organizing, leading, staffing, and controlling) the manager must perform. Although this is not a totally incorrect view of management, it is not sufficiently encompassing.

Management can also be viewed as a game. In its broadest sense, a game involves "procedures or strategies for gaining certain ends."[2] For example, the game of chess involves two players who attempt to capture the opponent's pieces with their own. The object of the game is to place the opponent's king in such a position that it cannot avoid being captured. The opponents move their pieces (resources) singly or in combination and use various strategies and tactics to win the game.

From this perspective, the desired end of the game of management is to use resources (people, money, ideas, equipment, tools) to gain certain ends

---

[1] Similarly, Eric Berne has described a variety of interpersonal games in his book *Games People Play* (New York: Grove Press, 1964).
[2] *Webster's New Collegiate Dictionary.*

desired by the organization. For a corporation, the object of the game is to increase wealth and profitability.

Two Sides of the Game

All games are played at two different levels. First, there is the *surface* or *outer* level, which involves the specified tasks or activities of the game.[3] For example, the game of chess involves the movement of pieces in order to capture the opponent's king and thereby win the game. The *inner* side of the game involves the mental and emotional (psychological) processes of the players: the extent to which one is willing to take risk, to be aggressive, and to be confident about the "moves" one makes. This is, in part, determined by the personalities of the players; for example, a Bobby Fischer has a very different style of playing the game of chess from the style of a Boris Spassky.

Winning any game depends not only on how well you play the outer or surface game of nominal activities but also on how well you play the inner game. One player may have a better technical mastery of the game, but may still lose consistently when faced with an opponent who has mastered the Inner Game. For example, a Roger Maris may have had a better textbook swing than a Pete Rose, but Rose still holds the record for base hits. Similarly, many sports teams lose not because they are technically inferior but because their opponents have intimidated them (are better Inner Game players).

Like other games, the game of management has an outer and inner component. The outer or surface game of management involves performing the *tasks* of planning, budgeting, decision making, time management, performance appraisal, and the like. These tasks or management functions are well known. Students learn about them in business courses, and they are the subject of countless books and articles.

If you talk to a manager and ask about his or her job, you will almost always hear the litany: "My job is to plan, organize, delegate, lead, and control." Yet, in spite of the fact that people know what they are supposed to do as managers, many still fail to do it. People fail to manage effectively because the basic management tasks we have cited are not merely technical functions to be performed. They each have a mental and psychological component as well. For example, people who are managers know what delegation is and that they ought to delegate, but many still do not delegate or do not do it well.

[3] This concept has been recognized in sports. See W. Timothy Gallowey, *The Inner Game of Tennis* (New York: Bantam Books, 1974).

Many of those who experience difficulties in delegation or any of the other management functions do so because they have not developed the intellectual and emotional mindsets that would allow them to feel comfortable performing such functions, even though they know what they ought to be doing. They have failed, in other words, to master the Inner Game of Management, which is an essential prerequisite to effective performance of basic management functions.

What Is the Inner Game of Management?

The Inner Game of Management is the game that takes place in the mind of the manager. It is the way an individual deals with the mental and psychological issues of self-esteem, need for control, and desire to be liked. These issues play an important role in the day-to-day performance of the manager's job. Mastering the Inner Game of Management involves understanding and accepting one's role as manager and developing the mental and psychological perspectives that are consistent with the requirements of this role.

A "role" is a set of expected behaviors. To a great extent, our concept of a specific role exists independently of the person who comes to occupy the role. This means that we expect people who have the role of manager, president, or engineer to behave in certain specified ways. Similarly, we expect people who occupy the role of accountant, secretary, or clerk to behave in certain ways.

These "role expectations" are culturally grounded and tend to be based on the position a person occupies in the organizational hierarchy. This hierarchy defines the typical career progression of people in organizations.

As can be seen in Figure 1–1, people typically begin in an "entry level position." Such entry-level positions involve the direct performance of work rather than the supervision of others' work. These positions include a wide variety of jobs such as accountant, computer operator or programmer, engineer, clerk, salesperson, machinist, and so on. People in these positions operate in "Doer's Roles;" that is, they perform technical work of some kind. The primary responsibility of the job is to perform or do specific tasks.

The next level in the organizational career hierarchy is the role of the first-line supervisor. This role will, of course, still involve the performance of technical work, but the individual who becomes a supervisor must make the transition to a role in which the primary responsibilities involve the management of people rather than the direct performance of work.

Positions at the level of first-line supervisor include such jobs as accounting supervisor, computer operations manager, programming manager, engi-

Figure 1–1. Organizational career hierarchy.

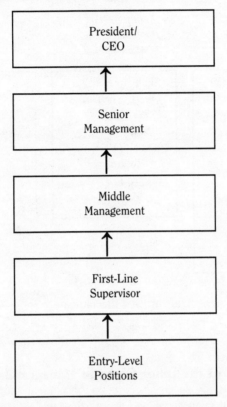

neering project manager, office manager, sales manager, and foreman. This is the first level at which an individual must begin to make a personal and professional transition to a different kind of role, one in which he or she is required to think and act like a manager rather than a technician or doer of specific tasks. It is analogous to making the transition from player to coach in athletics.

The next level of the organizational career hierarchy is middle management. This is the first level at which a manager must manage other managers.

The next level in the career hierarchy is senior management. At this level, the manager is managing several levels of managers. Positions at this level include Vice President, Senior Vice President, and Executive Vice President.

The final level in the organizational career hierarchy is President or Chairman. Depending on the organization, this is the chief-operating-officer

Figure 1–2. Factors influencing managerial effectiveness and success.

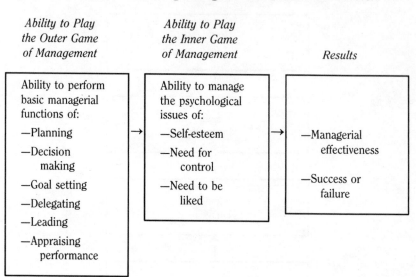

*Ability to Play
the Outer Game
of Management*

*Ability to Play
the Inner Game
of Management*

Results

Ability to perform
basic managerial
functions of:

—Planning

—Decision
making

—Goal setting

—Delegating

—Leading

—Appraising
performance

Ability to manage
the psychological
issues of:

—Self-esteem

—Need for
control

—Need to be
liked

—Managerial
effectiveness

—Success or
failure

or chief-executive level and involves the ultimate responsibility for running
the organization.

The Role of the Inner Game in Managerial Success

To be a successful manager as you move from one level to the next in the
organizational career hierarchy, you not only have to learn different skills
such as planning, organizing, and controlling (outer game activities); more
important, you need to develop different ways of thinking (Inner Game activities). Stated differently, the ability to perform the technical skills of planning,
delegating, selecting, and the like is affected by how well a person is managing the Inner Game issues. Taken together, these two things determine, in
turn, overall managerial effectiveness and success, as shown schematically in
Figure 1–2.

Ability to play the Inner Game, then, may be the critical variable that
determines whether or not a person succeeds or fails as a manager. In fact,
on the basis of our research and experience in working with managers, we
estimate that more than 90 percent of people who experience difficulties in
their management careers or ultimately fail as managers do so not because of
a lack of intelligence or motivation, or a lack of technical skills as a manager,

but because of a failure to understand and play the Inner Game of Management effectively.

Three Key Dimensions of the Inner Game

As shown in Figure 1–2, there are three key dimensions or requirements for playing the Inner Game of Management successfully:

1. Being able to manage your own self-esteem so that you derive satisfaction from the things managers are supposed to do.
2. Being able to manage your need for direct control over people and results.
3. Being able to manage your need to be liked so that it does not interfere with performing the managerial role.

We'll examine each of these three key components of the Inner Game in turn in the rest of this chapter.

Managing Your Self-Esteem

One of the key aspects of the Inner Game of Management is the extent to which a manager can effectively "manage" his or her own self-esteem. Self-esteem is a critical variable in how we interact with other people in all aspects of our lives, and it is no less important in how we think and act in managerial or other work-related positions. Self-esteem is basically the desire to value ourselves, to experience a sense of self-worth. This underlying need manifests itself in the need for achievement, confidence, independence, prestige, and recognition from others.

Unfortunately, the term *self-worth* is so benign or innocuous that it may prevent us from grasping the true nature and connotations of this need. It is, fundamentally, the need for self-acceptance; at the extreme, the failure to achieve it can lead to self-hatred.

The need for self-worth or self-acceptance is enormously powerful and complex. Individuals differ in how they derive their self-esteem. For some, it is extremely important that others openly acknowledge their success; for others, it is more important that they personally feel successful, regardless of what others might say. Some individuals must believe they're the best at whatever they are doing, or they feel it is not worth doing at all; others are satisfied just to have completed a task. Some individuals must do everything themselves in order to satisfy this need; others are happy to work as a member of a team.

The need for self-worth has the most fundamental and profound effects on people and their behavior, both at work and off the job. If we examine the behavior of people closely, we can explain a great deal of what they do in terms of the drive for self-validation. It can be a driving, all-consuming passion, and it can manifest itself in the most subtle aspects of human interactions.

Under ideal circumstances, an individual will have achieved a relatively high level of self-worth before entering the work force, so the developmental issues of self-acceptance will not intrude too much in the person's behavior at work. However, if an individual has not achieved at least a satisfactory degree of self-acceptance, then—unless the person has totally lost hope and given up—an enormous portion of his or her behavior will be inextricably bound up with issues involving the need for self-worth.

It is also important to note that a person's level of self-esteem or self-worth is variable rather than fixed. It's useful to think of it as something similar to a column of mercury in a thermometer. Just as there is an average seasonal temperature, there is some average level of self-acceptance, which can vary from day to day to some extent, depending partly on certain changes in the person's environment.

How Your Job Influences Your Self-Esteem

One of the most important factors influencing people's level of self-esteem is their job. People do not typically exist independently of their jobs or work roles. For most of us, the work we do helps define ourselves to others as well as to ourselves. People ask, "What do you do?" and we tend to answer, "I am an accountant (salesman, engineer, computer programmer, manager, professor)." They ask what we do, and we describe what we are, because our occupational or professional roles fuse with our overall identity. Such a fusion of organizational roles with individual identity can have important effects on a person's self-esteem.

In the doer's role—for example, as a salesperson, a computer programmer, or an engineer—an individual tends to derive self-esteem from his or her own performance. In such roles, people's personal achievements are the underlying source of their self-esteem. They derive satisfaction from meeting sales goals, being the best at solving complex problems, or pointing to specific programs they created.

In the manager's role, an individual must develop a different source of self-esteem. When you are a manager, it's no longer appropriate or necessary to be the best "bench engineer" or the best salesperson. The concept you have to develop instead is: "I want to be the best manager." The owner of an entrepreneurial firm must derive satisfaction from being the president and CEO, not just in title. He or she must thrive on being the orchestra leader who holds it all together and makes it happen, rather than on being the best virtuoso violin player.

A manager's job is to use resources, including people resources, to achieve organizational objectives. Thus, managers must increasingly derive their personal satisfaction from the performance of people reporting to them. This is analogous to a basketball coach who derives self-esteem from the team's ability to win a championship, rather than from his or her personal ability to play the game. Although the issue is relatively clear-cut in sports situations, it is more complex in other managerial situations where roles are not as precisely defined.

In order to be successful in these managerial roles, people must accept that part of their role involves greater emphasis on supervisory activities and begin devoting more time to this area. They must learn to feel comfortable performing such activities as planning (deciding what to do, when to do it, who should do it, and so on), reading materials and reports, managing meetings, and developing subordinates' skills. This is difficult for most people, since these skills are usually not well developed at the time of promotion. Further, the nature of the managerial role may be vague. A person realizes that he or she is "the boss" but may not understand what a boss does. These factors—underdeveloped skills and a vague role—may cause an individual to feel incompetent. In essence, people in these situations may feel that their self-esteem is threatened, and in order to protect it, they may simply "re-create" their old jobs by becoming "hands-on managers." This process can eventually lead to failure.

The failure of insecure "hands-on managers" is both ironic and tragic. It is ironic because the motivation for recreating the old job is typically to avoid failure in the new job. In brief, the individual is faced with the need to make a transition from what he or she does well to some role in which there is a chance of failure and, therefore, loss of self-esteem. Consciously or unconsciously, the person retreats to what he or she does best—where the chances of failure seem slight. However, the situation has changed. The new role is not the same as the old, and the very act of recreating the old job, as in the case of Gunther the Executive Chef, is a step toward failure and loss of self-esteem. The tragedy is that these failures *can* be avoided.

The basic prerequisite for making the successful transition to a managerial role is to shift your source of self-esteem from the old role to the new one. This, in turn, requires that you "manage" your sense of self-worth.

If you do not shift your source of self-esteem from pride in your own technical performance to pride in the overall performance of your "players" and develop the ability to feel comfortable performing as a manager rather than a "doer," a variety of problems can result. One problem is that you seem as though you are actually competing with your subordinates for recognition of who is "the best" at a particular job. While this may seem to be a strange idea at first, an example will help clarify it.

Randy Smith was a computer programmer at a major petrochemicals corporation. Since he was successful at his job, he was promoted. He began to recruit several talented programmers for his staff. At first, everyone turned to Randy for training and technical assistance, and Randy felt valued for his knowledge and training skills. After about one year, however, one of the new programmers, Jerry Duncan, bloomed. Jerry turned out to be a brilliant programmer who was able to derive simple but elegant solutions to complex problems. People began to turn to Jerry for help more often than they turned to Randy, and Randy began to feel uncomfortable because he was no longer the technical star of the department. He began to scrutinize Jerry's work and to find little things that bothered him. This brought the two into conflict. Jerry got upset with Randy and at one meeting got emotional and quit. Randy felt he was better off in the long run without Jerry, but many people in the department and the company felt it was a major loss to have Jerry leave. Soon, however, Randy filled the technical vacuum, and things went back to what they were before Jerry Duncan had joined the firm.

In brief, Randy's sense of self-esteem was tied to his technical, rather than managerial, skills. He was uncomfortable when Jerry Duncan seemed to eclipse his role as the star technician. Randy began to compete with Jerry for the esteem of the staff, and this initiated a sequence of events that ultimately forced Jerry into leaving the company. Randy solved his immediate problem but showed that he had not mastered the Inner Game of Management. He did not recognize that the change in his job from a doer to a manager required a corresponding change in the source of his self-esteem. To accomplish this change, Randy would have had to "manage" his own self-esteem. Unfortunately, he did not do so.

Randy's problems are certainly not unique, as we shall see throughout this book. Thus, learning to manage your self-esteem is a fundamental challenge you must meet if you are to master the Inner Game of Management.

Managing Your Need for Control

The second key aspect of the Inner Game of Management is the extent to which you can "manage" your need for control. Control is the ability to influence your environment. The amount of control you are able to exercise over your environment defines how "powerful" you are.

All of us have the need to be "in control of things"—that is, to be seen as "powerful." A feeling of having control over your life is essential for maintaining your identity and a positive self-image. The way the need to be in control manifests itself, however, can differ from individual to individual. Some people will settle for nothing less than absolute control over their environments. At the other extreme are those who believe that they can exercise little, if any, control over their external worlds and decide to "let the chips fall where they may." Somewhere in the middle of this continuum are those who realize that it is necessary to give up some control in order to achieve desired ends and who have also learned how and when to do so.

The need for control is as important as the need for self-esteem; indeed, it can sometimes be inextricably related to it. The need for control has its origins in childhood and in our perceived vulnerability to the world. If a person develops a sense of fear about the hostility of the world, a rational reaction is to try to control the world and its potential dangers and threats. The greater the degree of a person's sense of inadequacy (lack of self-worth), the more things will probably be perceived as threatening. This, in turn, will create the need for control, at work and elsewhere. Thus, most of us strive, to some extent, to control our environments in order to achieve self-protection.

It is important that we learn to manage our need for control, or else it can become an obstacle to our functioning effectively. The more things are perceived as threatening, the more we seek to control. At an extreme, if everything is perceived as threatening, then we must control everything. This is true not only at work but also off the job.

The ability to exercise direct control over results in the work environment depends, to a great extent, on the role one occupies. In an entry-level role, direct control over results is at the maximum. For an accountant, a computer programmer, an engineer, or a salesperson, the individual's performance frequently determines the results. However, as soon as the position of first-line supervisor is reached, the relationship between personal effort and control over results becomes more indirect and tenuous.

To play the Inner Game of Management effectively, a person must manage his or her own need for control. This, in turn, requires a person to accept a "decreasing degree of direct control" as a manager and not want to "be involved in everything." Becoming effective at giving up control involves learning how to delegate authority and responsibility, but the underlying prerequisite is that the individual must learn how to manage his or her need for control.

Delegation and the Need for Control

Delegation is a basic skill of effective management which involves assigning tasks and/or goals to others. In order to achieve managerial leverage, managers must delegate. Unfortunately, many managers do not delegate effectively and become swamped by work. Managers must, therefore, learn to delegate, not only to be effective but also to survive personally.

Learning to delegate involves more than simply mastering a technical skill. It involves developing a mindset which includes being comfortable with giving up a certain amount of control over results. When you perform an activity yourself, you have the highest degree of control over the outcome. As soon as something is delegated, however, outcomes are likely to be different than if you did it yourself, since most people to whom a task is delegated will tend to do things their own way. This leads to differences (some small and others large) from the way you would have done the task. Most of us have a great deal of difficulty in accepting this. We want the task accomplished, and we want it done in the manner in which we would have done it.

Odd as it may seem, these issues are illustrated quite vividly by the beliefs and actions of Woody Hayes, former football coach at Ohio State University. During his coaching days, Hayes was known for relying on the "ground game," also referred to as a "ball control strategy," since it provides the greatest degree of control over the game. Hayes' strategy was based on the premise that when you pass, three things can happen, and two of them are bad. The three things that can happen if a quarterback passes are, of course: (1) the ball will not be caught and the pass will be incomplete, (2) the pass will be intercepted by the opposing team, and (3) the intended receiver will catch the ball.

While it is correct that two of the three things that can happen are bad, Hayes' statement is not the whole truth. One aspect ignored by Hayes concerns the probabilities of each outcome. Another aspect is the relative gain from a pass versus that from a running play. Still another is the balanced offense that passing gives a team—the opponent cannot just concentrate on stopping the run. It is not surprising, then, to find that the Big 10 football conference (which tends to follow Hayes' philosophy) lost to the Pac 10 (which happens to follow a more balanced pass/run offense) in 17 of the 20 Rose Bowl contests during the period from 1968 to 1987.

The desire for control is not limited to the game of football, nor are the effects this desire can have on overall performance. There are important similarities between the psychology of ball control and the psychology of delegation in the workplace.

First, as was true with the decision to use a pass play, if we delegate a task, two out of the three possible outcomes will be "bad." If we delegate, the three possible outcomes are: (1) the task will not be done the way we would like; (2) certain aspects of the task will not be done correctly; (3) the task will be done correctly and just as we want it to be done. Like Woody Hayes, a lot of people cannot deal with the possibility that two out of the three outcomes will be unfavorable. These people tend to delegate very little or delegate just the relatively unimportant things (or at least those things they perceive to be relatively unimportant). Since this means that they will do all the important things themselves, they run the risk of becoming overloaded. They behave as doers rather than as managers.

Although delegating tasks may seem reasonable in principle, the practical difficulty involves the decision about what to delegate in an actual situation. For example, Stan Williams, the president of a medium-size financial planning firm, was fond of doing technical analyses for his clients by himself rather than delegating them. When asked why, he replied: "If I had someone else do them, I would be vulnerable if they left." While he was correct, he was incurring a cost by not delegating this task. The cost was the opportunity cost of his time—time he could have spent on other, potentially more valuable things. When this was pointed out to him, he did hire someone to do the technical analyses for him. Unfortunately, many people would not have done so. Their concern about being vulnerable would have outweighed the perceived benefits from delegation.

This phenomenon of unwillingness to delegate because of a perceived loss of control gets repeated many times in the behavior of many managers. Ultimately, they are overburdened and become ineffective, without understanding the underlying reasons. The surface symptom is the unwillingness to delegate, but the underlying cause is the unwillingness to give up control.

In order to master this aspect of the Inner Game of Management, you must train yourself to deal with a lower degree of control than seems comfortable. This means you must get used to the fact that some things will not be done your way. Similarly, you must accept the fact that some things, including important things, will go wrong. In brief, you must learn to manage your own need for control.

Another aspect of the need for control concerns the control over other people. While for some managers the need for control over others is a means to an end of self-protection, for others it can become an end in itself. The ability to control the behavior, or even the lives, of others can become addictive to certain people who define their own sense of self-worth or adequacy in terms of the power they wield over others. As one CEO of a major corporation stated: "Power is the ultimate aphrodisiac."

For such people, control over others is evidence of their own significance. It may be counterevidence to their own deep-seated feelings of pow-erlessness and inadequacy. In a management context, the need for this type of control must be managed, or a variety of problems will emerge, as described in Part II of this book.

Managing Your Need To Be Liked

The third key component of the Inner Game of Management involves the extent to which a person can manage the need to be liked by other people so that it does not interfere with his or her job responsibilities. Individuals not only want to be valued for what they do; at another level, they want to be accepted by others. Most people have a strong desire to "belong," to be accepted and liked by other people. This is a basic social need.

The need to be liked or accepted by others can also be related to the need for self-worth. If others like and value a person, that individual has external (and hence "objective") evidence of his or her perceived worth. For some people, being valued or liked by others can go beyond evidence of worth and can become the ultimate definition of self-worth. An example of this was Willy Loman, the central character of Arthur Miller's classic play, *Death of a Salesman*. For Willy, the need to be liked, and hence valued, was a lifetime obsession.

Depending on the individual, this need to be accepted by others can have more or less weight than other needs, such as the need for control. Some individuals will go to great lengths to avoid being rejected by others; others will believe that it is more important to accomplish the task than to please everyone. This means that at one extreme, the person will avoid con-flict at all costs; at the other, the individual will be more apt to face conflict and attempt to resolve it.

At some level, most jobs provide a way for people to satisfy their need for acceptance. The fact of organizational membership as a result of being employed represents acceptance to some people. Further, since most individu-als are members of small work teams, there is usually ample opportunity for people to develop the type of relationships which can satisfy the need to be liked (accepted). Some of these relationships will serve to satisfy other needs (such as the need for control), while other relationships will develop only if one is willing to abandon the desire to satisfy other needs. The trade-offs between the need for acceptance and other needs will vary, in part, as a result of the role one occupies within the organization.

In entry-level or technical roles, one is very much concerned with whether or not one "fits in" with the rest of the work group and is "liked" by the boss. Most people believe that organizational rewards and punishments are based partly on who one is associated with. Therefore, they feel it is best to try at least to get along with their supervisors. Most people also accept the idea that they should try to gain acceptance from other group members, since one's success at particular tasks may be contingent upon the efforts of those with whom one works. Further, many people believe that the best way to get fired is to make waves, and that the best way not to make waves is to be liked by others. This may involve subordinating some personal needs to the needs of the group or organization.

In a manager's role, an individual must recognize that not everyone is going to like him or her. A manager's job is to direct other people so that their actions are congruent with the goals of the organization. He or she is responsible for group performance and therefore is frequently placed in situations where there is conflict between what he or she (as the agent of the organization) needs the group to accomplish and what the members of the group want to do. When such conflict arises between a manager and a subordinate or a group of subordinates, the manager (as the source of conflict) may realistically fear rejection (loss of acceptance). No one likes to be rejected. However, to successfully play the Inner Game of Management, you must operate under the assumption that not everyone is going to like you and learn to face and deal with interpersonal conflict. Inability or unwillingness to deal with conflict may result in considerable costs to the organization, as the following case illustrates.

Sandra Davis was the owner of an executive search firm specializing in the financial services industry. Sandra had worked for several years with one of the largest national search firms before founding her own firm. As her business grew, Sandra hired people to help run the business. After a few years, she also added two senior-level people who she thought might ultimately become partners.

Unfortunately, Sandra found that her staff was not as committed to the business as she had hoped. Both of the two senior people were content to let Sandra do all the business development, and she found that she had to work even harder than before because of the firm's increased overhead. Sandra grew not only increasingly tired but also frustrated. She began to feel that she was working for her employees rather than the reverse. As this process continued, Sandra added more people to cope with the increased load, but nothing changed, except that her payroll costs were becoming disproportionate to the productivity of her staff.

She felt embittered by what was happening but was unable to deal with it. She was someone who did not like conflict. She tried to send subtle signals to people, but there was no effect. Sandra felt she was trapped in a situation she did not fully understand.

Her basic problem was that her need to be liked by people had prevented her from confronting her staff with criticisms of their performance. By avoiding conflict, she preserved the surface tranquillity of her organization. Everyone liked Sandra, in part because she never criticized anyone. Yet, Sandra was not being effective as a manager, because she had not learned how to manage her own need to be liked so that it did not interfere with the performance of her managerial functions.

Failure To Play the Inner Game Effectively

As discussed in this chapter, there are three critical components of the Inner Game of Management. To play the game successfully, you must:

1. Manage your need for self-esteem.
2. Manage the need for control so that you develop the capacity to feel comfortable with decreasing control.
3. Manage the need to be liked by other people so that it does not interfere with the requirements of the managerial role.

A person who successfully deals with these challenges of the Inner Game can be termed an Inner Game Master, someone who has literally mastered the Inner Game of Management.

When you fail to adopt a mindset that lets you deal effectively with one or more of these factors, you begin to play another game besides the one necessary to be successful in your role. On the basis of our research, we have identified a number of dysfunctional Inner Games that managers play when they have failed to adopt the mindset of an Inner Game Master. These dysfunctional Inner Games are demonstrated in a variety of syndromes, such as the Doer Syndrome.

In Part II of this book, we shall examine ten common syndromes that arise when people have not mastered one or more of the three key Inner Game dimensions. It should be noted that each syndrome results from some combination of problems with the three key Inner Game dimensions and that people can suffer from more than one syndrome simultaneously.

At the conclusion of each chapter, we shall give a brief analysis of how people can overcome the problems that characterize the particular syndrome. Then, in the final section of the book, we will examine, in detail, the ways in which these syndromes can be avoided or overcome, both through the individual's efforts and by management development programs provided by organizations.

Part Two

Ineffective Inner Games Managers Play

Chapter 2
The Doer Syndrome

Bob Miller was a successful salesman for Flair Fashions, Inc., a medium-size garment manufacturer. He was a very competent and competitive individual. He liked to win at any game he played.

Bob had graduated from the University of Southern California. While at USC, he played baseball. His team had played for the NCAA championship. It was just after graduation when Bob took a job as a salesperson with Flair Fashions, Inc. He was very personable, highly motivated, well organized, and almost immediately a success in sales.

Bob viewed sales as a game and applied the same self-discipline that had made him successful as an infielder at USC. He found that success at sales was reinforcing, and he began to earn a considerable income. He worked hard and spent between 55 and 65 hours per week on his job. The company was very pleased with Bob and felt he had a good future with Flair Fashions. Within two years after joining the firm, Bob had become its number-one salesman.

Four years after Bob joined Flair Fashions, the company reorganized its sales function and moved from a national sales organization to a divisional organization. Bob was offered the position of western regional sales manager. He accepted it—and just when everything should have been roses, it all began to sour.

Bob found that his new job was very different from being a salesman, a job he had mastered. As a salesman, he knew how to spend his time and liked the activities that went with selling. He enjoyed the process of selling and got a great deal of satisfaction when he closed a sale. He had viewed selling as a game and used his sales record as a score card. In this sense, it was similar to his being a player on the USC baseball team. The more sales he closed, the more fun he had and, of course, the more income he earned.

In his job as a salesman, Bob was responsible for his own destiny. When he faced a customer, it was his responsibility and performance that made a difference, just as when he had faced an opposing pitcher as a batter. Since he was good at what he did, he felt in control of his own destiny, although there were clearly times when he wished he had a better line from the merchandiser at Flair.

Once Bob was promoted to manager, he found that there were a great many new demands on his time. He was required to recruit new staff, visit his staff members in the field to help train them, hold quarterly meetings with all staff, attend a variety of operational and management meetings, and handle lots of paperwork. A further burden on his time was the fact that even after he was promoted to manager, Bob continued to service the key accounts in his territory, though this was not required by his role. He was concerned that if he neglected the relationships he had built up over the past few years, the company would experience a loss of business from these important accounts. He was so effective at this that he continued to be the company's number-one salesman even after he was promoted to a management position.

Bob found himself on the phone constantly, dealing with calls from his sales force and customers. He found that much of the time he spent in the new role required dealing with problems and handling crises. He jokingly began to refer to himself as a "fireman."

Bob had always prided himself on his ability to manage his time well. He had used a monthly plan in his job as a salesman, visiting customers on a regular cycle and allocating his time according to priorities and goals, which he set on a regular basis. However, he found that this system did not work as well in his role as a regional manager. In the new job, Bob found that regardless of how he planned to spend his time, a new crisis emerged every day. He also found that there were more and more telephone calls to return and he often had to play a game of "telephone tag" until he reached the party.

Gradually, Bob began to spend less and less time planning his work. He merely came to the office and responded to whatever problems and calls there were that particular day. To cope with the increased work load in his new job, Bob also increased the number of hours he worked. He began to work

10 to 12 hours each day, six to seven days per week. Still, he found himself falling farther and farther behind.

Just as he had in college, Bob responded to the increased demands on his time by focusing on some things and neglecting others. His paperwork, which Bob always found to be drudgery, kept piling up. He began to receive phone calls from Mike Kaufman, President of Flair Fashions, and others reminding him about overdue reports and asking why there had been no response to their memos.

Bob also encountered another unexpected problem: some of his salespeople did not seem to be motivated, or at least were much less motivated than he had been as a salesman. He spent time with them and gave them pep talks, but too frequently these actions had little effect. Since Bob was a positive guy who felt that people ought to be mature enough to know what was in their own interest, he tended to leave it at that even when it did not have the desired motivational effect on his sales staff.

Unfortunately, Bob had inherited a number of problem people when he took over the western region. Moreover, there seemed to be an endless number of petty squabbles among his salespeople and his office support staff. Bob found that he was forced into the uncomfortable position of being the intermediary in these disputes, and he resented this as a misuse of his time.

When sales growth did not meet planned regional targets, Mike Kaufman began sending Bob some signals that he was disappointed. The signals were gentle, but they were clear. To some extent, Bob felt that the implied criticism was unfair. He was working hard, and the problem was primarily with the mediocre staff he had inherited. He had to admit, however, that of all the new people he had recruited, only one was a winner and the decision was still out on the other two. He hoped that they would make it, and he tried to be encouraging whenever he spoke to them. Bob wished that he could spend more time with his new recruits, but he simply could not afford to.

In spite of the fact that Bob continued to be the company's number-one salesman, the results for his region as a whole did not improve. Bob responded by working even harder. It got to the point that he was putting in 16-hour days.

This pattern continued for 18 months. Bob was still the top salesman in the firm, but his region did not develop as the company had hoped. During this period, the firm's president, Mike Kaufman, met with Bob and tried to motivate him to focus on building the region. At each of these meetings, Bob agreed with everything Mike requested, but the results never seemed to improve.

Mike Kaufman had a very high regard for Bob, but he was concerned with the lack of development of the region. He began to second-guess the decision to make Bob a manager. He thought that Bob might very well be a victim of the Peter Principle—someone who was promoted to his level of incompetence. He began to consider replacing Bob as regional manager, but he knew Bob would take this badly and probably leave the company rather than go back to being a salesman. Finally, Mike felt he could no longer wait for Bob to improve. He offered Bob a new job as vice president of corporate accounts, which was intended to be a high-level sales job with a face-saving title.

Unfortunately, Bob was hurt and angry. He resigned from Flair Fashions and went to work for a competitor a few weeks later. The firm had not only lost its best salesman but wasted 18 months in building the western territory.

How Bob Miller's Inner Game Playing Created Problems

Bob Miller had been a successful salesman because he viewed selling as a game and because he was good at that game, just as he had been good at baseball. Although baseball was a team game, there was still a great deal of opportunity for individual recognition and success. For Bob, the opportunity to make a sale was analogous to going one-on-one with an opposing pitcher. Even after his promotion, he continued to service his key accounts. In part, he did this because he did not replace the game aspect of selling with a similarly satisfying game aspect of managing. Consciously or not, Bob was satisfying his self-esteem from his success in selling and being the best sales-man, rather than from being the best manager. He was deriving his self-esteem from selling activities that were based on his own performance rather than from the performance of his sales staff.

Bob also suffered from an inability to satisfy his control needs through the performance of his role as a manager. When Bob was a salesperson, he felt responsible for his own destiny. When he faced a customer, it was his skills that made the sale. He knew he was good at sales. He felt in control of things, even though the customer was free not to buy from him. After Bob became a manager, however, his control over sales became more tenuous. His destiny was now in the hands of others: his sales staff. While he was still responsible for the overall sales of his region, his ability to control sales was now indirect. He had to train the salespeople to make the sale. However, since this was uncomfortable for Bob, he still kept control over the key ac-counts by servicing them himself. Since he had a variety of new responsibilities making demands upon his time and since he wanted to ensure control over the key accounts, he put in more hours but still did not have time to do all that his job required. In effect, Bob was doing two jobs at once. This put him under great stress and made him unable to cope well with all the demands on his time.

The Doer Game That Managers Play

Bob Miller, whose Inner Game problems we discussed, was a classic sufferer of the Doer Syndrome. The Doer Syndrome refers to the tendency of a person who has been promoted to a managerial role to continue to think and act as a doer rather than as a manager.

As discussed in Chapter 1, a doer is someone whose activities involve the direct performance of some kind of technical work rather than the supervision or management of others. Doers typically occupy entry-level positions in the organizational hierarchy. These positions include a wide variety of jobs, such as accountant, computer programmer, engineer, secretary, machinist, and salesperson.

Once doers are promoted to managerial roles, however, they need to learn to play the Inner Game of Management rather than the Inner Game of a doer. This transition is analogous to making the psychological transition from a player to a coach in baseball or any other sport. Whenever this psychological transition is not successfully made, people play the Inner Game of Management by the rules of the Doer Syndrome and may experience problems that can ultimately result in failure in their new roles.

The Doer Syndrome is characterized by an inability to manage one's own self-esteem in a way that is consistent with the requirements of the role change from a doer to a manager; and an inability to manage one's need for control.

Individuals who suffer from the Doer Syndrome base their self-esteem on their own performance rather than on the performance of their staffs. Even after they are promoted to management positions, they continue to explicitly and implicitly evaluate their own performance in terms of their ability as doers rather than as managers. Consequently, these individuals tend to emphasize performance rather than managerial activities.

Doers tend to spend most of their time actually performing tasks rather than planning the work of others, delegating tasks, and supervising others' work. The underlying reason for their inability to spend their time like true managers is that they have not changed their role concepts. They still perceive themselves to be doers and thus link their self-esteem to the performance of doer tasks. Even after they are promoted, they continue to derive their self-esteem from the things they did as doers rather than the things they should be doing to be effective managers. These individuals may continue to be the number-one salesperson, accountant, secretary, or whatever and be proud of their accomplishments.

In fact, individuals who suffer from the Doer Syndrome may believe that to be the best manager, they *must* continue to be the best technician. They may, therefore, feel that they are in competition with their subordinates for the position of technical expert. They feel threatened by subordinates who possess greater technical expertise. Whenever this situation develops, it can be quite disruptive for the work group, because the manager spends most of the time trying to maintain technical expertise instead of recognizing the technical merits of his or her subordinates. If these competitive feelings are carried to an extreme, Doers may become Pygmy Syndrome sufferers. Individuals who suffer from this syndrome (to be discussed in Chapter 6) tend to hire weaker people, as one way of protecting their role as technical expert.

Individuals who suffer from the Doer Syndrome also suffer from an inability to handle decreasing degrees of control. As doers, individuals have a great deal of control over the results of their efforts. Once they are promoted to management positions, however, their ability to control results becomes more indirect. As discussed in Chapter 1, whenever control is given up, the likelihood that the task will be completed exactly as the individual himself or herself would have completed it is decreased. Doers are extremely uncomfortable with this situation and, hence, attempt to retain as much control as possible. They are, therefore, poor delegators, and they attempt to retain all decision-making authority. As we saw in the case of Bob Miller, this can lead to a situation in which the manager is greatly overburdened. This can, in turn, result in the manager's burnout or failure because there is no time to adequately perform the managerial responsibilities.

In brief, individuals who suffer from the Doer Syndrome need to change the concept of their role from a doer to a manager. The underlying psychological requirement to achieve this is to learn how to derive one's self-esteem from doing the things that managers do rather than from doing the things that one did as a doer. It also involves learning to give up a certain amount of control over results. Although this is a difficult psychological transition to make, it is possible, as we shall see in the next section.

Overcoming the Doer Syndrome

If Bob Miller were merely an isolated case of the Doer Syndrome, it would be sad but not that significant. Unfortunately, there are thousands upon thousands of Bob—and Barbara—Millers. Accordingly, it is very important that people understand how to avoid or overcome the Doer Syndrome.

We shall examine how to avoid or overcome the Doer Syndrome by studying the case of an individual who faced this problem and overcame it by learning to play the Inner Game effectively.

Terry Donahue: UCLA Football Coach

Throughout this book we have made the analogy between the job of coaching a sports team and the job of being a manager. We've chosen this analogy because we believe the two roles have a great deal in common. Drawing upon this similarity, we shall now use the case of Terry Donahue to illustrate how a person can learn to play the Inner Game effectively and thus avoid or overcome the Doer Syndrome.

Background

Terry Donahue is the most successful coach in UCLA football history; he led the UCLA team to more victories than any other coach. Even today, he is a relatively young coach, though he has been at UCLA for more than a decade.

Donahue began his career at UCLA as a football player. This is certainly a "doer" position and is analogous to any entry-level position in a corporation. He had always wanted to play football at UCLA. However, he was not recruited when he graduated from high school, so he became a walk-on at San Jose State College and later transferred to Valley College. Finally, he became a walk-on at UCLA. Donahue was a defensive tackle. At 6 feet, 190 pounds, he was not a very large tackle; yet, he was good enough to be a starter at UCLA, and he started for the Bruins in the 1966 Rose Bowl Game.

After college, Donahue became an assistant coach at the University of Kansas, under Pepper Rodgers. He returned to UCLA as an assistant coach when Rodgers came to UCLA as head coach. After Rodgers left UCLA, Dick Vermeil became head coach. After Vermeil's team won the Rose Bowl in 1976, he left to become the head coach of the Philadelphia Eagles, and Terry Donahue was selected as his successor.

Promotion to Head Coach

When Donahue became head coach at UCLA, he realized that he had a great deal of learning to do. He has said of this experience: "No one is born a head coach. You're an assistant coach, and then all of a sudden one afternoon, you're elevated to head coach. And when they elevate you, they don't give you a manual that tells you how to become a head coach. There isn't one. Maybe there ought to be."

Donahue went through a period of on-the-job learning of how to be a head coach. During this period he had to deal with the critical Inner Game issues that everyone must face to make the successful transition to a management role.

The Catalyst for Donahue's Transition. The basic catalyst for Donahue was not merely his desire to be a successful coach, for he had that motivation from the first day of his appointment as head coach at UCLA; rather, it was his experience of a considerable amount of frustration and pain in his job.

On the day Terry Donahue was appointed head coach of the UCLA football team, he said that it was a "dream come true." Four years later, the dream had turned into a nightmare. His wife told him that "there is no way you are enjoying your job; you are enduring it." The story of what Terry Donahue did to turn it around is an excellent case history of someone who overcame the Doer Syndrome and was able to make the transition to a management role.

Managing His Self-Esteem. The first thing Donahue had to learn was how to shift the source of his self-esteem from the activities of an assistant coach to the job of a head coach. As he stated: "When I first got the head coaching job here, I thought I got it because I was the best technical coach on the staff. . . I had been coaching two positions, the offensive and defensive linemen, and I assumed that my job was now to coach the whole team instead of just two positions."

In fact, Donahue got the job not because he was the best at coaching per se—though he was indeed an excellent coach—but rather because the man who selected him, the late J. D. Morgan, UCLA's Athletic Director at the time, saw something else in him: the ability to grow into a true head coach.

To do this, Donahue had to change the way he used his time, shifting from the things he liked to do (the things he was the best at) to some things he did not like to do (things which, at first, he was not so skilled at). As he stated: "I wanted to coach. That was what I was best at. That was what I liked." However, in his new job, he found there were a number of new responsibilities "pulling" at him. "There were many, many interruptions to my work," Donahue explained. During the season, he was expected to meet with the press. At other times, there were calls from the administration. He also had to deal with alumni—and, of course, there were student counseling problems to be dealt with. For example, there were times when he was running a staff meeting for his coaches to plan offensive or defensive strategy only to be interrupted by administrative duties, such as a call from the Athletic Director. He had to leave the meeting, and his assistants could not continue without him, because they could not really make any decisions. Donahue says: "I finally realized that the so-called 'interruptions' were really part of my job. I wanted to do coaching, which was what I loved, but my job had turned into a desk job."

Terry Donahue had to learn what his responsibilities were as a head coach. He had to learn to allocate his time among all the key responsibilities his job required. He had to learn to set priorities for allocating his time. He had to learn to like his new job. As he states:

"It took me a long time to learn to spread myself among the key areas of responsibility which comprise my job. There are really three key areas. One is the technical aspect—the X's and O's and the plays you run. The second is the administrative aspect, which involves everything from dealing with the school's administration to dealing with the media, speaking, dealing with students, answering correspondence, whatever, A to Z. And then the third is personnel. There are two types of personnel, those currently on your team and those you need to go out and bring to your team."

Donahue was able to manage his self-esteem sufficiently to accept the fact that he now had to spend his time differently, and he learned to derive his self-esteem from the things required by his new role. As he says: "The more you work as the head coach, the more your time is taken away from the purely technical aspects to other aspects. It took me a long time to learn to like those other aspects."

Managing His Need for Control. Another major task Donahue was able to accomplish was to learn to manage his need for control. It was obvious to Donahue that when he made the transition from player to assistant coach, he had less control over the outcome of the game. Since only players play the game of football, there was no question in his mind that he had to delegate. Coaches do not perform on the field. However, when Donahue moved from assistant coach to head coach, the transition was more subtle. He had to learn to delegate some things that he used to do as an assistant coach. As he states: "I didn't really have familiarity with how to delegate." As we mentioned, during the early years of his tenure as coach, Donahue would run the staff meetings with his assistant coaches, and he would sometimes be interrupted. When interruptions occurred, the assistant coaches simply had to wait for him to return, as they did not have any authority to make decisions. In effect, Terry Donahue was a bottleneck, because he could not be in two places at once.

Donahue made a variety of changes involving delegation of authority and giving up some degree of control; these were critical in his transition to a successful head coach. First, he delegated authority for the day-to-day technical aspects of the job to his assistant coaches—in this case, his offensive and defensive coordinators. As he explains: "I still determine the basic philosophy of offense and defense. For example, we always want a balanced offense with a mix of passing and running, but we will never throw the ball 60 times per game. However, I no longer call the specific offensive plays. That is the responsibility of the offensive coordinator, Homer Smith." Moreover, Donahue no longer runs the coaching-strategy meetings. As he states: "I will set the time of the meetings, and I will sit in on them whenever possible, but the coordinators can make decisions without me." This is clearly effective managerial practice, as it permits his assistants to make decisions without his presence and avoids the bottleneck problem encountered during his early years as coach. Donahue said that this aspect of his transition was the most painful. For this was what he really loved most about coaching.

Donahue concentrates on the head coach's job, and Smith and the other assistant coaches focus on their jobs. Donahue gave up direct control over crucial aspects of the game in order to devote himself to the other aspects of his role. To accomplish this, he had to manage his need for control.

One significant aspect of Donahue's willingness to give up direct control over the offense is that he accepted two different kinds of vulnerability. The first, of course, was the vulnerability that comes with delegating any critical aspect of organizational performance, such as the offense in football or sales in a business. The other was the possibility that Smith, rather than Donahue, would get the recognition for a successful offense. Although many managers suffer from this problem, Terry Donahue did not. His philosophy is that football is a team game and that each person has his role. Donahue's role is to manage the entire program, rather than to perform in any single area.

For Donahue to ultimately be as successful as he has been, he had to delegate some real authority, and he did it very well. He did it by managing his need for control.

In summary, Terry Donahue has been successful as a head coach because (1) he managed his self-esteem so that it was geared to his current role and (2) he managed his need for control sufficiently to be able to delegate crucial aspects of his operation to talented others. He has changed the way he allocates his time so that it is appropriate to his new role, and he has developed the skills necessary to be effective as a head coach. His abilities as a head coach were recently recognized by the National Football League's Atlanta Falcons. In late 1986, he was offered a multi-million dollar contract to become the head coach for that organization. He refused, stating that he had not yet finished what he set out to accomplish at UCLA.

He provides, in other words, an excellent model of the way to make the personal and professional transitions necessary to beat the Doer Syndrome. He is a winner—not just in football but also in mastering the Inner Game of Management.

Summary of Steps to Avoid the Doer Syndrome

In this chapter we have presented two case studies of people faced with the need to make the transition to a managerial role. In the case of Bob Miller, we found an individual who was successful as a doer but who failed to become a successful manager because he fell victim to the Doer Syndrome. In the case of Terry Donahue, we saw an individual who was successful in overcoming the Doer Syndrome.

In this final section we shall summarize the steps the Doer must follow to avoid or overcome the Doer Syndrome.

The first step is to make a definite commitment to change. This is an essential prerequisite for everything else. Although it may seem an obvious first step, it is, unfortunately, too often not done. Many people simply do not want to change. In the case of Terry Donahue, the catalyst to change was the recognition that he was enduring rather than really enjoying his job. Unfortunately, Bob Miller never made a real commitment to change, and so he ultimately failed as a manager.

Next, the Doer must learn to manage self-esteem so that he or she derives satisfaction from the current role rather than the previous one. The key issue here is psychological acceptance that one's role has actually changed, not just in title but in its requirements. How can this be done? Some people can simply "tell" themselves that their role has changed and, in turn, give themselves "permission" to perform the new role. For other people, this change can be accomplished only if the person is motivated by some painful experience such as actual or impending career failure. These people will be motivated to change because of problems experienced on the job. An individual's manager can serve as the catalyst to motivate a person to redefine his or her source of self-esteem.

Once a Doer has made a psychological commitment to redefine his or her source of self-esteem so that it corresponds to the new role, the next step is to adjust the way the individual is spending his or her time. A manager should be allocating time to activities that are appropriate for the role. For example, a Vice President of Sales should be spending time on planning, organizing, and developing the overall sales effort rather than on actual selling activities. Thus, a Doer must monitor his or her use of time in order to assess whether the use of time is appropriate to the actual level of the job. This can be accomplished with a formal time planning system that encourages the Doer to write down tasks and times for accomplishment.

The final thing to learn is how to manage the need for control. The effective manager must delegate, and the delegation must involve not only tasks but also authority. As one manager we know who has made this transition successfully states: "I recognized that I needed to learn how to feel comfortable delegating things. If I continued to run around and do things by myself, I would simply run myself ragged. To get out of the Doer role, I practiced letting other people do things themselves and avoided jumping in and taking over when they were doing something."

A classic problem facing victims of the Doer Syndrome is the feeling, "I can do it better and faster myself." While this may be true, to overcome the Doer Syndrome, a Doer must get used to the idea that others can perform tasks differently but still acceptably. One way to develop comfort with this is to experiment with assigning tasks to others and refrain from second-guessing or "correcting" their efforts. Simply accept what they do. The objective here is not necessarily to get the task accomplished in the best possible way but, rather, to develop comfort with someone else's doing a task. This process of experimentation ought to begin with relatively unimportant tasks and proceed to more complex, significant tasks.

In summary, to overcome the Doer Syndrome, an individual must:

1. Make a commitment to change.
2. Learn to see himself or herself as a manager rather than a doer.
3. Make changes in the way his or her time is used so that it corresponds to the person's actual role as a manager.
4. Learn to feel comfortable in delegating things to others.

A Doer who achieves these will have done much to improve his or her chances of management success.

Chapter 3

The Impostor Syndrome: The Superperson and the Ugly Duckling

Most of us know someone we went to school with, work with, or socialize with who seems always to succeed, no matter what he or she does. These people always appear confident, yet, when we remark about their success, they shrug it off by saying that it was all a matter of luck or that "anyone could have done the same thing." On the surface, it appears that the person is being modest. However, what most of us do not realize is that some of these people really believe what they are saying. They believe that they are "Impostors": they see themselves as inadequate, while those around them see them as successes.[1]

As a result of this discrepancy between their own and others' perceptions, Impostors experience a high degree of tension, or what psychologists refer to as "dissonance."[2] According to psychological theory, the dissonance

---

[1] P. R. Clance, in her book *The Impostor Phenomenon: The Fear That Haunts Your Success* (Atlanta, GA: Peachtree Publishers, 1985), identifies a phenomenon like the syndromes described here. The syndromes in this chapter are based on our research, and are only coincidentally related to what Clance describes in her book in spite of the similar labels.

[2] For a discussion of cognitive dissonance theory, see Leon Festinger, *A Theory of Cognitive Dissonance* (Stanford, CA: Stanford University Press, 1957).

created by such a discrepancy is unpleasant, so people will try to reduce it. This is accomplished by selecting one alternative over all others and then discounting the validity of the alternatives not selected. For Impostors, this means selecting either their own or others' opinions as the "correct" evaluation of their abilities and then finding ways to "prove" that the other evaluation is invalid.

Whenever Impostors subconsciously choose to believe others' opinions, they will work exceptionally hard to "prove" that they are successful. These people spend a great deal of time and effort trying to be perfect so that they can overcome their own feelings of inadequacy. As a result, they tend to be perfectionists who have an intense fear of failure. These individuals suffer from what we call the Superperson Syndrome. If, on the other hand, Impostors choose to believe their self-evaluations, they will subconsciously try to prove to others how inadequate they are. Individuals who choose this alternative tend to be risk takers, since taking excessive risks increases the possibility of failure. They also tend to feel, "I'm really worthless," and to adamantly discount any positive feedback as erroneous. These individuals suffer from what we call the Ugly Duckling Syndrome.

This chapter is devoted to a description of these two syndromes and an analysis of how they affect individuals' ability to play the Inner Game effectively. The first section of this chapter will describe the Superperson Syndrome and present the story of Mary Ellen Henderson, a Superwoman, who nearly failed because she could not play the Inner Game of Management effectively. In the second section, we describe the Ugly Duckling Syndrome and the problems that one of its sufferers, Doug Perry, encountered as he was promoted to higher levels in the organizational career hierarchy. In the final section of this chapter, we summarize the steps Impostors can take to increase their ability to play the Inner Game of Management effectively.

The Superperson Syndrome

Practically everyone is familiar with the story of Superman, the "being" from Krypton whose capabilities far exceeded those of normal humans. Superman was invincible; no weapon could harm him. Fortunately for humanity, he used his powers to serve rather than to destroy it. He did, however, suffer from one inadequacy: when exposed to Kryptonite (a fragment of his home planet, which had been destroyed), he became weak and completely vulnerable to attack. Fortunately, even when exposed to Kryptonite, Superman was always able to escape just in time to save the world from certain disaster.

While Superman is a character who lives in comic books, in cartoons, and in the movies, there are many real people who strive to be superhuman. While many of these individuals are "naturals" who possess a great deal of innate ability in some area, they are never satisfied, because they believe that they must constantly prove themselves worthy of the success others attribute to them. These individuals believe that they must be "the best" at everything they attempt to do. The driving force for this need is an intense, hidden fear of failure that they do not want others to discover. Failure is the "Kryptonite" that Superpeople fear being confronted with, because, at some level, they believe they could never recover if they were seen by others as failures.

The drive to be the best, along with a fear of failure, causes Superpeople to be high achievers in both their professional and personal lives. In fact, most Superpeople are such high achievers that they are perfectionists. As a result, many Superpeople are either procrastinators or workaholics—and neither of these strategies is conducive to high productivity. In the first case, the procrastinator spends an excessive amount of time worrying about doing the task rather than actively working to accomplish it. In the other, the workaholic spends an inordinate amount of time trying to complete a task which could have reasonably been completed in less time. It is easy to see that either of these tendencies can result in excessive stress and eventual burnout. In fact, many Superpeople suffer from sleeplessness and other stress-related health problems.

Even though it creates excessive stress in their lives, Superpeople strive for perfection, because they believe that if they are not perfect, they have failed and people won't "value them" or "like them." They fear failing because it will cause them to look foolish in the eyes of their family, friends, and co-workers. Consequently, whenever they can, they will avoid situations that present them with difficult tasks. More often, however, difficult tasks are unavoidable, because another characteristic of Superpeople is that they cannot say "No." These people view a refusal as an admission of failure: that is, they will be seen as failures because they are afraid to even attempt difficult tasks. They will, therefore, take on these tasks and work exceptionally hard to complete them. While they are usually successful, the price they pay is physical and psychological stress: they are prone to burnout from overwork.

The Superperson Game That Managers Play

There are many managers who play the Inner Game by the rules of the Superperson Syndrome. Since these individuals have a strong desire to achieve, they will work very hard to be "the best" manager. Many feel that they must be perfect immediately, all the time worrying that somehow they might fail. In an attempt to alleviate this worry, these people expend a great deal of energy in learning the technical aspects of their jobs: taking management development courses, reading self-help manuals, and listening intently to successful managers who talk about how they "got there." The Superperson is looking for clues on how to be the best manager.

Through the Superperson's efforts to learn about the managerial role, he or she may become very skilled at management's Outer Game functions. Unfortunately, most Superpeople will still be ineffective managers, because they have not adopted a way of fulfilling their needs for self-esteem and control that is consistent with the requirements of their new role. Their tendency to·play the Inner Game by the rules of the Superperson Syndrome greatly undermines their ability to succeed as a manager.

Superpeople suffer from a variety of symptoms of Inner Game problems, related to both self-esteem and control needs. First, they feel intensely uncomfortable because their role is so ill-defined. They no longer know what they need to do in order to be "successful." In an attempt to reduce the anxiety this situation creates for them, they will, as suggested above, try to find out what "good" managers do. They may spend so much time trying to figure out, before they act, what they need to do to be perfect that nothing gets done. They may, therefore, be seen as indecisive, since they often take so long to act.

A second symptom of ineffective Inner Game playing related to the desire to be perfect is the tendency of Superpeople to be ineffective delegators. Superpeople do not like to delegate tasks to subordinates because they believe that other people will not live up to their own standards of excellence. Consequently, Superpeople may be very directive in their style of management and/or may act as performers rather than as managers. In either case, Superpeople will spend more time than other managers working on tasks. As a result, they end up "doing" more and more, which in turn increases their personal stress. Their subordinates may come to believe that their manager does not trust them. The productivity and morale of the work group may drop, and the Superperson may soon find that he or she is a failure as a manager.

By spending an inordinate amount of time on performance activities so that their work group achieves "excellence," Superpeople place themselves in a situation in which they need to compete with their subordinates in order to protect their self-esteem. If they encounter a subordinate with greater technical expertise, their position as "the best" is threatened. These subordinates become "the enemy," much like one of the villains who challenge Superman's power. Whenever this occurs, Superpeople will try to outcompete their subordinates—and they may find that they have worked so hard at the competition that they ignored their other responsibilities and failed as managers.

Managers who play the Inner Game of Management by the rules of the Superperson Syndrome, then, have a variety of personal and interpersonal problems. As the following case illustrates, an inability to overcome this syndrome can have profound effects on one's ability to perform effectively in the managerial role.

Mary Ellen Henderson:
Superwoman

As she looked back on her life, 42-year-old Mary Ellen Henderson could see that she had always tried to be the best at whatever she did. In school, she was always a good student, always involved in club activities, and always well liked. She had strived for perfection in her school work and as a result received a lot of compliments from her teachers. However, her parents were always critical of everything she did; it seemed she could never be "good enough" for them.

Perhaps to prove her parents wrong, or perhaps to receive continued recognition from her teachers and peers, Mary Ellen had worked very hard in high school so that she would be accepted at a good college. With some amusement, she reflected back on the day when one of her high school teachers had so aptly predicted what lay ahead for her: "You should be the best that you can be, but quit trying to be such a perfectionist. Someday, it will get you into trouble."

"Yes," Mary Ellen thought, "I really did get into trouble because of my tendency to be a perfectionist. But I couldn't help myself." Here is Mary Ellen's story of how playing the Inner Game by the rules of the Superperson Syndrome nearly caused her to fail as a manager.

Mary Ellen's Early Years

Mary Ellen had always been a very ambitious person. She had been recognized for her achievements in school and the community and, as a result, was offered admission to many prestigious Eastern Universities. She decided on a small all-womens' college because she believed it would be more comfortable there and the "competition" would not be too tough. She had always feared academic competition, and even though she had had good grades throughout school, she could remember vividly her 12th-grade algebra teacher who had "ruined" her perfect 4.0 by giving her a B+ for the course. Although it had taken her some time, she had finally gotten over that experience, and with her acceptance into the university, she began looking forward to her college years.

Mary Ellen's first year at college was frustrating and confusing. She found it exceedingly difficult to do well in her math courses and since this was her chosen major, she began to have a sense of impending doom. She increased the amount of time she devoted to studying for her exams, but she simply could not get the A grades she desired. In fact, in at least one of her math courses, she was in jeopardy of getting a C. Mary Ellen recalled how miserable she was during that first year when she realized that she was failing and how she feared what her parents and friends back home would say. She considered dropping out of school, but realized that this would be the ultimate admission of failure. She decided that instead of dropping out, she would be better off changing her major. She chose computer science because it was interesting and challenging. Further, because she'd had a job where she learned the fundamentals of programming, she believed that she would have no trouble excelling in this major.

With the change in major, Mary Ellen was able to graduate in the upper third of her class. Her academic achievement as well as the subject matter she had selected for a major helped her secure a position as a computer programmer at a major East Coast firm. She was well liked by her co-workers and was well respected for her technical expertise. Her supervisor often complimented her on her work, and Mary Ellen was usually the one who volunteered if there was anything extra that needed to be done.

Mary Ellen felt secure in her position, although she was always fearful that she would be asked a question she couldn't handle. As a result of this fear, she made it a policy to keep up with the latest developments in software and programming and, consequently, became quite valuable to the organization in which she worked.

Everything seemed to be going her way. She had found a place where she could excel and receive the recognition she needed. She also, during her second year on the job, married her college sweetheart and settled into married life.

Promotion to Management

Given Mary Ellen's skill as a programmer, it was only a matter of time before she was promoted to supervisor. While she was happy about the promotion, she was also fearful that she would not be able to handle the new responsibilities. She did not know exactly what would be expected of her in her new role, and because she didn't want to appear stupid, she did not dare ask anyone. She knew that she had the responsibility to ensure that her subordinates were performing satisfactorily, but she wanted her area to be "the best."

Mary Ellen began her new job by trying to set priorities for her area, but often found that she had difficulty making a commitment to one course of action or another, because she feared that it might be wrong. She did not want her subordinates or supervisor to be aware of this, so she did the best she could. Her strategy was to provide subordinates with a great deal of direction as well as a great deal of criticism whenever they did not do something exactly as she wanted them to do it. Sometimes, she simply did things herself or found herself reworking what her subordinates had done.

Mary Ellen invested a great deal of time in her work, often staying after hours or taking materials home at night. She was always afraid that something had been overlooked, so her evenings were spent reviewing all assignments for the day. She worried a great deal about whether or not she was doing a good job and often found it difficult to sleep at night.

Six months after her promotion, Mary Ellen received her first performance review. The night before she was to meet with her supervisor, she couldn't eat or sleep and was somewhat frazzled when she went to his office the next day. She had feared the worst and was pleasantly surprised when her boss said that she was doing a good job. Her area was functioning well and was as productive as it had ever been. She was relieved and in an exceptionally good mood when she returned to her office. If she had only known what the next six months were to bring!

Once the feeling of her success had worn off and she had returned to "business as usual," Mary Ellen again began to fret over every detail of both her own and her subordinates' work. She was on her way to burnout, and her subordinates were on their way to rebellion.

Mary Ellen had been fortunate during her first six months on the job. Her body had adjusted to the added stress, and her subordinates had believed that the "problem with Mary Ellen" was that she was "learning the ropes of management." Unfortunately, during the next six months, things began to change. Mary Ellen began to suffer from migraine headaches and, as a result, was very irritable. Her subordinates began to complain that they were not given enough freedom to do what they wanted to do and that the department had lost its creativity. Her husband began to complain that she was always at, or thinking about, the office. As a result of her personal stress, her own productivity began to decrease along with her area's productivity.

She began to feel that if she didn't do something to overcome her problems, it would be only a matter of time before she lost her job, her husband, and her sanity. So, she decided to seek help.

How Mary Ellen Nearly Failed

Mary Ellen suffered from many of the classic symptoms of the Superperson Syndrome. Her self-esteem was tied so closely to her need to be perfect that she could not admit that she was fallible. This was evidenced in her reluctance to ask her superiors questions about how to perform her job effectively. It was more important for her to appear invincible than to admit to those around her that she didn't know what she was doing.

Since she was unwilling to ask questions or advice of others, she often spent a great deal of energy and time worrying about decisions she needed to make. Mary Ellen desperately wanted her decisions to be correct so that she could continue to be considered a success. However, since she could never be certain what course of action to take, she waited until she absolutely had to choose one alternative over others. Consequently, her decisions were not made in an effective and timely fashion. A further complication of this tendency to worry about decisions was that the worrying itself diverted her energy from other activities that were important to her success as a manager.

Mary Ellen's fear of failure also led her to try to control everything her work group did. She feared that if she delegated tasks to subordinates, they might not get the job done in an effective manner. The fact was that Mary Ellen would settle only for the "perfection" she expected from her own efforts. She therefore spent a great deal of energy either directing the efforts of her subordinates so they would perform the task "her way" (which was the only right way) or simply doing the work herself. This resulted in the tendency for Mary Ellen to act as a performer rather than a manager, and she probably also felt and acted as if she and her subordinates were competing to see who was the best.

Mary Ellen's excessive worry and work led to stress-related migraines and interpersonal problems not only with her workers but also with her husband. When she realized she was on her way to burnout and failure in both her work and her marriage, she decided to seek help. In the last section of this chapter, we will provide some suggestions on how Impostors like Mary Ellen can avoid or overcome their inability to play the Inner Game effectively. First, however, we will acquaint you with the other Impostor Syndrome: the Ugly Duckling.

The Ugly Duckling Syndrome

In Hans Christian Anderson's fable of the ugly duckling, the main character spends a great deal of his youth being ridiculed because he is so unattractive.

He eventually begins to believe that he is truly what others say he is: ugly and without friends. When he reaches adulthood, however, things begin to change. It seems that now everyone is attracted to him, and some even say that they are envious of his appearance. The duckling, now grown, cannot understand why others have changed their evaluations of him and decides that they must be unable to see him for what he knows himself to be: ugly. One day, however, he happens to view his reflection in the lake and cannot believe his eyes: instead of an ugly duckling, he sees a beautiful swan.

While this story is intended for children, we believe that it also has meaning for adults who suffer from what we label the Ugly Duckling Syndrome. Like the ugly duckling of the fable, people who suffer from this syndrome develop feelings of inadequacy during their childhood. These feelings often result from a perceived discrepancy between how the outside world evaluates the individual's abilities and how his or her family evaluates them. The individual chooses to believe the family's perceptions and, even in adulthood, is unable to accept the positive feedback others give him or her. In other words, unlike the ugly duckling in the fable, these individuals are never able to see and believe their own reflections which others provide.

One individual we know of, for example, was seen by his family as "the one with the common sense," while his twin sister was considered the "smart one." Even though this individual earned a PhD while his sister completed her Bachelor's degree with some difficulty, he never considered himself intelligent. Even at 35 years of age, he still believes that earning his degree was only a matter of "being in the right place at the right time." He believes that by some miracle his inadequacies have been masked, but that one day they will be revealed to the world and he will be humiliated. Until that day comes, however, he continues to keep up the facade that he has developed throughout his life: hoping that others' evaluations are correct, but believing that they are not. Others see him as "Mr. Perfect," but he sees himself as an Impostor or Ugly Duckling.

As this case illustrates, Ugly Ducklings appear to be quite successful to the outside world. To Ugly Ducklings themselves, however, the success others see is not real. Consequently, they tend to discount their accomplishments and to feel that they are undeserving of the praise others give them. They try to take on near-impossible tasks or organize their work in a way that dooms them to failure. Ugly Ducklings create a self-fulfilling prophecy: they believe that they are failures and consequently take action to make this judgment come true. The failure, when it does occur, is a relief rather than a disappointment. Ugly Ducklings, in one way, feel fulfilled, since now they can finally be seen for what they really are: failures.

The Ugly Duckling Game That Managers Play

Managers who play the Inner Game by the rules of the Ugly Duckling Syndrome believe that, through some fluke, they were recognized as competent in their jobs and were rewarded with a promotion. They do not believe that they are worthy of such success, and these self-doubts may become reflected in how they perform their jobs.

Ugly Ducklings, for the most part, have no problems delegating tasks. In fact, sometimes they delegate tasks they could and should perform themselves. One reason they delegate these tasks is that they see them as mundane. Many Ugly Ducklings prefer challenging tasks, since these tasks offer a high probability of failure. They prefer to operate in risky situations. An alternative reason why delegation is easy for Ugly Ducklings is that many of them believe that their subordinates are just as skilled at task performance and decision making as they are. They believe that since they are worthless, others must be at least as skillful as they are.

Fortunately for organizations, these strategies often result in effective delegation when the individual's subordinates desire a great deal of independence and are highly motivated to achieve the organization's objectives. When these conditions do not exist, however, the strategy employed by the Ugly Duckling may result in his or her failure as a manager.

Even if the Ugly Duckling and the organization are lucky enough to have subordinates who successfully accomplish tasks delegated to them, the Ugly Duckling can still fail as a manager because he or she is likely to avoid rewarding good performance. Ugly Ducklings have such a low opinion of themselves that they find it impossible to offer praise to others. These individuals believe that lack of criticism is the same as praise. Unfortunately, that's not the case—lack of praise can greatly decrease subordinates' motivation to achieve the organization's goals. Eventually, the work group may begin to perform poorly, and the Ugly Duckling may not even know why.

Ugly Ducklings are also ineffective decision makers. Some of them make decisions too hastily, without waiting until they have analyzed all relevant information. They do so because operating in such a fashion increases the chances of failure. In some cases, they make the right decision; in others, the decision results in disaster. The latter alternative offers the most reward for Ugly Ducklings, since in failing, they have proved to others how worthless they are.

Other Ugly Ducklings try not to make any decisions at all. These individuals, because of their low self-esteem, defer most decisions to their superiors and/or give subordinates a great deal of decision-making responsibility. Deferring decisions to superiors is a strategy Ugly Ducklings subconsciously use to show their supervisors how inadequate they really are. This practice results in ineffective decision making because the Ugly Duckling's superiors may be too far removed from the work group's daily operations to make appropriate decisions—and even if the decisions are appropriate, the delay that results from such deferral can lead to a loss in productivity. The other strategy, allowing subordinates to participate in decision making, is effective, but Ugly Ducklings often carry it to an extreme. They give subordinates so much decision-making responsibility that the work group never knows what direction it is supposed to be taking, because there is "no one in charge." Decisions are made slowly, if at all, and there is often a decrease in the group's productivity.

While all the problems related to the Ugly Duckling Syndrome can play significant roles in a manager's failure, perhaps the biggest problem for Ugly Ducklings is that they are never satisfied until they fail. They believe that they are failures, and therefore, no matter how successful they really are, they cannot enjoy their success. They believe the success is really undeserved. With each overt success, the stakes are raised: the next task or duty must be more difficult to accomplish and less likely to be achieved. As a result of this risk taking, there are many Ugly Ducklings who are great entrepreneurial successes—but there are just as many who fail miserably. Those who fail, however, may actually feel more secure in their defeat than those who are successful feel sure of their victories.

The following case will illustrate some of the characteristics of the Ugly Duckling Syndrome. It will also show how these characteristics can contribute to ineffective Inner Game playing and eventual failure in the managerial role.

Doug Perry: The Ugly Duckling

As Doug Perry thought back over his life, he realized that some of his problems had begun as far back as high school. He had always been a high achiever and considered a success—athletically, academically, and socially. However, he had always seemed to doubt his abilities in at least two of those areas. It was only when he became a "manager of managers" that these doubts and the way he tried to overcome them led to his ultimate failure.

Doug's Early Years

Doug Perry had always been a "star." A gifted football player and a good student, he was considered one of the most likely to succeed in his high-school class. Not only was he athletic and smart, but he was also well liked by his classmates. It was rare to find Doug standing, walking, or sitting alone. Doug earned the praise of his coach for his athletic ability, recognition from his teachers for his academic achievements, and the respect of his peers because he always seemed "so friendly."

To his family, however, Doug was "the jock" and nothing more. His sister, Janet, was the "academic" who was supposed to attend college to become a doctor. Whenever Doug brought home good grades, his parents seemed unimpressed. They conveyed the notion that the good grades were due to a favoritism afforded to "jocks" and that Janet was really the intelligent one, because she had to work for her grades. Similarly, the reaction of Doug's parents to his popularity at school suggested to him that this, too, was the result of the stardom he had achieved on the athletic field rather than his personal appeal.

As a result of his family's impressions of his achievements, Doug began to doubt his academic and social abilities. This doubt made him work even harder to achieve in these two areas, and he was rewarded with praise from his teachers and friendship from his peers. He always worried, however, that his parents might be right.

After graduation from high school, Doug attended the local college, where he majored in business administration and was again a football star. He maintained close relationships with many of his high-school friends, since they, too, attended the local college.

Doug chose business because he felt it would prepare him for a career in real estate, a profession he saw as lucrative and exciting. Doug believed that he could make a good living from this profession, especially in the growing suburbs of his community. He tried to take courses which would prepare him not only for a real-estate sales position but also, eventually, for a management role. He felt that someday in the future he would make a good manager, because he had frequently been praised by his coaches and teachers for his leadership abilities. Furthermore, people just naturally "looked up to him."

After graduation from college, Doug decided to seek employment at a relatively small firm with the potential for growth, rather than a larger organization. He felt that this type of company would present him with the greatest opportunities both in sales and in management. He looked forward to the challenges this job would present, but in the back of his mind, he worried whether he would be able to handle them. This would be the first time in his life that athletics was not a part of his image. He wondered whether people would still like him and whether he would be able to make it when he was no longer a "football hero."

Experiences As a Sales Associate

While it was something of a struggle at times, Doug became a fairly successful salesperson at Lake City Realty. He worked hard to learn all he could about the business and found that he often earned praise from his boss. Both clients and other sales associates said that they liked working with Doug. His customers said they felt that Doug really cared about them, and his fellow sales associates often sought his advice on matters of concern to them. As one of his peers remarked, "Doug was always willing to lend a sympathetic ear, no matter what the problem."

Even though Doug had apparently succeeded as a sales associate and was even well liked by those with whom he worked, he often felt that he was not as successful as everyone said he was. He feared that one day, he would not be able to live up to the expectations others had for him. He feared that one day he would just "blow a sale" because he did something wrong or look foolish because he didn't know the answer to a very basic question about the property being sold. He also feared that one day he might give one of his work friends the wrong advice, thereby destroying the friendship which he greatly valued.

While such fears were always in the back of his mind, Doug did become a successful sales associate who legitimately earned the praise of his peers, superiors, and customers.

Doug's Promotion to Branch Manager

Five years after Doug entered Lake City Realty, he was promoted to branch manager. Doug's interpersonal skills seemed to make him an ideal candidate for this position. However, the president was concerned that Doug might not have the technical skills necessary to perform the administrative side of his new position. The president voiced this concern to Doug, and Doug assured him that he could handle that aspect of his new position.

Doug devoted a great deal of energy in the first few months of his managerial career to learning how to be a "good manager." He was particularly concerned with developing the administrative skills he would need to accomplish this goal. It was also important to him in his new position that he remain on a friendly basis with his employees, so he devoted a great deal of energy to helping his subordinates deal with their work-related and personal problems.

A few months after Doug assumed his new role, the president called him in to say that he was "very happy" with Doug's performance. Doug's hard work and dedication had apparently paid off. He was seen as competent at recruiting and training sales associates in the skills necessary to be successful in their jobs. He was also viewed as successful in meeting the administrative requirements of his role, such as planning, budgeting, and evaluating employees. Doug seemed to have a good relationship with his sales force, and the performance of his branch, in terms of revenues, was slowly becoming one of the best in the company. Doug seemed to have what it took to be an effective manager. Even in the face of success, however, he was uncomfortable. He could not believe that he was really as good as the president said he was.

Doug became particularly worried about his own abilities as a manager when, during his second year as a branch manager, the president asked him if he would assume the manager's position for one of the two new branches the firm was acquiring. The new position would present Doug with new challenges, since he would have to start from ground zero in terms of staffing the branch and developing a sales force. It meant that he would have to leave the branch which he was now managing quite successfully.

The challenge to achieve new heights in management was tempting, but Doug also felt a little apprehensive: he feared that he might not be able to handle the responsibilities. He decided that the challenge presented by the new position far outweighed his fears, so he accepted the position and moved into the new Main Street branch of Lake City Realty.

As manager of the new branch, Doug was again a success. He worked long and hard, and within six months, he had the office fully staffed with both new as well as experienced sales associates whom he had recruited. Revenues were increasing practically weekly, and it appeared that the branch would show a profit by the end of the year. The sales associates were working well together, and the president was again pleased with Doug's progress.

Promotion to "Manager of Managers"

Three years after Doug assumed the role of manager of the Main Street branch, the president decided to implement a new organization structure. In this new structure, there would be two regional managers, each with the responsibility for supervising the managers of six branches. The president felt that the most likely candidates for these positions would be people with highly developed interpersonal skills who could act as liaisons between top management and the branch managers. The president thought, "Doug is someone with these skills."

The president summoned Doug to his office and explained that the new job would be one in which Doug would be "managing managers." He would be responsible for working closely with branch managers to ensure that they were meeting or exceeding their goals. The president cautioned Doug that this management position would be very different from the kind he had been accustomed to, since he would no longer be involved in the day-to-day operations of the branch offices.

Doug weighed the costs and benefits of this move. Again, the position sounded challenging, but somehow Doug feared that he was not completely capable of handling the responsibilities it involved. After all, he knew nothing about the skills needed to manage managers. He was apprehensive, but decided that he wanted the position. He told the president that he wanted the position and added, "I know that I can handle it." However, he secretly wondered whether or not he could.

According to the president's directive, one of Doug's first duties as a regional manager was to introduce Management by Objectives to the branch managers, as a way of increasing their accountability. Unfortunately, this was not an easy process, since most branch managers were not accustomed to being held accountable for their actions and greatly resisted this change in procedures.

Doug knew that he would be evaluated on his ability to motivate branch managers to adopt this new method, so he wanted to work very hard to achieve this goal. He attempted to counter the resistance he was given by meeting with each branch manager individually. The purpose of these meetings was to outline "branch plans" on which the managers would be evaluated and to discuss any difficulties that the managers were having. The format for these sessions was a "friendly discussion," during which Doug listened and responded to each manager's problems and then provided them with a series of directions for beginning the implementation of the program outlined, given their particular problems.

Doug worried that the managers "weren't getting it," but he was doing the best he could. After all, he couldn't do the managers' jobs for them. Unfortunately, Doug found that more often than not, the managers were not making progress in the direction which had been agreed upon at their meetings with him. In these cases, managers would often say, "I didn't know that we had agreed on my doing that. I thought that we were just talking and that I had the freedom to act as I felt necessary." Whenever this occurred, Doug would again review the branch plan with the manager and attempt to resolve any problems the manager was having. He made an effort to draw upon everything he had learned from his previous experiences about being a good manager.

Doug hoped that the problems he was having would be resolved, but felt uncomfortable because he didn't know how to handle the conflict situations these managers were placing him in. What the president called Doug's "business over lunch" style of management was ineffective in resolving these conflicts. It was not helping improve his region's performance and actually might have been detracting from it.

Over the course of the next year, Doug spent many sleepless nights worrying about how to improve the performance of his region. He met with managers frequently, but nothing he did seemed to make a difference. He believed that he was doomed to failure. Fortunately, the president recognized that Doug was having problems, and after a year, he called him in to discuss them. The president said, "Doug, I am unhappy with what's occurring in your region, and I'm sure you are, too. Performance is poor and morale is low. I also understand that you've been having difficulties with some of the managers. Tell me about it."

Doug replied, "I just can't seem to motivate them to use the MBO approach. They have goals, but they are not meeting them. I have had numerous individual meetings with each manager to discuss problems and outline a plan of action to resolve them. The managers go back to their branches and immediately abandon whatever we've talked about. Then, they make excuses like, 'I didn't know that I was supposed to do that.' "

The president told Doug that he was aware of this lack of follow-through on the branch managers' parts, but that he was also aware of Doug's own lack of follow-through. The president reminded Doug of his memo which told the president that Tammy Fuller, manager of the Elm Street branch, would be terminated if her branch's performance did not improve. The memo had been received nearly nine months ago. The branch's performance had not improved, but Doug had not terminated the manager. "You cannot manage by making idle threats," the president said. "People need to know that you mean what you say and that you will follow through on plans and agreements you make."

Doug replied that he had just wanted to give people a fair chance to better themselves. "Perhaps," he said, "this philosophy has caused me to be too lenient in providing direction and evaluation." He told the president that he would improve the region's performance within the year. On the inside, however, he wasn't so sure that he would be able to accomplish this.

The next few months were very stressful. Doug tried to be "tough" while devoting more effort to ensuring that managers understood what their own problems were and how to resolve them. In so doing, he began to forcefully impress upon branch managers what the consequences would be of their continued unwillingness to meet their goals.

The Aftermath

Unfortunately, Doug's good intentions seemed to have little impact on the region's performance. In fact, they only seemed to worsen the relationships between Doug and the branch managers and to lower morale even further. The managers felt that now Doug was trying to "bully them" into better performance by using threats. These threats were often ignored, since many managers believed that Doug would still not be able to follow through on what he said he would do. The managers also began to find ways to place the blame for poor performance on Doug's shoulders. Some managers even went to see the president with complaints that Doug's style of management was the source of low morale and low performance in the region. It appeared that Doug was about to be revealed as the failure that he believed himself to be.

A year after the president's meeting with Doug to discuss his problems, the president felt the need for another meeting. Neither the region's performance nor Doug's relationship with the branch managers was improving. Doug knew this and had already decided to resign before he went into the meeting. Doug began with: "I know what I'm here for. My region is still performing poorly, and morale is lower than it was last year. I have tried everything that I can think of, but nothing seems to work. I guess I'm just not cut out to be a regional manager. I want to resign."

The president said that he agreed with Doug's evaluation. He also said that he felt that with his interpersonal skills, Doug was a valuable asset to the company, and that he wanted him to remain with the firm. "I have a branch manager's position open and I'd really like you to take it," the president said. "You and I both know that you are the best person for the job."

Doug agreed that his skills as a branch manager were very well developed. He remembered how much he had liked his job as a branch manager and what a struggle the last two years had been. He did not like the idea of being "demoted," but he did not want to leave the company that he had devoted so much of his working life to. After some thought about the costs and benefits of remaining with the company, Doug decided it would be best to accept the offer and began to look forward to the responsibilities of his "new" old job.

How Doug Perry's Inner Game Playing Led to His Failure

Doug Perry could not see himself as a "success" in either the technical or the interpersonal aspects of his job, because he was predisposed to think of himself as a failure. While on the outside he appeared to fight for recognition of these skills, on the inside, he never felt successful. He suffered from the Ugly Duckling Syndrome.

Doug was successful as a branch manager because his subordinates liked and respected him. He was able to motivate them by a kind of charismatic leadership that he did not even know he possessed. His subordinates looked up to him, and if he asked them to do something (that is, delegated a task to them), they did it because they believed that he knew how to make both the branch and its employees successful. Even though Doug's branch and its personnel were indeed successful, he still believed that he was doomed to failure.

When he became a regional manager, the promotion represented another opportunity to reveal his true identity as a failure. The likelihood of this failure was increased, somewhat, by the high conflict situation in which Doug found himself upon his promotion: his primary responsibility was to motivate branch managers to adopt a managerial practice that they disliked. Doug began attacking this problem by using the same methods that had worked for him when he was a branch manager: he simply asked branch managers to make the change and provided suggestions for ways in which they might accomplish it. When problems developed, he listened to the branch managers' explanations and helped design solutions. Unfortunately, in this new situation, his strategy did not meet with success. Branch managers did not make the needed change; in fact, they began to walk all over him. Doug could not adopt the mindset he needed to be successful as a regional manager, because he subconsciously wanted, and perhaps even expected, to fail.

When Doug realized that he was having problems, he decided to quit. This is a typical response for Ugly Ducklings, as it represents the ultimate admission of failure. The action tells the world: "You expected too much from me, and I was not capable of living up to those high expectations. I am a failure, and this proves it."

Even though, in some respects, such recognition of failure fulfills the need of Ugly Ducklings to be recognized for what they believe themselves to be, we contend that many very competent people fail in management positions because they falsely believe they must fail. Failure becomes a self-fulfilling prophecy so that every action is subconsciously aimed at this goal. We are convinced that such failure can be prevented if individuals learn to play the Inner Game of Management effectively. In the next section, we will summarize the steps necessary to avoid or overcome the problems associated with playing the Inner Game by the rules of the Superperson or the Ugly Duckling Syndrome.

Overcoming the Problems Associated with the Impostor Syndromes

In this chapter, we have discussed two very different, but related Impostor Syndromes: the Superperson and the Ugly Duckling. Both syndromes result from a discrepancy between how people view themselves and how others perceive them. It is the resolution of this discrepancy, in favor of either one's own or others' perceptions, that produces the Superperson Syndrome on the one hand and the Ugly Duckling Syndrome on the other. In order to play the Inner Game of Management effectively and thus overcome these syndromes, individuals must learn to satisfy their self-esteem needs through the requirements of their organizational roles.

For Superpeople, this means developing the ability to feel comfortable in a role that may be ill-defined; learning to make decisions in a timely fashion and not constantly fearing that they will make mistakes; and accepting that they do not have to be the best performer, but that they should strive to be "the best manager." Perhaps the most important lesson Superpeople need to learn is that it is all right to make mistakes.

How can a victim of the Superperson Syndrome accomplish these changes? Since Superpeople are afraid of failure, the basic strategy is to reduce the risk of failure. One method of accomplishing this is to ask their superiors about the criteria that will be used to evaluate them. If Superpeople know how they will be evaluated, they may feel less anxiety and therefore be able to overcome the tendency to do everything themselves. Supervisors of Superpeople, then, can help their subordinates by advising them that they will be evaluated on their managerial effectiveness rather than on their ability to actually perform a task.

Superpeople also have a tendency to procrastinate because they fear making mistakes. To overcome this tendency, they should practice making decisions in a timely fashion. Management development programs can help Superpeople develop these skills by providing case-oriented training in making decisions rapidly.

A Superperson also typically has a problem of self-flagellation when he or she makes mistakes. Accordingly, Superpeople need to learn not to beat themselves up after making mistakes. Supervisors can help here, too, by not criticizing a Superperson, but providing support and stating that the person is a valued employee.

In brief, the underlying drive for Superpeople is to be the best at whatever they do. Accordingly, they need to focus on becoming the best managers, rather than continuing to try to be the best doers. It will help them to find out the parameters of the job that will be used in their evaluation, and also to learn how to make timely decisions. The bottom line is that they must learn to be comfortable with making mistakes. Mistakes cannot be avoided, and Superpeople must give themselves permission to occasionally make a mistake. To do this, they must learn to evaluate themselves on their "batting average." A batting average is the percentage of successful performance, and no sport or task requires a perfect batting average. A Superperson must learn to accept this notion.

Unlike Superpeople, Ugly Ducklings need to *improve* their sense of self-worth and feel more confident of themselves and their abilities. They need to learn how to be effective decision makers. For some individuals this may mean waiting until all relevant information is in before acting, while for others it may mean trying to make decisions without superiors' or subordinates' input. Ugly Ducklings also need to learn to feel comfortable praising their subordinates for good performance. Most important, Ugly Ducklings must find ways to overcome their belief that they are failures and to accept others' evaluations as reality.

To make these changes, Ugly Ducklings must practice looking for the positive things they have accomplished. This can be as simple as listing accomplishments. Ugly Ducklings also need to avoid the tendency to minimize whatever they do. One way to do this is to make a list of goals they want to accomplish, and make sure that they'll feel satisfied if the goals set are actually achieved. Then, Ugly Ducklings should evaluate whether the goals have been accomplished. If so, they need to learn to allow themselves to be pleased with what they have accomplished. In brief, Ugly Ducklings need to learn to enjoy their success.

Ugly Ducklings also need to practice providing constructive criticism as well as praise to subordinates. Both are necessary if they want to motivate subordinates and be effective leaders. They need to find something to praise in a subordinate's work and talk to the person about it. Similarly, they need to identify things in people's work that could be improved and then talk to them about it. After such encounters with subordinates, Ugly Ducklings should evaluate the interaction and their own feelings about it. This will help them feel more comfortable the next time such situations present themselves.

Ugly Ducklings also need to learn to be more assertive about what they want people to do. This involves feeling comfortable exercising control. Accordingly, an Ugly Duckling should practice asking people to do things and, if they do not perform, practice giving constructive feedback.

Superpeople's and Ugly Ducklings' abilities to play the Inner Game are also impaired because they are unable to satisfy their control needs through their managerial roles. Superpeople need to learn to give up a certain amount of control to their subordinates and to accept less than "perfect" performance. Ugly Ducklings need to learn to take more control as managers. Superpeople need to learn how to delegate tasks to subordinates, while Ugly Ducklings need to learn what tasks are appropriate for them to perform themselves.

Recognizing that these problems exist is the first step. Once they acknowledge their problems, Superpeople and Ugly Ducklings can develop strategies that will change them from Impostors into Inner Game Masters.

Chapter 4
The Godfather Syndrome

In his classic novel *The Godfather*, Mario Puzo presents the story of Don Vito Corleone, an Italian immigrant who rises to a position of great power in the criminal underworld. Vito Corleone was a "Godfather" to all the people in his sphere, in the sense that they could turn to him when they needed help. All that was required to get his assistance was that the applicant proclaim his "friendship." This proclamation meant that the applicant openly expressed his indebtedness to the Godfather. It also meant, however, that the applicant, by his very request of the great man's favor, *acknowledged* that he was personally less powerful than the Godfather and, therefore, required his protection as well as his favor.

The very setting in which requests for favors were received, as well as the manner in which they were received, served to communicate and reinforce this implicit acknowledgment of inferiority and submission on the part of the applicant. So long as the applicant was properly "respectful" of the Godfather, the Godfather would be generous. Indeed, he would let little or nothing stand in his way of solving a man's problem.

In brief, the Godfather required submission and acknowledgment of his power and superiority in return for his patronage and personal generosity. When a person failed to be submissive or properly respectful, the Godfather would be angered and treat the individual with contempt. He might even try to humiliate the individual as a way of forcing him into submission. In Puzo's novel, for example, Amerigo Bonaseras, the undertaker, is reluctant to become indebted to the Godfather and is therefore treated with coldness and subtle hostility by Don Vito Corleone. Finally, Bonaseras quite literally bows his head and murmurs: "Be my friend. I accept." In making the statement "I accept," Bonaseras explicitly acknowledges that he has now accepted Don Corleone as "El Patron," or Godfather.

As illustrated in this case, Vito Corleone was very skilled at controlling people by making them dependent on him. This is symbolized by the jacket of Puzo's novel, on which the Godfather is depicted as the person "pulling the strings" of people as though they were mere puppets. Vito Corleone was able to control people in this fashion by putting them in positions in which they had to acknowledge his power and superiority and thus could not or would not challenge him. If a person was not submissive or properly respectful, the individual was eliminated from Vito Corleone's organization. This threat of punishment or exile was enough to keep even people like Luca Brasi, the Godfather's "strong man," under Vito Corleone's control.

Puzo describes the relationship between the Godfather and Brasi in the following passage: "The Don received Brasi as a king greets a subject who has done him an enormous service, never familiar but with regal respect. With every gesture, with every word, Don Corleone made it clear to Luca Brasi that he was *valued*."[1] However, in spite of his value to the Godfather, Brasi made Vito Corleone somewhat nervous. As Puzo states: "The man was like a natural force, not truly subject to control. He had to be handled as gingerly as dynamite. The Don shrugged. Even dynamite could be exploded harmlessly if the need arose."[2] In brief, the Godfather required all his people, regardless of their value to him, to be subject to his control. Even a Luca Brasi, a pillar of his strength, needed to be loyal and subject to his control or he would be eliminated.

The Godfather Game That Managers Play

Although Vito Corleone is a fictional character, there are many examples of Godfathers in legitimate business.[3] At the surface level, a Godfather is anyone with power who has the ability to reward or punish others at his or her whim. In the case of Vito Corleone, this involved matters of life and death. In the typical business case, it involves matters of people's self-esteem and their livelihood. Even in the latter case, it is significant power indeed.

[1] *The Godfather* (New York: Signet, 1969), p. 25.
[2] Ibid, p. 26.
[3] Although this chapter deals principally with male Godfathers, the reader should be aware that there are also women who suffer from this syndrome.

Underlying this image of significant power, however, is a deep-seated insecurity. Individuals who suffer from the Godfather Syndrome may believe themselves to be unworthy, or they may simply see themselves as possessing some weakness which, if revealed to the outside world, could be exploited by others to "destroy them." In an effort to reduce their insecurity, Godfathers develop strategies for increasing others' dependency on them for satisfaction of their needs. This dependency results in Godfathers being able to control others' fates through rewards, the withholding of rewards, or punishment. It is through such control that the Godfather is able to compensate for his own feelings of inadequacy. Such control also decreases the threat that the Godfather's perceived weaknesses will be revealed.

For these reasons, then, Godfathers are "into" control over people with a vengeance. At one extreme, they merely want to pull people's strings to remain in control as a means of self-protection; at the other end of the continuum, however, these managers are addicted to control because they like to humiliate people as a way to decrease their own feelings of inadequacy.

This need for control leads Godfathers to insist that their subordinates acknowledge their superiority. To ensure that this occurs, they develop two basic strategies. The first involves hiring weak people or maintaining people on the payroll who are loyal to the Godfather but not highly competent. In this case, the Godfather is able to exercise a great deal of control because these individuals respect his ability and look to him for direction. The second strategy involves hiring people with good credentials whom the Godfather wants to "own." By hiring strong people and by being able to control them, the Godfather can show, by implication, that he is a significant person.

Whatever type of subordinate the Godfather has, however, the only reward he expects in exchange for providing services to others is that they openly express their loyalty and respect for his power. This serves three purposes. First, such expression serves to increase the Godfather's sense of self-worth, because it shows how important he is in others' lives. Second, if the Godfather has loyal subordinates, the chances are minimized that the inadequacies he is trying to hide will be revealed. Finally, by having loyal subordinates, the Godfather is able to provide himself with strong protection from outsiders who may attempt to injure him. In essence, loyal subordinates act as buffers against an outside world which the Godfather perceives as extremely hostile.

The Godfather, in fact, views all people as potential enemies (as able to reveal his inadequacies) until they prove otherwise. Thus, he is seen as secretive and may be described by others as someone who is difficult to know. Something about him always eludes his subordinates, and this increases his unpredictability, keeping them off balance. Those who work under and with him are never sure what to expect and may fear that they will inadvertently injure him in some way and draw his wrath. For the Godfather, however, hiding "behind a veil" is an effective strategy, because it prevents subordinates and any potential enemies from consolidating too much power. Thus, the threat to his power and position is minimized. He is able to protect his inadequacies from being revealed, while at the same time satisfying his need for control.

Variations of the Godfather Theme

Thus far in this chapter we have described a generic Godfather. There are, however, two basic types of Godfathers: the Malevolent Godfather and the Caretaker Godfather. We will now describe each type.

The Malevolent Godfather

The person who suffers from this version of the Godfather Syndrome is the type of individual most people associate with Mafia chieftains. These people play to win and are ruthless in their dealings with both their friends and their enemies. They believe that all people are "worthless" and seek to prove this by steadily humiliating and degrading the people over whom they have control.

This type of Godfather may be charming and able to court people to join him when he wishes. However, there is a perverse twist to this very process: the very act of "acquiring" a person leads this Godfather to devalue that person. The rationale is similar to the classic Groucho Marx quip: "I would never want to join a club that would have me for a member."

Once the Malevolent Godfather has acquired people, however, he derives a great deal of amusement from playing with them. He likes to pit people against one another in a sort of "organizational chess" game and then watch what happens, never really caring what the outcome is. The "game" is all that matters.

The Malevolent Godfather is an angry person, and the anger is deeply seated in his personality. Although there are often similarities in some of the surface behaviors of the Malevolent Godfather and the Caretaker Godfather, the major difference is in their motives, as you will see by comparing the following case with that of Walter Polk, the Caretaker Godfather (to be described later in this chapter).

Conrad MacArthur: The Malevolent Godfather

Conrad MacArthur was the president of a manufacturing company which he had built from virtually nothing to more than $500 million in annual revenues in less than a decade.

"Connie" was a self-made man who had considerable personal force and who could be charming when he wished. He had not attended college and, as a result, was ambivalent about education. Connie began his career as an insurance salesman for a major life insurance company and had considerable success at sales and later at sales management. He had easily been a $10-million producer. After a few years, Connie had the opportunity to buy a company with a unique product in the emerging electronics industry. Even though he personally knew little about the industry, his firm was an immediate success.

In a few years, Connie became a very wealthy man who acquired all the trappings of wealth: a home in the suburbs and a vacation home in Palm Springs, California; several cars, including a Rolls, a Porsche, and a Mercedes, as well as two antique cars; winter trips to California and summer trips to Europe.

Along with a home and cars, however, Connie also liked the fact that he had "acquired" people to help him build his company to $1 billion. He obtained several "advisers" who were eminent men in their own right; he attracted these people by offering them extremely lucrative positions on his board of directors. He also hired a number of "heavyweight" managers, who came with good reputations and very high salaries. Connie was generous; he typically paid salaries that were 50 percent higher than what even these well-regarded people could earn elsewhere. All of his advisers and managers were clearly overpaid. But there was a deeper motive than mere generosity. Connie wanted to "own" these men.

He enjoyed the fact that someone like him, a person who had not graduated from college and who had been an "insurance peddler," could now hire—and fire—lawyers, CPAs, consultants, and former presidents of major corporations. In fact, as a way of emphasizing the power he had over others, Connie was known to "make people carry his bags." In other words, he made people perform petty services for him as a subtle means of degrading them. His request might be as simple as fetching something he had forgotten, to literally having an executive carry his suitcase at an airport. Although it is always a complex task to assess someone's underlying motives, a number of Connie's associates perceived that there was more to his requests than the request per se.

Connie also enjoyed playing organizational chess with his people. He tended to distrust people, so he played them off against each other. He typically used a one-on-one style to meet with people and get information about operations and other people. The information acquired at these meetings could then be used to increase his influence over people, or at the minimum, to help bring employees into the "war game" that he staged for his own amusement.

While Connie, for the most part, felt in control of his company, he was nonetheless uncomfortable in large meetings. At these gatherings, he tended to become somewhat stiff and formal, but was also known to explode if things displeased him. Connie was an earthy man who, when he "went nuclear," peppered people with expletives. A number of the very good people Connie had recruited left the company because they would not tolerate this verbal abuse, but a greater number stayed. They tended to figure out what set Connie off and avoid it as far as possible.

Connie was also known to take occasional "shots" at people in meetings. He seemed to select first one person and then another, almost at random. There was, however, a subtle pattern to his attacks: they were intended to keep people off balance. He kept after people so long as they put up a defense or fought back, but if an individual indicated weakness or submission, Connie did not press his assault.

The result of this management style was an extremely fragmented, highly political organization. People tried to "psych out" Connie, but he was smart enough to continue to be relatively unpredictable.

In spite of these tactics, Connie had developed strong loyalty among a large number of his staff members. Since the company was successful, he could reward people generously with bonuses and salary increases. People were encouraged to travel first class, and the company had lavish banquets and dinners. Connie took good care of "his people."

Unfortunately, the company was strong in one sense but not in another. Since the company had been first to market its product and the product was a success, it prospered in spite of its day-to-day mismanagement. While the market was strong, business practices did not seem to matter. However, as the market for the product matured and competitors brought out "knock-off" versions of the product, the company's underlying strength began to erode.

Although Connie hired people in engineering, research, and manufacturing and spent lavishly on research and development with great fanfare, the organization moved very slowly. A few minor products were developed, but nothing of consequence grew out of these efforts.

Still flush from his company's earlier success, Connie decided to buy other companies that had developed new products but that lacked the capital necessary to manufacture and market their developments. He hired an acquisitions specialist to put deals together. Again, the company spent lavishly, and a few good products were acquired.

The politics of the company, however, worked against effectively capitalizing on the new acquisitions. Since people were pitted against each other, they tended to focus on the things that would benefit them personally rather than on the things that would benefit the company as a whole. They did not cooperate and play as members of a team.

Ultimately, even Connie's "war chest" of resources began to empty. The banks, which had willingly lent Connie many millions of dollars on his way up, moved in and took over the company.

Connie resigned "to pursue other interests." The game was over. Conrad MacArthur, who had experienced meteoric success, now experienced meteoric failure because he had failed to master the Inner Game of Management.

How Conrad MacArthur's Inner Game Playing Led to his Failure

Although he was certainly not a Mafia chieftain, Conrad MacArthur had a great deal in common with Vito Corleone. Connie had fallen into the Godfather Syndrome, in which he was more concerned with pulling the strings of his people than in really building and managing his firm as an organization.

Connie fell into the Godfather Syndrome trap of winnowing out strong people. Instead of trying his best to staff his company with the strongest possible people, Connie "bought" people who had the right credentials but who were, in reality, submissive to him. The really strong people, who refused (explicitly or implicitly) to submit to his abuse (which was indeed a ritual of submission), left the company. Those who remained did so because they were compensated generously—but since they remained for financial reasons, they tended not to jeopardize their situations by confronting Connie or taking any risks. This led to inaction throughout the company, and although the company looked strong to the outside world, that was actually a facade.

Connie also fell into another trap of the Godfather Syndrome: he tended to reward loyalty and respect rather than competence. This meant that the company had a large number of trusted and loyal people who actually did very little that was productive. Since these employees were well aware of their own lack of productivity, they tended to discredit the real workers in the company, and many of the latter became demoralized. The company drifted into indolence. Productivity, rather than being rewarded, was actually punished, because productive people were a threat to the political pals.

All these aspects of the Godfather Syndrome can be viewed as a defensive strategy on the part of Conrad MacArthur. The wisdom of the strategy may be debatable, but it is at least an understandable strategy.

There is, however, another, darker side to Connie's behavior as a Godfather that had a great effect on his Inner Game of Management. Unlike Vito Corleone, Conrad MacArthur seemed to enjoy his power over others as an end in itself. Specifically, he seemed to derive a deep pleasure from humiliating people. This was reflected, for example, in the gratuitous "shots" he took at people in meetings. He rationalized that he was simply keeping people off balance, but in fact, he enjoyed watching people squirm.

The Caretaker Godfather

Compared to the Malevolent Godfather, the Caretaker Godfather is relatively benign. His basic need and motive is to care for his people. He is like a benevolent autocrat, or parental figure.

The Caretaker Godfather is a strong person to whom others naturally look for help and support. This Godfather enjoys providing this assistance in return for people's acknowledgment of his capacity to provide, of his generosity, and of his strength. He is, in effect, the classic "good provider" for his family.

This type of Godfather does not necessarily want to humiliate people, and he may only inadvertently make them dependent upon him. He is merely being strong for them and providing what they tell him they need.

The people who depend on the Caretaker Godfather benefit from his support, while he, in turn, derives satisfaction from being a caretaker of others. It satisfies his sense of self-esteem to be valued for his ability to provide for others. If, however, this type of Godfather comes to believe that his people are not giving him proper respect, or if he believes that, even though he is providing them with ample resources to satisfy their needs, they are still not loyal to him, he will feel betrayed and will lash out at those who have betrayed him. In essence, the actions of others can be responsible for transforming the once benign Caretaker Godfather into an angry Malevolent Godfather.

Vito Corleone, the Godfather of Mario Puzo's novel, was, despite his criminal nature, a relatively benign Godfather. His central concern was to provide for his family. Similarly, benign Godfathers can be found in many business organizations, as you will see in the following case study.

Walter Polk: Corporate President

Walter Polk had grown up in the home-improvement business. Over the years, he had witnessed the industry's ups and downs. On a personal level, however, it seemed that life only continued to get better.

Walt was 20 years old when Apex, Inc., hired him, but he soon became one of the company's top young salespeople. For someone his age, he was making a very comfortable living. His success extended into his personal life. During his third year with Apex, Walt married and purchased his first home.

Although he never became the number-one salesperson, Walt's abilities did not go unnoticed by Apex. Four years after coming to Apex, Walt was promoted to store manager. During that same year, he also became a father for the first time.

Experiences As a Store Manager

Walt made the transition from salesperson to store manager with little difficulty. One reason for this may have been his experience in the home-improvement business—his technical knowhow—but another may have been the fact that he was the type of person people just naturally liked. His subordinates liked him because they knew that they could turn to him whenever they needed help with a personal or technical problem. In Walt's eyes, his salespeople were much like the children he had at home. He wanted to be a "father" to them, yet he also wanted them to learn what to do when left on their own. He didn't mind, however, helping them whenever they came to him with questions or problems, which they often did.

Walt's style of management seemed well-suited for the organization in which he was working. His store traditionally had one of the highest sales records and lowest turnovers. People liked working for him, and the company considered him a valuable part of the organization.

Although Walt was satisfied with his job as store manager at Apex, he was aware that there were other challenges to be met. In 1970, he was asked to join Bailey Home Stores as a regional manager. Working for Bailey appealed to Walt: it was a well-respected local firm that was just beginning to expand its operations. The job at Bailey represented a challenge: unlike at Apex, there was room for Walt to make a "real" contribution in shaping what the firm was going to become. Walt thought, "There are many opportunities in such a firm, and I want to take advantage of them."

Walt Leaves Apex for Bailey Home Stores

With some regret, Walt resigned from his post at Apex and began as a regional manager at Bailey. Bailey Home Stores could not have recruited a person more suited for its style of management. It considered itself a "family" where everyone knew everyone else and where people looked to their managers for direction as if they were their fathers. Walt liked being in this position. He liked being a father both at home and on the job, and he was good at it.

Through his experience, he knew what was best for the stores he supervised, and he was willing to tell his employees what to do and how to do it. People readily accepted this style of management, since it was what they were accustomed to.

Walt's region became one of the most successful in the company. Revenues were high, and people seemed to like working for him. Other regional managers seemed to respect his managerial ability. In 1973, the board of directors chose to recognize Walt's successful management by offering him the presidency of the company. This was a dramatic step for a 34-year-old person to take, but Walt accepted the promotion with little hesitation.

Experiences As the President of an Entrepreneurial Company

As president, Walt assumed the role of "father" to all of the firm's employees. His roles as store manager and regional manager had prepared him to manage in this way—only now he would be responsible for more staff and have a greater number of people reporting to him. He was given the responsibility for making all decisions in the company, from day-to-day operations to long-range planning. He accepted this role and had confidence in his abilities to make the right decisions at the right time.

Walt soon found that he had to become even more directive than he had been in his position as branch manager, since he was now the company's ultimate decision maker and people depended on him more than ever. Although he was directive, he was directive in a "parental" way, as evidenced by the closeness that he seemed to have with all his employees. Walt had an open-door policy and welcomed the opportunity to talk with anyone who wanted or needed his advice. Employees liked this policy so much that even though store managers were assigned the responsibility of overseeing their individual stores, many salespeople felt more comfortable going to Walt with their problems. They knew that Walt would be sympathetic to their needs and expend a great deal of effort in helping them. Walt always seemed to know what to do, and people depended on him.

Unfortunately, the nature of the company began to change. At about the time that Walt was beginning to get accustomed to his role as president, the company began experiencing an unprecedented surge in growth. In a period of five years, revenues increased from $1 million to nearly $10 million and the number of employees increased from 50 to nearly 200. Neither Walt nor anyone else was prepared for the stress and strain on the company which the rapid growth caused. Walt was now faced with a company that, like a teenager, had become too "grown-up" to be told what to do.

Walt attempted to continue acting as the "father," but he was becoming increasingly frustrated with his inability to perform this role effectively. The firm had grown too large for him to oversee and control all of its operations. Too many decisions needed to be made quickly, and he did not always have the time to critically evaluate the information necessary to make rational decisions. When decisions were made, they were often made too slowly to be effective. Another problem was that Walt no longer had time to help people with their problems, and he felt that, somehow, he was neglecting his responsibility to the firm's employees. There were simply too many demands on his time. What was worse than the personal fatigue these demands were causing was the fact that the company was experiencing its own growing pains, which Walt felt could jeopardize its success.

Walt was frustrated with his inability to solve the company's and his personal problems. No one at Bailey seemed to know how to get out of the "rut" that they were operating in—a rut that could be fatal to their company. People were beginning to feel that Walt no longer cared for them, since he could no longer take a personal interest in everyone. Walt was beginning to feel that he had lost control of the firm, that he could no longer handle the responsibility entrusted to him, and that, perhaps, he was not the person to manage this firm any longer. "Perhaps," he thought, "the organization has outgrown me."

How Walter Polk's Inner Game Playing Created Problems

Walter Polk was a very typical Caretaker Godfather. He enjoyed and derived a great deal of satisfaction from being able to take care of people. He was able to find or create situations in which others would be dependent upon him, and it was in these situations that he satisfied his self-esteem needs. Further, this dependency gave him a great deal of control over others' fates and thus helped satisfy his needs for control.

People liked having Walt take care of them, and he liked doing it. This is because the subordinates of Caretaker Godfathers such as Walt truly believe (usually correctly) that the Godfather has only their best interests in mind. They believe that he knows what's best for them and are therefore very willing to follow his lead. They find that they can reap the most rewards in this fashion, and they really don't mind being under someone else's control, because their managers rarely "explode," as often happens in the case of Malevolent Godfathers.

Unfortunately, as illustrated in the Walter Polk case, the Caretaker Godfather style of management is most appropriate only in small firms; if a firm is successful and begins to grow, the Caretaker will soon find that he can no longer control everything and everyone in the firm. He begins to feel that he has lost control and is failing. His subordinates begin to lose faith in his ability to manage, because when he is looked to for direction, he is too slow to provide it or the direction he provides is inadequate, since he can no longer be aware of everything that is happening in his department or the firm.

It is at these critical junctures in the life of the firm and the lives of those managers who suffer from the Caretaker Godfather Syndrome that some vital changes must be made. We will discuss these changes in the final section of this chapter; but first we present a discussion of the organizational consequences of this syndrome.

Organizational Consequences
of the Godfather Syndrome

The consequences of the Godfather Syndrome go well beyond the personal indignities of the individuals who are subjected to it; there are also profound consequences on organizational effectiveness and competitiveness.

Organizations built by Godfather types are highly political firms. They are staffed by people whose primary criterion for selection is personal loyalty and submissiveness to the Godfather, rather than competence. They are organizations in which great amounts of energy are devoted to political infighting between people seeking the Godfather's favor. Such contests serve to keep people off balance and, in some cases, are staged by the Godfather for his personal amusement.

In effect, the organization built by a Godfather is his personal, private playground. Beyond a certain point, profit may not interest him. For example, one president of a company, who could afford whatever he wished, liked to be "entertained" by vendors seeking his favor. In return for lavish entertainments, he would purchase materials for his company. However, his purchases bore no relation to his company's needs, and it was estimated that the company's inventory of raw materials would last for 12½ years at the current rate of consumption—yet the Godfather was buying still more.

An organization built by a Godfather is also unlikely to have an orderly plan for management succession to replace the Godfather. Most Godfathers guard their organizational power with great care. Since they do not want to give up any of their power, they use a variety of defensive ploys to prevent any other potentially strong leader from emerging in the organization.

The Godfather may keep all his lieutenants separate so that only he understands the strategy of the total business. Another tactic is to set up a competition among several potential successors. The result is that all the rivals may destroy each other—or even if one does emerge as the victor, he will be bruised and have several bitter losers to contend with.

Yet another tactic is to appoint a series of heirs apparent and dispense with each after a few years. Since the potential rewards of the Godfather position are so great, it is usually not a problem to find a ready supply of eager aspirants. Still another ploy is to give the potential replacements for the Godfather enough rope to hang themselves as they perform high-risk tasks and jobs. The Godfather simply watches while the would-be successors disqualify themselves.

The net effect of all these ploys is to prevent the organization from developing and retaining strong managers other than the Godfather. Truly strong managers typically leave and go to other companies. This leaves the Godfather as the sole strongman in the firm, which is his objective. However, it also leaves the company vulnerable if he should fall ill or have an accident, or when he ultimately must be replaced.

Overcoming the Godfather Syndrome

Given the nature of the Godfather Syndrome, what can one do to overcome it? The central challenge in overcoming the Godfather Syndrome is to learn to manage the needs for self-esteem and control.

Self-Esteem Management

The Godfather is typically a very strong individual in his own right. Objectively, he does not really need to dominate everyone else within his sphere. The first challenge, then, is for the victim of this syndrome to recognize that being a powerful person does not necessarily mean dominating others. His self-esteem does not have to be linked to being seen as the strongest or most dominant person. Instead, the individual must learn to derive satisfaction from helping others grow stronger.

The Godfather tends to dominate people almost by reflex. He derives satisfaction from the *process* of domination as well as from the result—power. To overcome this syndrome, the Godfather must reverse the process. The Godfather must learn to accept the idea that his need for dominance is *not* an indication of true strength but a manifestation of underlying weakness and insecurity. Thus, the Godfather must recognize that his true strength will be manifest when he controls his own insecurities and suppresses the urge to dominate.

It must be recognized that overcoming the urge to dominate will be a probabilistic process; it cannot be managed by "turning a switch." The person trying to overcome the Godfather Syndrome is likely to "slip up" from time to time. However, if he is making progress in increasing the likelihood of controlling the need to dominate others, he should take pride in his increased self-mastery.

It is important for the Godfather to achieve self-acceptance. The person must learn to be comfortable with who he is and what *he* has achieved. He must avoid destructive comparisons with his subordinates. These people are *not* in competition with the Godfather; rather, the Godfather manager is in competition with them.

The process of achieving self-acceptance is extraordinarily complex; there is no simple formula. One essential ingredient in this process is to derive satisfaction from personal achievements. A step toward this can be as simple as preparing a list of accomplishments. As the list grows, so should the person's degree of self-worth. Since Godfathers are usually "numbers-oriented" people, they like to "keep score." Typically, they keep score by using organizational revenues, but we suggest that they include other achievements as well.

It is relatively easier for the Caretaker Godfather to overcome this syndrome than it is for the Malevolent Godfather to break free from it. The Caretaker truly cares for his people, and if he feels that he is weakening them by his behavior, he may be motivated to change in order to strengthen them. The Malevolent Godfather, on the other hand, gains a great deal of satisfaction from humiliating others; therefore, it is more difficult for him to give up his behavior.

In either case, if the Godfather's behavior is to change, the changes should be made in small increments. The fundamental change a Godfather must make is to decide that he is going to make his people grow stronger. He must then formulate a plan for their gradual development—a plan that has to include transferring increasing amounts of authority and power to them.

We are fairly pessimistic about the ability of the Malevolent Godfather to change his behavior, though change is not impossible. The underlying motives driving this type of Godfather relate to a relatively low sense of self-esteem, which in turn requires the humbling of others. The ultimate requirement for changing the behavior of this type of Godfather is a change in his level of self-esteem. The Godfather must learn to accept himself. He must learn to value himself for what he is and for what he has accomplished, not for his superiority and power over others. This is a difficult task, but it can be accomplished.

Managing the Need for Control

In addition to managing his need for esteem, the Godfather must learn to manage his control needs. If the need for control is mostly defensive, as for the Caretaker Godfather, it can gradually be diminished as his sense of self-esteem increases. However, if the need for control or manipulation is linked to a need to humiliate others (as is true of the Malevolent Godfather), it is unlikely to change.

In brief, since the Godfather has learned to control everything, he must now learn to give up control over things. To succeed in this, a Godfather should practice delegating things to people. This should include the delegation of tasks and authority. The Godfather should practice not interfering with the people to whom things have been delegated. One possible way to do this is for the Godfather to take a vacation and delegate things to people to do in his absence. After the vacation period, the Godfather can then stay away from the office and let people work on their own. Step by step, he can increase his comfort with less control.

Another way for a Godfather to get used to the idea of giving up control is to practice not going to all meetings. Moreover, he should practice not asking for information about everything. The objective is to learn to be comfortable with incomplete information.

In sum, to overcome the Godfather Syndrome, an individual must learn to manage his or her own self-esteem and the need for control in ways other than by dominating people. Godfathers are typically strong people, and they must learn to use their strength to manage their own needs.

Chapter 5
The Napoleon Syndrome

As the name of this syndrome implies, its distinguishing characteristics are derived from a profile of the Emperor Napoleon Bonaparte, who ruled France and most of Europe during the early 19th century.[1] Napoleon's ambition, it is said, was to become emperor of the entire world. He was a man driven by an intense need for control. He wanted to be seen as powerful in order to compensate for the fact that he felt physically inferior (because of his short stature) to other men. In other words, Napoleon suffered from an inferiority complex.

The term *inferiority complex* was coined by Alfred Adler,[2] a contemporary of Sigmund Freud, to describe the way people feel when they believe that they are somehow handicapped with regard to power. According to Adler, this feeling of inferiority is overcome through either "compensation" or "overcompensation." When a person tries to compensate for a perceived weakness, he or she takes constructive steps (such as taking classes to improve certain skills). Overcompensation, on the other hand, usually results in maladaptive behavior. The individual cannot accept himself or herself with the weakness and desperately tries to compensate for it by gaining superiority over others. In fact, this desire may be so intense that it becomes the driving force in the person's life.

[1] For a discussion of Napoleon's life, see J. N. Larned, "Napoleon: A Prodigy Without Greatness," in *A Study of Greatness in Men* (New York: Houghton Mifflin, 1911).
[2] For a description of Adler's theories, see H. L. Ansbacher and R. R. Ansbacher (Eds.), *The Individual Psychology of Alfred Adler: A Systematic Presentation in Selections from His Writing* (New York: Harper & Row, 1956).

Napoleon was a classic sufferer of an inferiority complex. Throughout his life, he attempted to compensate for his weakness (his small stature) by gaining and using power over others. In his quest, he had no concern for others: they were useful to him only as creatures who openly recognized his success. In fact, he often created situations where individuals would have no choice but to overtly acknowledge his superiority. Whenever he held sessions with his advisers, for example, he always sat while requiring them to stand. He also required that all those in his presence, even his wife, address him as "Your Majesty." He went so far as to falsify history in order to glorify himself, and formed an educational system whose primary goal was to teach children about the Emperor's greatness and their need to be obedient to his wishes. He came to believe that he was invincible, and even in exile he still forced his court members to perform services for him which showed that they respected his authority.

The Napoleon Syndrome in Management

Some managers play the Inner Game of Management by the rules of what we have described as the Napoleon Syndrome. While these managers are certainly not "kings," they do tend to behave in some ways much like Napoleon Bonaparte did. Their intense need to be recognized as powerful causes these individuals to play the Inner Game of Management ineffectively, and unless they recognize that they have problems, they, like Napoleon, will meet their Waterloos.

The Napoleon Syndrome is closely related to the Godfather Syndrome, described in the last chapter. Like the Godfather, individuals who suffer from this syndrome have high needs for control and low self-esteem. They want to have power over others, but unlike the Godfather, they do not relish "taking care" of others. Their self-esteem is so low that they must focus all their effort on satisfying their own needs; hence, they do not care about what others need. Consequently, like the Malevolent Godfather, they can be very abusive to others. While this abuse is tolerated by those whom the Godfather "controls" because benefits accrue to those who tolerate it, the Napoleon's abuse of subordinates eventually results in his or her downfall because they will no longer subject themselves to the abuse. In other words, the Godfather motivates people through both rewards and threats of punishment, while the Napoleon uses only coercion to "keep subordinates in line."

For whatever reason, Napoleons feel weak and inadequate when compared to other people. These feelings of inadequacy often have their basis in real or imagined physical shortcomings (say, short stature or a speech impairment). However, some people who display this syndrome do not have an obvious weakness. In the latter case, the stimulus for this syndrome is largely psychological.

The feelings of inadequacy that produce this syndrome are usually developed in childhood. As a result, Napoleons devote a great deal of their lives to achieving positions of authority which they believe will allow them to fully compensate for the low self-esteem they feel. The managerial position, because it carries with it a great deal of legitimate authority, represents a prize in these individuals' eyes. They feel that in such positions they can begin to exercise a great deal of control over others and gain their respect.

Managers who suffer from the Napoleon Syndrome bask in the glory of holding a position where they can wield power over others. These managers like to create situations that allow them to keep subordinates "in their places." This usually involves, in one way or another, subtle or blatant threats of retaliation against those who don't follow the Napoleon's directives. Whether or not the Napoleon is able to really carry out these threats is irrelevant. The point is that he or she is able to create situations in which subordinates are led to *believe* that the manager will actually do what he or she is threatening. These beliefs are fostered through the use of several strategies intended to buffer Napoleons from the outside world so that they will not be revealed for the tyrants they really are.

One such strategy is to hide behind a facade of caring. Napoleons will say to their subordinates, "This is what's best for you," but in reality, they do not care whether or not it's good for their subordinates. What is more important is whether or not the proposed course of action will benefit the Napoleon. Subordinates sense this lack of real caring, but are usually unable to articulate it because they fear that challenging their superior may have adverse consequences.

Another strategy Napoleons may use is to surround themselves with "weak" people. They exploit subordinates' weaknesses to increase their sense of self-worth and levels of control. Through emphasizing others' weaknesses, Napoleons are able to appear stronger themselves. Further, because subordinates' weaknesses are made more salient by the Napoleon, they will be less likely to challenge the Napoleon's authority—they fear that this would bring only more abuse.

When hiring weak people is not possible, Napoleons may use a strategy of selectively filtering information to subordinates and superiors. They may construct elaborate channels of communication so that no matter what information reaches either superiors or subordinates, it will be favorable to the Napoleon and serve his or her purpose. Many times, subordinates are afraid to go over the Napoleon's head, and superiors are unable to perceive problems until they have escalated to a very high level, because their only source of information about the work group is the Napoleon. This strategy serves to keep the Napoleon in a position in which he or she can feel quite powerful because of the control exercised over others.

In brief, Napoleons are those individuals who try to compensate for their low self-esteem through abuse of their power positions. They like to exercise control over subordinates by threatening to punish them if they do not obey, and they are most satisfied when they are in positions of authority that give them the opportunity to exercise this power. The following case study illustrates the dynamics of the Napoleon Syndrome and shows how a manager can lose his or her job because of it.

Nicholas Dalton: Napoleon

Nicholas Dalton always hated being reminded of his childhood. When he was growing up, the other kids had always made fun of him because he was so incompetent in practically every game he tried to play. He was always the last to be chosen in the pick-up games at the local park, and it had always seemed that whichever team "got stuck with Nick" uttered a loud groan. The fact was that Nick was pigeon-toed, and this affected his running—which, of course, affected his prowess at practically every sport. He was called "clumsy" and "the penguin" because of the way he walked. As a result, he grew up being very conscious about how he looked to other people. In the back of his mind, however, he began at an early age to plot his revenge: some day he would find a way to get back at the people who had made fun of him.

While Nick's gait was somewhat impaired, he had always been very good with his hands and was considered to be fairly intelligent. He loved metal shop in high school and excelled in mathematics. As a result, he was encouraged by his teachers to become an engineer. Nick thought a great deal about what he wanted to do and decided that he would be a good engineer. He also believed that there was a lot of opportunity in mechanical engineering, the field he felt he would be best in.

After graduation from high school, Nick was accepted at the local college of engineering and received an academic scholarship as a result of the high recommendations his high-school teachers gave him. He did, indeed, excel in mechanical engineering and after graduation was offered positions in a number of companies.

He decided to work for MyersTech because it was a growing company with opportunities for promotion to management positions. This was important to Nick, since he had aspirations of someday being "the boss" in charge of a particular area. He thought he would make a good supervisor and decided to work hard to make his dream a reality.

Experiences As an Engineer

Nick did, indeed, work hard at his position as engineer. He was known throughout the company as a "quiet guy who could get the job done." He liked to work independently, but if someone needed help, he was more than willing to offer his expertise. Some of his fellow workers often remarked that while Nick was always willing to help them with problems, he tended to treat them as if they were children who had no conception of what the problems were that they were attempting to solve. They often felt that he was "talking down to them," but dismissed it because Nick always seemed friendly.

Promotion to Management: The Beginning of the End

After about four years with the company in various engineering positions, Nick was promoted to a management position. He had worked hard for MyersTech, and management wanted to recognize the contributions he had made by naming him group leader of one of the areas. All the people who were to work under Nick knew of him, but none had ever worked with him before. Nick looked forward to getting to know his people and to helping them achieve the goals the company had set for them. Nick also felt an intense sense of achievement: he finally was in a position where he would be respected by others.

At first, Nick went about his job with relatively few problems. His team worked well together and seemed to produce at a level consistent with that of the rest of the company. In his position as manager, Nick was responsible for supervising ten individuals, who were working independently on their own aspects of the group's project. Managing this group required that he meet with people individually as well as with the group as a whole. The individual meetings offered Nick the opportunity to "get to know" his people, but his subordinates weren't always sure that his interest was totally benign. After about a year on the job, they began to feel that it definitely was not: he was beginning to abuse the power his position afforded him. However, since most of his subordinates were afraid that he would somehow retaliate if they spoke against him, it took some time before his behavior caused him problems.

Nick was never overtly abusive or threatening to his subordinates. Instead, he would do subtle things that were intended to "keep subordinates in their place." He would often, for example, refer to the women in the group as "the girls" and the men as "my boys." He would sometimes "talk down" to one member in front of the others by beginning with something like, "My dear girl (boy)." This irritated most group members, but they brushed it off with: "That's just Nick. He's our boss, so we have to tolerate it."

Nick also used less blatant means to intimidate his subordinates, but in many cases, the victim would not even know that he or she had been "put down" until much later. A case in point occurred between Nick and one of the senior engineers, Elaine Richards, shortly after the beginning of his 18th month as a group leader.

Elaine had been working for some time on a problem that was both complicated and crucial to the rest of the team's project. When Nick called her into his office to discuss her progress, he began with: "I've read your report, and I'm afraid you've been wasting your time. It's clear that you haven't grasped the critical elements of the problem. You need to try it again." Then, Nick proceeded to outline exactly what Elaine should try and where she could go for answers to the questions he believed "she *must* have." He left her little room for a response and simply, according to Elaine, "laid down the law." Elaine felt powerless to question his authority, since "he knew what he was doing." She simply said that she'd try what he had suggested and thanked him for his time. Nick was satisfied that now she knew what to do.

About an hour later, as Elaine was relating the incident to a fellow worker, she began to realize what had happened. She knew that she hadn't quite gotten the problem, but much as had happened in the past, the solution she'd been forced to adopt was totally Nick's. Elaine thought, "It's always Nick's solution that is the correct one; nothing the rest of the group does is ever right. It has to be Nick's way or no way." Elaine was bitter when she thought how she had, again, "bought in" to his game. "Next time," she said to herself, "I'll stand up to him."

Elaine was not the only one who was beginning to discover Nick's "hidden agenda." Others in the work group were beginning to resent him as well. Lunch times were often spent "plotting" his downfall or complaining about Nick's latest encounter with group members. The group's morale and productivity began to drop. Fortunately for them (but unfortunately for Nick), Nick's superior, Russ Taylor, began to take notice. In fact, he had been a little wary of Nick's performance as manager from the day his promotion was announced. He had thought, "This guy just seems to get off on power." Problems really began to surface at the end of Nick's second year as group leader when Elaine asked if she could privately meet with Russ about some problems she was having.

Elaine seemed quite nervous and apprehensive about the meeting. She kept asking Russ about the confidentiality of what she would say in the meeting and who else besides Russ knew about the meeting. She told Russ she was afraid that if Nick found out she was even contemplating a meeting with him, he would find an excuse to fire her, or at least make her life miserable. Russ assured her that no such thing would happen and that, if forced to, he would protect her by transferring her out of the department.

During the course of the meeting with Russ, Elaine related what she could about Nick's behavior. She told him about her personal experiences as well as the incidents that other group members had discussed with her. Russ told her that she was one of four people who had recently come to see him about Nick and that he had not been aware of the extent of the problem until recently. He assured Elaine that the problem would be resolved and that things would get better.

The next day, Russ called Nick to his office to have a chat. "It's come to my attention," he began, "that there are some problems in your work group. Why don't you tell me about them?"

Nick was taken aback. He couldn't believe what he was hearing. Nick said, "I don't know what you mean. My work group is doing just fine. Everyone seems to get along well, and I believe performance is comparable to or better than that of any group in the company."

Russ then told Nick that there had been a number of complaints about him by his subordinates. Nick told Russ that the complaints were probably from a few disgruntled employees who were asked to do something they didn't want to do. He said: "I treat my employees as if they were my children or brothers and sisters. I look out for them, and I only ask them to do what's in their best interest."

"That," Russ replied, "is the problem. Your employees are adults and do not need the kind of advice you're giving in the manner you're giving it. It appears that this whole thing has gotten out of hand. I would like to say that you can try to make things better with your work group, but I'm afraid your employees dislike you too much. I'm going to have to ask you to resign."

Nick did not know what to say. He had failed as a manager, and he hadn't even known that it was happening. He had lost a position that he had worked for all of his life. Nick Dalton was a victim of the Napoleon Syndrome.

How Nicholas Dalton's Inner Game Playing Led to His Failure

Without even realizing it, Nicholas Dalton was a Napoleon. A driving force in his life was to attain a position where he could be seen as powerful. Once he'd attained that position, however, Nick's need to exercise control over others in order to compensate for his own inadequacies caused him to disregard a very important component of the successful game of management: being able to satisfy the organization's needs while at the same time satisfying subordinates' needs. Nick was so obsessed with satisfying his personal needs that he ignored those of his subordinates. He pretended that everything he did was in his subordinates' best interests, but in most cases it was clear that his actions were intended only to aggrandize himself.

Nick was very skilled at creating situations which would promote his superiority at the expense of others' sense of self-worth. One strategy used to accomplish this was to make others feel "weak" with regard to their knowledge of a particular problem. This was illustrated by his interaction with Elaine. Once Nick was successful at showing others their inadequacies, he would provide a solution to their problem intended to show his superiority. In getting subordinates to accept his solutions, Nick essentially decreased their self-esteem while increasing his own.

One reason Nick was able to go on with his behavior was that, while he was condescending, he was never blatantly abusive to anyone in front of the work group. Subordinates were therefore never sure whether or not they had been put down and hence did not want to challenge Nick in front of other group members. Their self-esteem was in jeopardy if they appeared too sensitive to Nick's comments and criticisms.

It wasn't until subordinates began to discuss their feelings among themselves that they discovered their shared perceptions of Nick. Once subordinates realized that they were not alone in their feelings, they were able to redefine the reality of the situation and to overthrow Nick. They were able to see him for what he was: a "little man" with a big need to have power over others.

Nicholas Dalton is not the only Napoleon in business organizations. There are many like him. Fortunately, many Napoleons are able to overcome their problems if they acknowledge them before they become too critical. The following case illustrates how one Napoleon, Jonathan Kelley, was able to work toward becoming an effective manager when he recognized his tendency to play the Inner Game by the rules of the Napoleon Syndrome.

Jonathan Kelley: The Napoleon Who Became President

Jonathan Kelley had always been small for his age. He remembered back to when he was a child and, each year when the school picture was taken, he was always right in the front row with all the girls. He remembered thinking that, some day, he would be a very important person in spite of his height. Amazingly enough, by the time Jon was in his forties, his prediction had become reality.

Jon's Early Years

Even though Jon Kelley was short in stature, he was big on brains and had a good business sense. This didn't necessarily mean that he was a genius. He had to work for whatever he got, but he usually got what he wanted. In high school, for example, he worked very hard to get good grades so that he would be eligible for a scholarship to attend the state university. He also worked after school and on weekends so that he could save for college.

After graduation from high school, Jon entered the university and majored in business administration. He liked accounting and finance courses best but developed a keen interest in personnel issues as well. Upon graduation from college, he went to work as an accountant with a medium-size regional firm. Jon liked his job and made a good living, but kept thinking that there was more to life than just manipulating numbers for various clients.

After three years with the accounting firm, Jon decided to return to school and earn an MBA. By this time, he had gained the respect of his peers and superiors; his application packet, which he sent to some of the best business schools in the country, included very good letters of recommendation. He had also done exceptionally well on his entrance exams and, not surprisingly, was offered admission to many of the schools to which he applied.

Jon decided to go to Harvard because it was "high-powered" and a Harvard degree carried a great deal of prestige. He worked hard in the MBA program and during that time became interested in investment banking. Jon discovered that what he had been missing in his last job was the opportunity to "be an expert" in something. He liked solving problems, and he wanted to be recognized for possessing expertise in some area. He saw the research function within the field of investment banking as the way to satisfy these needs.

Investment banking firms were interested in Jon because he had what they believed to be good work experience (his time in the accounting firm plus a summer internship with a major East Coast firm). Consequently, Jon was offered three positions. He chose to go to work for the company at which he had interned, since he was familiar with its operations and liked the people who worked there.

Experiences in the Investment Banking Firm

Jon's position with the investment banking firm was that of a research analyst. He was very adept at finding the answers to difficult questions and soon became known as the resident expert in the research department. Many turned to Jon for quick and accurate answers to questions they had. Others, however, were reluctant to go to him, because he had a subtle way of making them feel inferior. These people couldn't quite put their finger on it. They decided it was a problem of working styles, and instead of confronting Jon with it, they would just avoid having to deal with him.

Jon's technical expertise earned him not only a terrific salary but also rapid promotions. Within four years of entering the firm, he had been promoted to assistant department head of research. In this position, Jon continued doing the same things that he had done in his previous position, but was given the added responsibilities of assisting the department head in recruiting, selecting, and training new personnel to staff the department and of designing and implementing the department's strategic plan. Jon was required to attend a variety of company meetings, and he knew that it would be only a matter of time before he was promoted to department head.

Jon's promotion to department head came during his seventh year with the company when his department head left the firm to "pursue other interests." The new position carried with it full responsibility for planning, budgeting, and staffing the department, and Jon enjoyed the independence it afforded him. He remained the technical expert in his group, and many of the younger staff members admitted that they were somewhat in awe of Jon's abilities.

In his new position, Jon did not really have a great deal of interaction with his subordinates, since they worked autonomously on projects. The only opportunities to interact with them were when they asked questions of him or when Jon provided feedback on completed assignments. Jon's style of providing feedback in these situations disturbed some people. If individuals adequately completed an assignment, Jon would seldom say anything. If, however, the project was not completed satisfactorily or was not on time, Jon could become very hostile. His philosophy was that people who failed to fulfill their missions deserved "a kick in the ass" and that he was the one responsible for giving it to them. This belief was put into action in a variety of ways. Sometimes it was public humiliation in the form of throwing the report back on a person's desk and telling him or her to do it again and do it right. In other instances, it would consist of a semiformal "performance evaluation," during which Jon would, not in so many words, tell the individual that he or she was "worthless."

In any event, Jon's subordinates decided that the best way to avoid these encounters was to either do a good job or "play on Jon's ego." This latter strategy consisted of constantly asking for Jon's approval on certain courses of action. As a result of the fear Jon incited by his behavior, his department was one of the most productive in the company. Jon's superiors believed that he knew how to manage people to get results. Consequently, Jon became a very successful manager in their eyes and was rewarded appropriately.

Experiences As a Board Member

Shortly before Jon's 34th birthday, he was invited to join the board of directors of StarProducts, a medium-size consumer products firm. He gladly accepted the invitation, because the position would afford him the opportunity to have input into the decisions affecting the company. He felt that he had enough business experience to be an asset to StarProducts and help it become even more successful than it already was.

Jon's behavior at the board meetings, however, led some of the other members to conclude that Jon's primary concern was not with the company but with gaining a reputation for his own abilities. His style in the meetings often suggested that he might be on some kind of "power trip." Jon's style was to sit quietly until everyone else had expressed his or her opinions and then "let them have it" with his usually more than thorough critique of what others had said. He would conclude with a statement of the best course of action, which was usually *his* solution. More disturbing to some board members than Jon's unwillingness to participate in the debates like everyone else was the fact that during his critique he usually managed to include a few put-downs intended to show others how "superior" he was to them.

On one occasion, for example, the group was debating the merits of refinancing a particular project. When Jon finally took the floor, he reinforced his arguments for the "stupidity" of the refinancing project suggested by another member by beginning with: "One of the first lessons I learned in business school was that in evaluating projects, one should perform a cost/benefit analysis, and it's clear that Mike has ignored this in his argument. Let me tell you what a cost/benefit analysis of this project says . . ." It was a subtle message, but Mike Tuborg knew that it was a put-down. He was a self-made local businessman who had barely finished high school. Jon knew this, and he used the fact that Mike felt uncomfortable about it to his advantage. In fact, Jon often played on what he knew to be others' perceived weaknesses. Such behavior was tolerated by other board members, however, because Jon did possess a great deal of specific expertise which many board members lacked.

Jon Becomes President: Napoleon Takes Charge

At the beginning of Jon's tenth year as a board member, the president of StarProducts decided to retire, and the search began for a successor. The retiring president suggested that Jon might be a logical choice, since, by that time, Jon was a senior member of the board and had had a great deal of experience with the problems, products, and personnel at StarProducts. He had always been regarded as a "mover" who knew what it took to make a business successful. Further, the company had been suffering from declining profits and internal problems for nearly two years, and the retiring president believed that Jon would represent a strong force in resolving these problems.

Some members of the board were reluctant to give Jon the job, because, from their experience with him, they feared he might abuse his position. However, they knew the company needed new direction and believed that Jon could provide it. So, for the good of the company, it was agreed that Jon should assume the presidency.

Jon was ecstatic about his new job, and the investment banking firm, while sorry to see him go, expressed its warmest wishes for his continued success. Jon saw the new position as his opportunity to gain the respect he'd always believed he deserved. In fact, one of the first things he did to ensure that he would be afforded proper respect was to introduce himself to the personnel at StarProducts as "Jon Kelley, your new president." This was his way of saying that he expected to be addressed in this fashion and that anything else would be considered inappropriate. Employees got this message quite quickly. In the past, no one had addressed anyone, not even the president, by anything other than the person's first name. Use of his title signaled to employees that changes were on the horizon and that things were going to be very different at StarProducts from now on.

This was, in fact, the message Jon wanted communicated. He believed, and the board supported the notion, that it was time for StarProducts to become a professional firm. It needed someone to "turn it around," and Jon believed that he was the person to do it. The company needed to "tighten its belt" and redefine its operating systems to be more in line with the professional organization it was becoming. This meant that certain people needed to be terminated, budgets needed to be cut, and policies and practices needed to be changed. These changes would not be easy, but Jon believed he was taking a necessary course of action and didn't really care whether or not people liked it, since the changes were for the good of the company. He issued his directives for change in the form: "This is what we're going to do, so do it."

Some of the senior vice presidents began to complain almost immediately about the changes. They were particularly concerned about the proposed terminations and said it was impossible to fire individuals who had been with the firm for as much as ten years. Jon simply responded with: "It's for the good of the company, so I expect you to do it." To reinforce his message, he terminated those senior managers he believed would not be able to make the changes he demanded. This action symbolized that, "If you don't do as I say, you could be the next one out the door." Senior managers soon realized that Jon meant business and that to survive at the company, they needed to do as he said.

Jon believed that, along with getting rid of "the deadwood," it was important to establish an organizational hierarchy with well-defined reporting relationships. This would give management the ability to exercise better control over the results of the company's operations. Further, it would give Jon ultimate authority for company decision making, thus providing him with a great deal of power.

Jon knew all about how to use such organizational power to his advantage. He believed that the best way to maintain a position of power was to retain control of critical bits of information. When only he knew the answers to certain questions, he was afforded a great deal of power. To Jon, then, the best way to maintain control was to "keep people guessing."

He put this philosophy into practice in dealing with the senior vice presidents, the board, and other employees. His strategy was never to reveal the entire picture to anyone, but instead to provide only bits and pieces of it. The amount of information any one person received depended on his or her position in the organizational hierarchy. Those at the top of the hierarchy received more information than those at the bottom, and the information that was not to be filtered to the next lower level of the hierarchy was clearly labeled "confidential."

The use of confidential information created a lot of anxiety among employees, who speculated about what certain information might mean for their jobs. Managers were often frustrated, because even when they were directly asked about an issue by their subordinates, they sometimes could do nothing but say, "I can't tell you about that right now because it's confidential." Even more frustrating for managers, however, was the fact that they often found themselves playing a version of "Twenty Questions" with Jon in an attempt to get the big picture for themselves. The problem was that, often, Jon would be so evasive that they, like their subordinates, would simply have to resort to speculating about what certain bits of information meant.

Subconsciously, Jon got pleasure out of seeing what people would come up with whenever he withheld information. Sometimes, managers would come into meetings prepared to discuss an issue in light of the information they had, only to find that, during the course of the meetings, Jon would suddenly reveal a crucial bit of information that would make their opinions irrelevant. This served as a way of keeping certain managers in their places. It was Jon's way of showing that he was the boss.

Since he was "at the top," few people could challenge Jon's authority.

Consequently, he was given a great deal of freedom to manipulate people in subtle ways. Besides discrediting others' opinions in meetings, he also often felt it necessary to override lower-level decisions as a way of showing who was in charge. Whenever this occurred, the new decision was usually accompanied by a put-down of the original decision maker. Much as he had done as a board member, he would discover an individual's weakness and use it as a way to control him or her. In one instance, for example, he overrode a middle manager's decision to purchase some equipment from a particular vendor. The memo he sent to the manager to explain his reasons for taking another course of action included a statement about the manager's abilities. It said, "Your decision to purchase the equipment from Z-Tech suggests to me that you have not researched the options available. Clearly, In-House offers a higher-quality product for a better price. You should have been able to find this out for yourself. I expect a better analysis of the options available the next time."

As a result of such memos and direct confrontations with Jon, employees began to live in constant fear of being publicly or privately humiliated by him or, worse, fired. They believed that while Jon might really care about the company, he didn't care about them. They believed they were only replaceable tools with which Jon intended to accomplish his mission: to make the company a professional organization. To deal with this situation, employees adopted the policy of "telling Mr. Kelley what he wants to hear," or "making every effort of doing what Mr. Kelley wants." Consequently, the information reaching Jon suggested that everything was going reasonably well. However, it seemed that the company was not making the type of progress he expected it should.

Jon began to feel that even though he appeared to be accomplishing what he intended to do at StarProducts, there were still some very real problems. Morale seemed to be declining, and with it productivity. Jon knew that people wouldn't like what he was doing, but hoped that eventually they would just accept it and learn to live with the changes. This did not seem to be occurring. Jon realized that he could no longer handle the situation himself, so he decided to seek the advice of an outside consultant. After an evaluation of the situation, the consultant determined that the company did indeed have problems, although Jon had made significant strides in the right direction. Part of the company's problems, however, were a direct result of the difficulties people had adjusting to Jon's management style. Jon wanted to make the company a success, so he decided to listen to what the consultant had to say and try to change his style. He began to make a real effort to overcome his tendency to play the Inner Game of Management by the rules of the Napoleon Syndrome.

How Jonathan Kelley's Inner Game Playing
Created Problems

Unlike Nicholas Dalton, Jonathan Kelley was the epitome of a successful manager. He was able to play the Inner Game of Management by the rules of the Napoleon Syndrome and still succeed, in part because he was a master at the Outer Game. He had great technical skills and was recognized as an effective manager and leader by his peers and superiors. However, like other Napoleons, Jon eventually reached an organizational level where his inability to play the Inner Game began to cause problems for himself and for those with whom he worked. It was at this point that he decided to seek help.

Jon was, like Nick, a classic Napoleon. He attempted to gain positions in which he could exercise power over others. In these positions, he tended to be both subtly and blatantly abusive. His peers and subordinates tolerated him, in part because they respected his expertise. They also tolerated him because, like Nick, Jon was skilled at making them feel that they had to tolerate him to avoid punishment. This punishment usually involved exploiting another's weakness, which Jon was very skilled at discovering.

When Jon became president of StarProducts, he was afforded more responsibility and power than he had ever had before. The company was in a state of disarray and needed a strong leader like Jon—someone who would make and enforce the changes necessary to resolve its problems. Unfortunately, while Jon knew what needed to be done and attempted to implement the necessary plans, he failed to consider the effects his policies would have on the people within the company. He was so concerned that his policies be carried out that he did not consider the effects they would have on the human side of the organization. Jon was insensitive to others' needs, and as a result of this insensitivity, morale began to drop, and along with it productivity.

Jon liked the feeling of being in total control, especially with regard to information. He believed that by controlling access to information, he could protect his position. Unfortunately, such a practice led many employees to believe that Jon did not trust them. This feeling that Jon did not trust them, combined with his insensitivity to their needs, led them to believe that the best way to maintain their jobs was to either "stay out of Jon's way" or "tell him what he wants to hear." These beliefs, when put into practice, led to a situation in which Jon never really knew what was going on in the company. Hence he could not determine why the company was not attaining the goals he had set for it more quickly.

When Jon realized that certain problems were occurring that he did not understand, he decided that it was in the company's best interest to seek outside advice. It was at this point that he discovered that he would need to make some changes in the way he managed if he was to continue to be successful. He could no longer treat people like the playing pieces in his game. He needed to overcome the Napoleon Syndrome. In the next section, the conclusion of this chapter, we describe the steps that Jon took, and that other Napoleons can take, to overcome the Napoleon Syndrome.

Overcoming the Napoleon Syndrome

The Napoleon Syndrome results from attempts to overcome a low self-esteem through gaining positions of authority where a high degree of control over others can be exercised. Therefore, sufferers of this syndrome must learn how to manage their needs for self-esteem and control.

Napoleons must learn to recognize that they are abusing the power that their position affords. As described in the cases presented in this chapter, many Napoleons believe that whatever power they are exercising is for the good of the organization or their subordinates. Therefore, one of the first questions Napoleons need to ask themselves is: "Is what I'm doing really for the good of the organization, or does it simply make me feel better?"

This is not the only question Napoleons need to answer. They also need to be concerned about the manner in which they carry out their responsibilities. As illustrated in the cases, both Nicholas and Jonathan were very skilled at putting their subordinates down in the course of performing their managerial duties. Much of the time, such behavior is unnecessary and can ultimately be quite destructive. Napoleons, therefore, need to be aware of situations in which they tend to behave in this fashion. Once aware of these situations, they need to find ways of avoiding the tendency to increase their own self-esteem at the expense of others.

One way to do this is to simply become more sensitive to others' needs. Napoleons need to learn how to motivate subordinates through reward rather than punishment. They need to learn how to avoid the tendency to exploit others' weaknesses and, instead, begin motivating subordinates by exploiting their strengths. Once they are able to recognize others' strengths, Napoleons need to learn how to help their subordinates develop their abilities.

The final thing that Napoleons need to do to overcome their problems is to find ways of increasing their own self-esteem so that they do not have to compensate for their low self-esteem by abusing the power they hold over others.

How can a victim of the Napoleon Syndrome make the required changes? Frankly, if the symptoms of the syndrome are so severe that the person derives a great deal of pleasure from humiliating others and has no empathy for others' feelings, we believe the best course of action is some form of psychotherapy. This is because, for these people, the likelihood that they can change by themselves is almost zero. The situation is analogous to that of a smoker who wants to quit, but who is so addicted that he or she does not have the willpower to stop smoking.

However, just as there are smokers who quit "cold turkey," there are Napoleons who can recognize that they have a problem and take steps to change. Basically, these individuals need to learn to practice self-control in situations in which there is a tendency to humiliate people. Whenever such situations arise, the Napoleon needs to develop strategies to avoid putting people down. One strategy is to learn to say nothing at all. Another is for the Napoleon to practice saying something positive about people and trying to make them feel good about themselves rather than putting them down with "gratuitous shots."

Napoleons may also try to reverse the process of humiliation of others by giving someone in their organizations either "permission" or the responsibility of providing feedback on how they are behaving. For example, how is the Napoleon behaving in meetings? By legitimizing the process of feedback, the Napoleon can get an independent assessment of what progress he or she is making in overcoming this syndrome.

Another thing the Napoleon can do is to hire strong people who will not tolerate this kind of behavior. This serves two purposes. First, the Napoleon will find that when he or she attempts to humiliate strong people, it will backfire. They will challenge the Napoleon's authority and may actually end up humiliating him or her. Therefore, the Napoleon will learn, out of necessity, how to avoid humiliating others. Second, the Napoleon will learn that there are rewards to be gained by managing others without humiliating them. Strong subordinates will increase the ability of the Napoleon to meet the organizational goals assigned to him or her and thus objectively increase the Napoleon's managerial effectiveness. Provided the Napoleon has learned to develop self-esteem from the managerial role, he or she will find it no longer necessary to humiliate others.

In brief, to become effective Inner Game players, Napoleons need to take systematic steps toward controlling their tendency to humiliate others and practice being positive rather than destructive people.

Chapter 6
The Pygmy Syndrome

Barry Adelson graduated cum laude from Ohio State University and then studied law at Columbia Law School. He received his LLB and went to work for a large, prestigious law firm in New York City.

Although Barry had made Law Review while at Columbia, his forte was business development rather than the technical aspect of law per se. He was more than technically competent. He was also a charming, outgoing individual who tended to be included in a wide variety of social occasions. Since people liked Barry and felt comfortable with him, a significant number of his acquaintances became his clients.

As Barry's professional practice increased, his influence in the firm increased accordingly. He was known as a "rainmaker," a lawyer who brought business into the firm and made it available to the other lawyers who serviced his clients in special areas. As a result of his business development activities, Barry found it increasingly difficult to provide the technical services required by his clients. The clients themselves did not seem to care who provided the back-office services, as long as Barry was the primary person with whom they had contact. They viewed him as a "good businessman" because of his pragmatic and incisive way of thinking.

This process continued for a number of years, and Barry was eventually made a partner in the firm. Although he was pleased with the status and financial aspects of his role, he was vaguely dissatisfied with his life as a partner. He had grown further and further away from the technical aspects of law. He now had a number of "associates"—junior lawyers who worked for him—who were superior to him in technical knowledge. Although he had graduated from Columbia and had had an excellent record at Ohio State, his firm was now recruiting young men and women with both undergraduate and law degrees from prestigious Ivy League schools. These were well-scrubbed, polished, bright, articulate, and well-trained people, who, quite frankly, intimidated Barry. Although he was a partner and they worked for him, he frequently felt that it was he who had to justify himself to them.

Sometimes, for example, when he held staff meetings to review their case work for one of his clients, it was obvious that he had barely had time to read the briefs they had prepared. This caused him some embarrassment, as did those instances where he failed to grasp an esoteric point in a case. Since Barry was spread increasingly thin among his responsibilities of client "handholding," administrative meetings of the firm, and other matters, the potential for this embarrassment was great. What was worse than his own feelings of discomfort, however, was the fact that when Barry committed one of those legal *faux pas*, he would sometimes notice a quick glance between staff members, which he interpreted as a look of reproach and condescension.

Barry responded to this situation in a variety of ways. For a few years, he ignored the perceived insults, although he seethed inside. But finally he lashed back. One afternoon, when he was particularly fatigued after having returned on the "red eye" from California, where he had spent four days in excruciating negotiations concerning a corporate acquisition, he exploded at one of his associates who seemed to smile patronizingly when Barry made a minor slip. Barry, who had been bottling his rage for quite some time, made this unfortunate young man the scapegoat for his anger. He lectured the associate, Roy Lockwood, who was one of his most talented, in front of the group and then left the meeting, leaving his staff amazed. The behavior was out of character for Barry, who was typically jovial and good-spirited.

At first, Barry felt embarrassed at his loss of control, but he also felt a twinge of pleasure at having turned the tables on the young "snotnose." Nothing further was said about the incident, but it did have a lasting effect. Pandora's box was open: having exploded once, Barry found it increasingly easy to let out his anger and frustrations. The nature of his staff meetings changed. He was no longer on the defensive. His demeanor, once as charming with his staff as with his clients, now changed. Barry used sarcasm, cold stares, changes in voice tone, and put-down remarks to "tame his young lions," as he put it to a colleague. He was tired of their "bullshit attitude." He was the one paying the bills by bringing in the revenue, and they had better realize it. Privately, one of Barry's colleagues remarked that he seemed to be enjoying "taming the lions" a bit too much. Indeed, Barry was finding his newly exercised power over his young associates to be addictive.

There were other changes as well. A number of his talented associates began to leave the firm. Roy Lockwood was the first to go. Each case seemed to have different reasons, and there was no apparent link to Barry's changed style, but the amount of staff turnover had clearly changed. Barry attributed the change to the "new breed" of youngsters graduating from the law schools, who simply lacked the old-fashioned virtues of loyalty.

Since he had a large and prestigious firm, Barry found it relatively easy to recruit new associates. Inexorably, however, the overall quality of his staff had subtly begun to deteriorate. At first, he merely found it more difficult to attract as many of the first-rate graduates. After a few years, he found that the top graduates simply declined his firm's offers. He found that he had to hunt around his firm for some individuals who were having difficulty with other partners and who could be coaxed to join his team. Unfortunately, these were typically people with just a little less on the ball than Barry had grown used to from previous years.

The strength of Barry's operation had always been a delicately balanced machine in which he brought in the business and then had it serviced by his staff, which could be relied upon to perform capably. Now Barry found that he had to worry about his staff's technical performance and, consequently, had to spend a greater proportion of his time in technical review. He was spread increasingly thin, and the percentage of mistakes increased. As the mistakes increased, so did Barry's explosions, which, in turn, led the best of his staff to leave. It was a vicious, vicious process.

Things continued to deteriorate for Barry. One project involving a large, complex acquisition was so botched that it led to the loss of a major client as well as an old friend. It also had the effect of tarnishing Barry's reputation among all his clients.

Gradually, Barry began to lose clients and, in turn, his power base within his firm. He was an unhappy man, who wondered what had gone wrong.

How Barry Adelson's Inner Game Playing Created Problems

Barry Adelson failed to play the Inner Game of Management effectively because he had a relatively low sense of self-esteem, in spite of his accomplishments. He felt threatened by the competence of his own subordinates, and he felt in competition with them as legal technicians. These feelings led him to behave in ways that ultimately were self-destructive. Specifically, Barry began to throw his weight around and abuse his subordinates. This, in turn, led the most competent to leave, and Barry was left with a set of weaker people who tolerated his abuse.

Barry continued to think of himself as a legal technician rather than as a manager, even after he became a partner. In this sense he was a victim of the Doer Syndrome. However, he was intimidated by his subordinates' technical skills as well as their outstanding academic credentials, and he allowed his own insecurities to diminish his worth in his own eyes. In brief, he continued to think of himself as a technician because of his insecurities regarding his self-worth.

There was, however, another, more complex issue involved in Barry's ultimate problems. This involved the social interactions between Barry and his staff. He perceived his staff to be mocking him in meetings, and he may have been correct (though it is possible that the subtle insults Barry perceived were more imagined than real). His staff members' reactions may have been their way of gaining control over a very tenuous situation in which they found themselves. As associates, they were not permanent members of the firm; they were subject to Barry's authority and, finally, his recommendation of them for partnership. Although it may well have been a case of "biting the hand that feeds you," some of the associates may have been sufficiently immature to peck at Barry's vanity without realizing the degree of his sensitivities.

To some extent, the slights Barry perceived as directed at him by his subordinates were based upon his own ambivalence about the value of his role. Instead of becoming aggressive and pushing his people, Barry needed to "educate" them about the value of his role vis a vis theirs. Even if they did not understand the nature of his contribution and the pressures he was under, the strategy of lashing out was counterproductive in the long run.

It should also be noted that the problems Barry had were certainly not his alone. It was not totally his responsibility to educate junior associates about the value of a business-development partner; this was the responsibility of the firm and its managing partners. The firm should have dealt explicitly with the changing role of partners during their careers. In fact, the ambiguity Barry felt was not unusual; most lawyers share the same feelings. They are trained to be lawyers rather than businessmen, and many would rather avoid the grubby realities that come with having to practice law as a business. But the firm simply ignored the reality of its need for business developers and held an almost academic model of the lawyer as the professional ideal. This contributed to a climate in which smirks could be made by junior lawyers, who didn't appreciate that they could practice as legal technicians only so long as there were Barry Adelsons available to feed them business.

Although the firm could certainly have helped minimize the problem to some extent, the ultimate responsibility was still Barry's. He needed to control his reactions to his staff. He needed to continue to hire strong people and retain them. He needed to stop competing with his subordinates. In brief, he needed to master the self-esteem dimension of the Inner Game of Management.

The Pygmy Game That Managers Play

Barry Adelson, who had had such a promising start in his career, was just one victim of what we call the Pygmy Syndrome. This syndrome refers to the tendency of a manager to feel threatened by talented subordinates and, consequently, to surround himself or herself with people who are relatively weak. By selecting only such people, the manager can feel like a "giant among pygmies."

The basic Inner Game problem underlying the Pygmy Syndrome is the victim's lack of self-esteem. For a variety of reasons, people who are victims of this syndrome feel inadequate. Their sense of personal inadequacy is kept under control so long as they perceive themselves as the best at something in their own immediate environment. Whenever this position as technical expert is threatened by more competent subordinates, the manager who suffers from the Pygmy Syndrome will find ways to eliminate the competition by either firing these subordinates or causing them such humiliation that they resign.

The Pygmy Syndrome has several related symptoms. One of the most fundamental ones is that the manager tends to surround himself or herself with weaker people. There are different degrees to which this symptom exists. For some managers, every subordinate must be weaker in all areas. Others can surround themselves with talented individuals, but even those talented subordinates must have some weakness that the manager can exploit to "control" them. This strategy, also used by Napoleons, involves creating situations in which subordinates are so intimidated by their managers that they will not challenge their authority.

Another symptom is that the manager tends to compete with his or her subordinates. For example, a sales manager will compete with the staff for recognition as the best salesman. A manifestation of this might be the statement: "I'm still the best guy in the field." Similarly, an engineering manager may compete with people for recognition as the technical guru of the group. A department chairman at a university may compete with young assistant professors for recognition as the leading researcher on the faculty. In each of these examples, although the individual's role has changed to that of a manager, he or she is still viewing himself or herself in terms of criteria appropriate to the former technical role.

If managers who suffer from the Pygmy Syndrome have their authority challenged in any way by subordinates, they may react with great hostility, as we saw in the case of Barry Adelson. This is particularly true when they hold positions that carry a great deal of organizational power. In these cases, the positional power acts as a buffer: these individuals believe that no one would dare question their authority because of the power they are afforded by their organizations. They can, therefore, be very abusive toward their subordinates with little risk to themselves. In other cases, sufferers of the Pygmy Syndrome may simply resign from their positions rather than attempt to "fight off" their challengers. This is how Tom Wilson, the subject of our next case study, handled a situation in which he believed he was being challenged.

Tom Wilson: Team Leader

Tom Wilson was a senior design engineer for Datatronics Corporation, a rapidly growing high-technology company that specialized in the design, development, manufacture, and sale of communications test equipment. Tom had graduated as an electrical engineer from UCLA and began his career at a large computer mainframe manufacturer. He had worked as an electrical design engineer for two years before joining Datatronics.

Tom had learned a great deal at the mainframe manufacturer, but liked the more informal environment and challenge presented by joining Datatronics. The firm had been a start-up company that had achieved rapid success in a specialized niche in the telecommunications test equipment market. Tom was convinced that the firm had excellent prospects.

As a hobby, Tom liked to play with software applications on his personal computer at home. Although he recognized that he was no genius, he had good analytical skills and was a good problem solver. He followed an orderly, systematic approach in what he did, and this enabled him to effectively develop new software modules to adapt existing packaged products to his personal needs.

After working for the mainframe manufacturer for two years as an electrical design engineer, Tom was invited to participate in a special project involving the design of a "new box" with related software for the telecommunications market. Since Tom had both hardware and software skills, he was a natural addition to the project group, which consisted primarily of people with either hardware or software skills and interests.

Because of his unique mix of skills and interests, Tom found himself serving as the communication link between the hardware design people and the software development people in the project. He had become, in effect, the informal leader of the group and the facilitator of the group's work.

When the project was completed, 18 months later, it was an immediate success, and it led Datatronics Corporation to establish the project group as a formal research and development department, called the Telecommunications R&D Test Group. Tom was asked to take the job as manager of the department. This was, in part, a reward for and recognition of his role in the group's success. Tom's selection was also based on the belief of Dan Mc-Carthy, Vice President of Engineering, that Tom was the most logical choice for the job. Dan was a results-oriented engineer himself, who believed that Tom's performance in the project marked him as someone with good potential.

Although Tom did not have any formal training as a manager, he seemed to do well in the role. He had sufficient technical skills in both the hardware and the software areas, and people came to him to help resolve problems. Even though he was not the best technician in either group, he came to be known as "Mr. Fixit," the problem solver who chipped in whenever the group reached an impasse.

Tom took a great deal of pride in his role as department manager and spent many hours, both on and off the job, in continuing his own technical education. He felt it was important that he stay abreast of new concepts and developments in his area. As the number of projects increased, the demands upon Tom's time also increased, and he found himself being spread too thin to have the time to keep up with new technical developments. In the back of his mind this bothered him, but things were going well in his group.

For about two and a half years after Tom was promoted, the team continued working well together under his leadership. It was getting results. Dan McCarthy was pleased with Tom's performance and his own decision. Everything was going very well in Tom's eyes. He believed that he had become a successful manager.

Then, one day, an unexpected problem arose. It all began when a new member, Kevin Turner, was added to the group. Kevin was a very bright young man who had recently graduated from one of the nation's top schools in computer science, having received many honors during his studies. Kevin had worked as a research assistant with some of his professors and had published two articles, whose titles, let alone their contents, Tom could barely understand. It seemed that Kevin was something of a mathematical genius who was steeped in the latest hardware and software concepts and methods.

In many respects, Kevin was much like Tom. He was highly motivated and, like Tom, had chosen Datatronics because of its informal environment, its growth, and the creative opportunities it offered its employees. Dan believed that Kevin was a great recruiting coup and that Tom would find him to be a "real asset."

During the interview process, Tom was very impressed with Kevin. He had an almost instantaneous grasp of the development efforts at Datatronics. It was clear that Kevin was highly intelligent, and even though he was graduating only six years after Tom, his command of state-of-the-art concepts and methods was awesome. Tom felt a little intimidated by Kevin and his obvious abilities and outstanding credentials.

Even though Kevin was very talented, he had a number of personal traits that made him difficult to deal with. He often seemed to be daydreaming at work, and his hours were somewhat irregular. He would stay up until 3 A.M. or 4 A.M. working on a problem one day and then sleep in half of the next day. Since this was an unpredictable occurrence, it was difficult to hold project meetings with the expectation that Kevin would actually show up. This idiosyncrasy was resented by some people in Tom's group who chose to keep more regular hours. However, no one doubted Kevin's abilities or even his contributions to the group.

Kevin's training in computer science had given him the same linking-pin capability that had formerly been possessed only by Tom Wilson. Since Kevin's training was more recent and more in-depth than Tom's, it was clear that he was a valuable resource to the team. People tolerated Kevin even if they did not feel close to him.

Unfortunately, Tom began to feel increasingly uncomfortable about Kevin. He felt that in small, subtle ways, Kevin was undermining his position and authority in the department. First, there was the need to schedule team meetings around Kevin's unpredictable schedule. This was a necessity because Kevin was now viewed as a major player on the team. Next, there was the fact that Kevin had come to be seen as the technical guru of the department. People tended to go to him rather than to Tom with their technical problems. Moreover, Kevin was notoriously delinquent with his status reports. Although Datatronics tended to be informal in interpersonal relationships, formal status reports were part of the company's culture and management practices, yet Kevin's were always overdue. Tom frequently had to request them, and Kevin always had the same excuses: "I was too busy doing the work itself to spend the time on the reports," or "I was too tired after an 'all-nighter' to prepare a written report on my work." Some people accepted these excuses as just one of Kevin's idiosyncrasies, but a few others made it an issue when Tom pressured them to get their reports in on time.

All in all, Kevin had made Tom's life more complicated and stressful. Tom had great difficulty in controlling Kevin, and he began to wonder whether Kevin was really after his job.

Tom found himself increasingly preoccupied with Kevin and how what Kevin was doing might undermine his position. He also found himself hoping that Kevin would leave Datatronics. Tom began to try to scrutinize Kevin's work to a greater degree. Unconsciously, he was hoping for Kevin to make some mistake, to embarrass himself.

In group meetings, Tom tried to ask probing questions concerning Kevin's work, but they were designed more to embarrass Kevin than to facilitate the team's work. It began to be clear to people that there was some friction between Kevin and Tom, although Kevin himself seemed oblivious to it.

Tom also tried to keep up with Kevin by continuing his own technical development at home during evenings and on weekends. However, after four months of this he gave up. Kevin was simply far better as a computer systems technician than he was.

As time went on, Tom began to find himself increasingly depressed about coming to work. Dan McCarthy sensed that Tom was concerned about something and asked to meet him for lunch. At the lunch, Dan tried to find out what was wrong. He asked whether Tom was having problems at home, and Tom said, "No." Although Dan tried to probe the situation, Tom just insisted nothing was wrong, and they left the luncheon with Dan telling Tom how good a job his group was doing and that it was a credit to Tom. Unfortunately, what Dan didn't know was that Tom had been looking for another job and that it would be only a matter of time before he resigned.

How Tom Wilson's Inner Game Playing Created Problems

One reason Tom Wilson was experiencing problems and distress in the management role was that his self-esteem was threatened: when Kevin entered his department, Tom was no longer the technical expert. Tom believed that to be a good manager, he must be the technically most competent member of the group. This belief led him to conclude that Kevin had informally taken over as leader, because his technical knowledge was superior to Tom's. In Tom's mind, he was in competition with Kevin for the role of technical expert, which he equated with the role of manager. Tom had not learned, or at least had not mentally accepted, that a good manager need not be the technically most competent member of a group or department.

Tom believed that it was only a matter of time before his inadequacies were revealed and he was replaced. So, like many sufferers of the Pygmy Syndrome, he decided simply to find a new job in which he could reestablish his technical expertise.

Unlike Tom Wilson, some victims of the Pygmy Syndrome are better able to control the amount of competition they face. We will see an example of that in this chapter's final case study, which describes the problems encountered by Warren Harris when he played the Inner Game by the rules of the Pygmy Syndrome.

Warren Harris:
Company President

Warren Harris began his career as a salesman for a computer firm, a position in which he excelled. He rose rapidly to sales manager. In this job, he continued to sell while, at the same time, managing a sales team. In spite of his managerial responsibilities, Warren remained among the top salesmen in the company.

Warren found that he did not like being a manager as much as he liked being a salesman. He therefore decided to start his own company in which he could once again be a salesman—but in this case, a salesman of his own product and company. He realized that he could never hope to compete directly with the large computer companies, but he had the idea of developing a machine with related software for a specific industry.

During the early years, he had to bootstrap the operation, but his tireless efforts and his sales skills enabled him to get the company off the ground. Moreover, he was able to sell some venture capitalists on his concept and get sufficient funding to finance significant growth.

Warren's technical background was strong for a salesman, but was not really very deep. He tended to overrate his technical capabilities and interfered in the design aspects for products. Consequently, he found it more comfortable to hire design engineers who were not particularly assertive and would take his direction. Similarly, Warren tended to hire sales managers who were weaker than he. As a result of these actions, he was able to dominate the entire company.

Although Warren felt comfortable in his unchallenged position, there was a significant cost to the company. Because of Warren's concept of himself as a strong, decisive manager, he tended to make decisions quickly. Borrowing from the best-selling book *The One Minute Manager*,[1] some of Warren's people said he went the one-minute manager even better. He became known as the "thirty-second decision maker" or, more derisively, as the "hip-shooter." This style, which Warren saw as strong and decisive, was seen by many subordinates as comical and absurd. Yet, these were people who valued their jobs and understood that their boss would brook no challenge. Thus, they remained silent.

---

[1] K. Blanchard and S. Johnson (Eds.), *The One Minute Manager* (New York: Berkeley, 1985).

How Warren Harris's Inner Game Playing
Created Problems

Warren Harris's sense of self-esteem was tied to his view of his own technical skills. He was uncomfortable with people around him who challenged his ideas, and he took such disagreements personally, as a challenge to his manhood or self-esteem. Consequently, he tended to hire people who were relatively passive and unwilling to challenge him. They played the game of letting Warren dominate the play. Unfortunately, Warren failed to understand his real skill, which was in strategic vision and the willingness to assume entrepreneurial risk.

Like many others, Warren Harris failed to master the Inner Game of Management. To master this game, Warren would have had to manage his sense of self-esteem. He would have had to hire strong people. In the next section, we describe the steps people like Warren Harris can take to avoid or overcome the Pygmy Syndrome.

Overcoming the Pygmy Syndrome

The key Inner Game issue facing people who are victims of the Pygmy Syndrome involves the need to manage their self-esteem. People who are victims of this syndrome, in effect, adopt a defensive strategy to protect themselves from perceived threats to self-worth. In contrast to the Malevolent Godfather or the Napoleon, the victim of the Pygmy Syndrome is acting with the goal of self-defense, not the control or humiliation of other people for the purpose of feeling important. Although the goal is understandable and benign, the managerial consequences of this syndrome are still problematic for the manager, the subordinates, and the organizations which employ them.

The first step in overcoming this syndrome is self-recognition. These managers must assess their behavior and feelings in order to determine whether they are victims of this syndrome or of the Napoleon or Godfather Syndromes.

The next step involves a personal plan for self-inoculation against the doubts and fears that cause this syndrome. Pygmy Syndrome sufferers must make a commitment to changing their behavior. Above all, they must make a conscious effort to hire strong people and get out of their way. The basic weakness of the manager who is a victim of this syndrome is hiring weaker people; therefore, an important action step to overcome it involves making sure that the individual is surrounded by a strong staff.

Once they've hired the right people, these managers must learn to overcome their tendency to compete with subordinates for technical supremacy. That is, they must learn to accept and feel comfortable with subordinates who are technically more competent. Accordingly, another step for a manager to overcome the Pygmy Syndrome is to train subordinates so that they can surpass the manager's skills in certain areas. For example, an engineering manager can train a subordinate in some engineering speciality until the subordinate surpasses the teacher. The purpose is for the victim of the Pygmy Syndrome to get used to the idea that it is O.K. to have people on the staff whose technical skills exceed his or her own. The manager will see that this is beneficial and does not undermine his or her authority. By increasing this process over time, the victim is building up "antibodies" to the feelings of inadequacy which provoke the Pygmy Syndrome.

The manager should also practice letting people make their own decisions without his or her intervention. This must be done even if the manager feels that their decisions will be wrong.

A final suggestion is for the manager to encourage people to challenge him or her. The victim of the Pygmy Syndrome should practice listening to people without trying to debate with them or trying to prove them wrong.

If all these things are done, an individual can make significant progress in overcoming or avoiding the Pygmy Syndrome.

Chapter 7

The Dr. Jekyll and Mr. Hyde Syndrome

In "The Strange Case of Dr. Jekyll and Mr. Hyde," Robert Louis Stevenson[1] describes the plight of the kindly Dr. Jekyll, who stumbles upon a potion that allows the evil side of himself, Mr. Hyde, to emerge and wreak havoc upon his community. Dr. Jekyll, although mostly a good and upstanding citizen, realizes that there is a part of him that runs counter to this image. He comments, in fact, "that man is not truly one, but truly two,"[2] and it is this dichotomy that leads him to attempt the separation afforded by the potion he creates.

The potion allows the Dr. Jekyll and Mr. Hyde sides to separate completely, transforming Dr. Jekyll from a handsome man into a small, ugly, gnarled person in his role as Mr. Hyde. The separation is so complete, in fact, that Hyde has his own quarters, servants, and clothing. However, when the bad side becomes blatantly outrageous, the good side feels remorse, and since Dr. Jekyll is all too aware of Hyde's exploits, he vows to keep the bad side hidden: "I swear to God I will never set eyes on him (Hyde) again. I bind my honour to you that I am done with him in this world. It is all at an end."[3] Unfortunately for poor Dr. Jekyll, by this point, the evil side of himself has

---

[1] R. L. Stevenson, *The Strange Case of Dr. Jekyll and Mr. Hyde* (New York: Franklin Watts, 1967).
[2] Ibid., p. 86.
[3] Ibid., p. 29.

taken such control that he is forced to use the potion to help the good side prevail. Eventually, even taking the potion cannot control Mr. Hyde. When this point is finally reached, Dr. Jekyll commits suicide, because he can no longer tolerate the person that he has become.

The Dr. Jekyll and Mr. Hyde Game That Managers Play

Dr. Jekyll and Mr. Hyde do not exist just in literature. There are many managers who suffer from this classic role split in which they become tyrannical Mr. Hydes whenever they are acting as the boss but are described as possessing a pleasant personality whenever they are not in their work roles. Often, the split is so complete that those who experience only the person out of his or her work role are unable to believe that the individual they know as friendly and easygoing is uncaring and domineering when directing the actions of subordinates.

Individuals who suffer from this syndrome have high needs to be liked as well as high needs for control and self-esteem. In the doer's role, they are able to satisfy all three needs relatively well. They are able to have ultimate control over the results of their efforts and are rewarded for their personal performance (thus satisfying their selfesteem needs). Further, doers are able to satisfy their need to be liked through the comradery which co-workers often share.

Once they are promoted to a management position, however, control over results is reduced and their ability to succeed in the role is dependent on the efforts of others. The ability to satisfy their need to be liked also changes. No longer are they part of a work group; rather, they are leaders. To a Dr. Jekyll/Mr. Hyde, this means that, to succeed, he or she can no longer behave as "one of the guys or gals."

Sufferers of the Dr. Jekyll and Mr. Hyde Syndrome believe that their need to be liked by those whom they supervise is inconsistent with satisfying their needs for control and self-esteem in their new role. They know that a manager's main responsibility is to exercise control over the actions of subordinates so that organizational objectives are achieved. If they are successful in doing so, they will be seen as effective in their organizational roles, and, as a result, their self-esteem will be enhanced. They believe, however, that to be able to exercise such control, they cannot be too friendly with their subordinates. Hence, they find ways to separate their need to be liked from their needs for control and self-esteem.

The "potion" that these individuals use to separate Mr. Hyde from Dr.

Jekyll is the prescription that they have for becoming successful in their work roles. The basic ingredient of this prescription is finding ways to exercise ultimate control over the actions of subordinates. Many Dr. Jekyll/Mr. Hyde managers believe that this can best be achieved by learning and enforcing the organization's rules, since "no one can argue with the rules." They may, however, also attempt to control subordinates' actions by enforcing their own standards for technical excellence. Their philosophy thus becomes, "the organization's/my way or no way."

Subordinates who deviate from these standards are usually publicly reprimanded. Hence, subordinates of a Dr. Jekyll/Mr. Hyde tend to describe their manager as "unreasonable and domineering" or in other, more colorful terms. Since they are exposed only to the Mr. Hyde side, they believe that their manager does not really care about their needs.

Even though their subordinates do not necessarily like them, individuals who suffer from the Dr. Jekyll and Mr. Hyde Syndrome are usually at least initially successful at performing the requirements of their roles. Since subordinates want to avoid the abuse that results whenever they don't play by either the organization's or their manager's rules, they tend to do the job as they are instructed or to leave the organization. The Mr. Hyde side is allowed to continue abusing subordinates because, as was true of Napoleons, sufferers of this syndrome have developed strategies for controlling their subordinates' realities so that their authority is not challenged.

The basic strategy these individuals use is never to allow their superiors or peers to see their Mr. Hyde side. Whenever they are successful at this strategy, superiors and peers find it difficult to believe a subordinate who complains that his or her manager is abusive and unreasonable. Since superiors and peers see only the pleasant Dr. Jekyll, they attribute subordinates' complaints to an inability of the subordinate to function in the work group, rather than blame the problem on the manager. Only when the problem escalates to a very high level do superiors and peers accept subordinates' definition of reality. At this point there may be no choice but to ask the manager in question to leave—in essence helping him or her commit organizational suicide.

Fortunately, in many cases, individuals who suffer from the Dr. Jekyll and Mr. Hyde Syndrome realize that they have a problem before it becomes so severe that their job is jeopardized. This realization is usually triggered by a critical incident such as the departure of one or more subordinates for reasons such as "personality problems." The Dr. Jekyll/Mr. Hyde may begin to wonder whether he or she has anything to do with the problem and may discover that subordinates feel abused. This may come as quite a shock, since the individual may believe that he or she was only behaving like an effective manager. When Dr. Jekylls/Mr. Hydes discover that their tendency to "be all business" has led to interpersonal problems for their work group, they can begin to work toward changing the way they manage so that they can function as effective managers.

In the following cases you will see how the tendency to play the Inner Game by the rules of the Dr. Jekyll and Mr. Hyde Syndrome led to problems for Maxwell Cooper, a contractor, and Noreen Jackson, a bank manager. We shall also examine the case of L. Robert Patton, who was hired to play the role of Mr. Hyde as president of a company. In the final section of this chapter, we discuss ways in which the problems this syndrome presents for its sufferers can be avoided or overcome.

Maxwell Cooper: Contractor

Maxwell Cooper had known all his life that some day he would run his own company. It was a dream that he had saved and planned for ever since he was a small boy. He remembered how he used to pretend that he was a big oil tycoon living in a huge mansion built from the profits of his businesses. Even though this dream of grandeur became tempered, somewhat, as Max grew up and discovered the reality of who he was and what was possible given the situation he found himself in, he never lost sight of his ultimate goal. When it finally became a reality, however, Max found that being the "boss" was much more difficult than it first appeared. People did not always do what they were supposed to do, and no matter how he tried, things just never seemed to work out exactly as he had planned. Sometimes he wondered whether or not he was cut out to be a manager, but he concluded that he just had a tendency to hire the wrong people. Max often thought, "I wonder where the problem lies."

Maxwell's Early Years

Maxwell Cooper was the son of a fairly successful contractor in a growing community. He always respected and tried to emulate his father and, consequently, always had some scam going that was intended to make him a millionaire. When he was a child, it was neighborhood "carnivals" at which, for a small admission price, kids could play a variety of games and possibly win a token prize. In high school, he had designed T-shirts with various class and club logos on them and sold them during homecoming. One thing was for sure, as soon as Max completed one project, he was looking for another at which he could make some money.

Max spent a lot of his time scheming, planning, and partying with his numerous friends, often neglecting his school work. This didn't seem to matter, however, for while he was not an exceptional student, he was at least average and therefore could attend college if he chose. His father, in essence, demanded that Max attend college, saying, "I never had the opportunity, and I want you to at least try it." Since Max respected his father's opinion, he (somewhat reluctantly) enrolled in a state college whose reputation suggested that school work came second to parties.

Max did not really know what to major in, so he groped around, taking whatever seemed to be the easiest courses. He joined a fraternity during his freshman year and enjoyed the social events this membership provided. Max chose psychology as a major, because his frat brothers said that it would be the easiest major. He didn't really care about school but tried to endure it for his father's sake.

Max looked forward to the summer breaks when he could return home and work for his father's company. He liked the comradery that being with "the guys" afforded him. He worked hard, but after work the guys also played hard. Max had decided that he'd "tough it out" at college, but that as soon as he finished, he would return home, work for his father, and save so that he could obtain his contractor's license and start his own company.

It took Max nearly five years to complete his degree. When graduation day came and he could finally leave college behind, he was somewhat relieved. Now he could begin doing what he had always wanted to do: working toward becoming his own boss.

Max Becomes the Boss

After graduation, Max went back to his home town and worked for his father. During his third year after college, he began studying for his contractor's license, and when he obtained it a year later, he was ready to start out on his own. Since he didn't want to increase competition for his father's business, Max decided to establish his company about 50 miles inland from his father's firm. He had watched the development of the surrounding community and knew that there were many opportunities in the area he selected. He knew that with his father's recommendations, he would have relatively little difficulty generating business. Max took with him some of the younger people with whom he had worked at his father's company. They liked Max and believed that they could have a "good time" working for him.

The first few months after Max started his company were rough. He had to work hard to establish himself as a competent contractor and harder still to attract clients. Within a year, however, he was well on his way to becoming a successful businessman.

Max was indeed a shrewd businessman and a natural salesman. His clients liked him, because he had a unique way of dealing with people which led them to believe that he not only knew what he was doing but really cared about their opinions. He seemed quite knowledgeable and was also receptive to his clients' suggestions. He was willing to take the time to talk to them and address their concerns, and people seemed to appreciate this. Max always seemed so pleasant, even when he was under a great deal of stress to complete a project. He often spent leisurely lunches with his investors, describing a project's progress and outlining the plan for completing various stages.

His clients, however, were unaware of Max's other, darker side which he often showed to his subordinates. Max had traditionally been a one-man operation and had a great deal of difficulty getting accustomed to telling other people what to do. He had seen how his father had handled this situation and had always felt that people had taken advantage of him. Specifically, Max saw how his father's employees "loafed" and seemed to do things their way on their own time schedule. His father, a gentle person, typically ignored this and therefore got the reputation of being a "soft touch." Max, therefore, had decided that the best way to manage was to be firm and to the point about what needed to be done. Sometimes, however, Max was too much to the point.

Max's subordinates found Max to be very knowledgeable but, at times, very "nit-picky." Max could sometimes be very pleasant, but could just as easily "nail someone to a post" because he did not perform some job exactly as Max wanted it done. It sometimes seemed that Max was looking for what was wrong with a job, rather than complimenting people on jobs well done. He was like a tornado whenever he was on site, and if the foreman of the job knew Max was going to be around, he informed the other workers so they'd be on their best behavior. To avoid encounters with Max, workers attempted to learn exactly what Max wanted and did things his way. Any other way would no doubt result in public humiliation at Max's hands.

Max did not like being so hard on his employees. This was not his nature. He liked having a few beers with the guys and joking about this and that. However, now that he was the boss, he felt that it was his responsibility to keep people in line, and he could think of no other way to do this but to be as firm as he could be. After all, he had seen how workers had treated his father, and he did not want to be treated that way.

In response to Max's demands, his employees began to believe that they should not do anything without first checking with Max. Consequently, they began asking Max about even the most trivial details of a job. This irritated Max, since he believed many of the questions were ridiculous—anyone who had been in the business for even a year should know the answers. He could not, in fact, understand why certain questions were being asked and wondered if, perhaps, he had hired people without the necessary skills. It never dawned on him that he might be the cause of his subordinates' behavior.

As a result of the constant questioning and need for Max to describe in detail whatever he wanted subordinates to do, he was beginning to fall behind in his deadlines and was becoming exceedingly anxious. He began to put in 15-hour days and spent all his time on the construction site. This was causing him to neglect his business-development duties, and he could see that it would be only a matter of time before his entire business fell apart. Max began to worry that his company would be a failure.

How Maxwell Cooper's Inner Game Playing
Created Problems

Maxwell Cooper had always been very sure of both his technical and interpersonal skills. He was well liked and seemed to know how to get a job done. As a doer, he was extremely self-motivated, as evidenced by the numerous business projects he undertook. He also seemed to be skilled at "selling" whatever product he developed. Although he preferred working alone and managing himself, he was also able to enjoy the comradery that working for his father provided.

When Max became the boss and had to actually manage other people, things began to fall apart for him. He was still a very successful businessman in terms of being able to sell his product, which now had become basically "selling" himself and his technical abilities. He was friendly and seemed really concerned about his clients' needs. Unfortunately, Max's pleasant personality remained hidden from his employees.

Max, like many sufferers of the Dr. Jekyll/Mr. Hyde Syndrome, believed that if he was too friendly with his employees, they would not respect him. Max had basically decided that he needed to be tough if he was going to succeed. This meant enforcing his rules and standards and not tolerating any deviations. He believed himself to be the technically most skilled individual in his company and therefore expected his employees to follow his directions.

Max, then, attempted to control the behavior of his subordinates so that it would meet his technical standards. In exercising this control, however, he became abusive and unreasonable. In an effort to counter this abuse, Max's subordinates adopted a common strategy used by those who work under a Dr. Jekyll/Mr. Hyde: they decided that the only way to protect themselves against public humiliation was to "check with Max" before doing anything. This resulted in time delays on jobs and in Max's having to spend a great deal of his time on-site to ensure that projects remained on schedule. The time spent "on-the-job," of course, detracted from Max's business-development responsibilities, and he began to realize that, if something wasn't done, his company was going to fail.

Noreen Jackson, the subject of the next case, also came to the realization that there were serious problems within her work group that needed to be resolved. In her case, however, it was a very specific instance that alerted her to the possibility that she might be the cause of the problems her work group was experiencing.

Noreen Jackson: Bank Manager

As Noreen Jackson thought about her achievements, she was pleased with what she had done in her life. In a period of a few years, she had moved up from a part-time bank teller to branch manager. She had become a leader in her organization—someone to be respected. Unfortunately, Noreen could not enjoy her success, because she sometimes felt that the pressure of success was driving her to be a person that she no longer liked or understood. Sometimes, she couldn't believe the way she acted toward other people on the job. Eventually, she felt that such behavior was going to get her into trouble.

Noreen's Early Years

Noreen had begun her banking career as a part-time teller in her home town's savings-and-loan institution. She had taken the job to help defray her junior-college expenses. At first, she felt somewhat uncomfortable having to deal with customers one right after another and worried that she would make a serious mistake. But she liked the relative independence the job afforded her, and since she was taking business courses in school, it seemed to be a terrific opportunity to gain some experience in the "real world."

Upon graduation from junior college with her AA, Noreen decided to move with a friend to Chicago. She asked the branch manager of the bank in which she worked if he knew of banks in Chicago where she might be able to get a job, and he was able to help her obtain a teller position at a small Chicago bank.

Experiences As a Bank Teller

Prior to her first day on the job, Noreen was afraid that she wouldn't be able to handle working in a "Big City" bank. She didn't know whether the training she had received at the local savings-and-loan had really prepared her for such a position. She found to her amazement, however, that she knew a lot more about banking than some of the tellers who had been with the bank for a year or more. She knew what was expected of her and was skilled at performing her job. Noreen was one of the few tellers who "balanced" every night. Not only was Noreen competent at her job, however, but she was well liked by her co-workers. Noreen really liked her job, and she liked the fact that everyone at her branch treated each other as if they were family. She and the other tellers, in fact, often went out after work to "just let off steam."

Noreen's skill and professionalism at her job, as well as her interpersonal skills, earned her both praise from her supervisor and raises. Her performance reviews suggested that she had the skills necessary to become a manager, and after her third year as a teller, her supervisor recommended that she be promoted to branch manager. Since her own supervisor was being promoted to a corporate executive position, he recommended that Noreen take over the small branch in which she had been a teller. He believed that she knew the branch operations fairly well after spending so much time there.

The role of branch manager brought with it not only a pay increase but also the responsibility for running the entire branch. Noreen's main job was to supervise the branch's eight tellers. This meant that now she was going to be "the boss" to some of the people who were her friends. She did not know whether she could handle telling her friends what to do, but decided that if they were her friends, they would support her in her new role.

Noreen Becomes a Manager: Ms. Hyde Is Unleashed

The first few months after Noreen accepted the position were spent in training sessions intended to provide her with the skills she would need to perform her job effectively. These sessions were a real revelation for Noreen. She learned a lot about what managers really do—things she had not been aware of before. She listened intently and took notes while the instructors described the responsibilities of branch managers and how they should be carried out. Noreen hoped that when she returned to her branch, she would be able to put into practice what she learned. One thing was paramount in her mind: that she had to be as professional as possible in her new role.

When Noreen returned and assumed her role as branch manager, she somehow felt that she had been alienated from her friends at work. She wasn't sure whether it was just her own perception of the situation or whether it was really that people began to treat her differently. "Unfortunately," she thought, "this part of the job was not discussed at the training sessions, so I'll have to do the best I can." The problem was that Noreen desperately wanted to continue being "one of the girls," but what she had learned in her training sessions suggested that this was not the appropriate way to behave as a manager. She believed that if she remained too friendly with people on the job, they would take advantage of her and she would fail. She decided that the best strategy for protecting her feelings and preserving her friendships was to rely on the rules of the organization for guidance. She thought, "People can't argue with the rules, and if they do, they *have* to see that I am only doing my job by enforcing them."

Unfortunately, trying to enforce the rules as a way to manage resulted in more problems than Noreen had expected. She found that her subordinates frequently stretched or bent the rules to meet their own needs, and this really frustrated her.

As a result of this frustration, Noreen would sometimes simply "go off" for no apparent reason and humiliate someone in front of everyone else. In her mind, however, she was trying to get people to see that they were not doing what they were supposed to do. She usually did not intend to hurt other people. It was almost as if she couldn't help herself. Whenever this happened, she would usually cool off quickly and ask to speak to the person alone. In these sessions, she would apologize for embarrassing the person in front of others and restate her request that the person comply with the rules. In an attempt to avoid these encounters, she even tried writing and circulating a series of memos that outlined policy and procedure, asking each subordinate to read and initial them.

Outside of work, at first, everything was pretty much the same. Noreen continued to go out at least once a week with her employees. As time went on, however, her appearance at these sessions grew less and less frequent. Her subordinates believed it was because Noreen was trying to emulate the other managers who did not socialize with their subordinates or that she was, in fact, spending her time with them. The fact was that Noreen was growing exceedingly uncomfortable with playing one role in the office and attempting to still be friends after work. She often amusingly thought of herself as the cartoon sheep dog who spends his entire day beating up a coyote (because it's his job)—and then, when the clock strikes five, the two say, "Good night," and go to have a drink together. Noreen believed that she simply could no longer play this "nice gal" role after work, given what she went through during the day with her subordinates.

Perhaps the beginning of the end for Noreen came when her best friend, Judy Dobbs, quit. Noreen's subordinates had felt, for some time, that Noreen always seemed to pick on Judy more than anyone else. This was no doubt partially due to the fact that Judy would stand up to Noreen whenever she was being unreasonable. This would, of course, infuriate Noreen, who believed that if Judy were truly her friend, she would respect her authority and do as she was told. They would end up practically yelling at each other and eventually settle the dispute behind closed doors. The final encounter between Judy and Noreen came toward the end of Noreen's second year as manager.

Judy had shown up at work one day 15 minutes late. The prior week, Noreen had circulated a memo stating that employees were expected to be at the bank and ready to work no later than 9 A.M. While this had always been the "official" start of the work day, many tellers had traditionally bent this rule. Sometimes they arrived at the bank as late as 9:20 A.M. No one had ever seemed to care, as long as all the preparation for the bank's daily opening was completed before 10 A.M. After Noreen's memo, however, most tellers arrived at work usually no later than 8:50 A.M. Judy, however, insisted that the enforcement of this rule was "ridiculous" and had told Noreen so. When Noreen refused to relax the rules, Judy made it a point to be late every day as a form of protest.

When Judy arrived that morning 15 minutes late, Noreen approached her and said, "I see you're a little late this morning. Did you have car problems?"

Judy replied that she hadn't had any problems at all. She said, "Why do you ask?"

Noreen said that Judy had obviously seen the memo regarding being on time to work, since she had initialed it. Judy replied that she had seen it and that she had felt it was unnecessary. She said, "We've always gotten here within a few minutes of nine o'clock. Sometimes we're 15 minutes early; sometimes we're 15 minutes late. Sometimes we stay after work a half hour or more to complete a job, but I notice that that isn't even taken into consideration in your memo. Frankly, I don't see what difference it makes what time we get here as long as we're ready for the customers by ten o'clock."

At this point, Noreen lost her cool. She said, rather loudly, "Oh, come on, Judy. I know you've been late every day since I sent out that memo, and I know you're just doing it to get to me. Well, I'm just doing my job. This is corporate policy, and if you continue being late every day, it may be grounds for your dismissal. Please don't let it happen again."

Judy was really angry now. "The nerve of Noreen to treat me like some kind of child," she thought. She responded with, "Well, I think this whole thing is stupid. All these little rules make life absolute hell around here. If you'd just let us do our jobs the way we used to, your life and ours would be much easier."

At this point, Noreen insisted that they go into her office. Twenty minutes later both emerged looking like they had gone into battle with no one the victor.

After this incident, Judy believed that Noreen had "really lost it," so she decided to talk to Noreen's supervisor about the problems the tellers were having with Noreen. She began: "I think that we have a communication problem in our branch. Noreen wants things done a certain way, and she just never listens to what we have to say. She wants the rules followed to the letter, and doesn't take into account that sometimes this is impractical or unreasonable."

Noreen's supervisor, Clarence Carpenter, said that he was not aware of any problems with Noreen. She had always seemed like a competent manager and appeared to "get the job done." He had met her, and she seemed to have a very pleasant personality.

Judy responded, "I used to think she had a pleasant personality, too. Ever since she became branch manager, however, she's become extremely difficult to get along with on the job."

Clarence told Judy that he would look into the matter and would do something about it, if he felt it necessary.

Unfortunately for Judy, the meeting with Clarence seemed to have little impact on the situation. Judy believed that Clarence could see only the surface level of Noreen's behavior, and at that level she was performing quite well. The situation continued much as it had before, and Judy felt there was little recourse left to her but to look for another job. She wanted to preserve what little there was left of her friendship with Noreen.

When Judy quit, Noreen asked her why, and Judy said that it was because she and Noreen had a personality problem. They simply could not work together as manager and subordinate. This disturbed Noreen, and she began to wonder whether other subordinates felt the same way. When, within six months of Judy's resignation, two other subordinates left the branch, Noreen realized that perhaps she was at the base of the problem, and she decided to seek help in changing her behavior and in becoming a more effective manager.

How Noreen Jackson's Inner Game Playing Created Problems

Noreen wanted to succeed in her job and desperately wanted to be liked by other people. In the doer's role, Noreen was able to satisfy both these needs. Even though she was somewhat insecure about her technical skills as a teller, she was liked by her co-workers and was praised for her ability to perform her job effectively.

Unfortunately, once Noreen was promoted to a management position, she came to believe that if she was to be successful, she would have to quit being "one of the girls." In other words, she believed that being liked by her subordinates was inconsistent with being able to carry out the requirements of the managerial role. She believed that if she continued to be too close to her subordinates, it would be difficult to ask them to do things, in the interest of the organization, that they did not want to do. Noreen believed that if a manager falls into the trap of allowing subordinates too much freedom in performing their jobs, then he or she is doomed to failure. She therefore decided that the best way to ensure that she would be able to carry out her responsibilities was to forget about satisfying her need to be liked through her work role. She found other ways, outside her work life, to satisfy her need to be liked. That way she could protect her self-esteem need (through reducing the likelihood that she would fail as a manager).

Unlike Maxwell Cooper, Noreen did not believe that she was her work group's technical expert. She therefore believed that she could not control others' behavior through telling them how, technically, to do their jobs. She could, however, succeed as a manager and satisfy her need for control by learning and enforcing the organization's rules. And this is indeed what she did.

Noreen's tendency to enforce the rules became so extreme that she ignored the needs of her subordinates, and they, in essence, rebelled against her. This is a fairly typical reaction of those who work under a Dr. Jekyll/Mr. Hyde. These subordinates cannot understand how their managers can be so insensitive, and when the situation becomes too severe, they either quit or appeal to their manager's supervisor to resolve the problem. Noreen's subordinate and friend, Judy Dobbs, attempted to use the latter strategy to alleviate her work group's problems. Unfortunately, as is true in many cases, Noreen's supervisor was exposed only to her Dr. Jekyll side. He found it difficult to believe Judy and therefore did not actively investigate the situation. Judy had no recourse but to resign.

While Judy's resignation was an unfortunate occurrence, it did serve as the catalyst for Noreen to realize that, perhaps, it was Noreen and not Judy who was the source of the interpersonal problems in the branch. In fact, it appeared that Noreen had, for some time, been aware of the way she was treating her subordinates. She had justified her behavior by appealing to the requirements of her role. Judy's resignation, however, led her to believe that something was very wrong with her interpretation of her role and that, if she wanted to continue being a successful manager, she would have to make some changes. In the final section, we suggest what people like Noreen Jackson can do to avoid or overcome the Dr. Jekyll and Mr. Hyde Syndrome. First, however, we shall examine a variation on this Syndrome.

A Variation on the
Dr. Jekyll and Mr. Hyde Syndrome:
Robert Patton, the "Hired Gun"

Another situation in which the Dr. Jekyll and Mr. Hyde Syndrome may be encountered is where an individual's natural personality must be concealed in order to perform his or her role effectively. Specifically, when a CEO of a company does not like to deal with conflict himself or herself, the solution is often to hire someone to play the role of Mr. Hyde.

The CEO, who is often a victim of the Salesperson Syndrome (discussed in Chapter 9), decides to bring in someone to play the role of the "bad guy" or heavy. This manager is supposed to act like Mr. Hyde. He or she is supposed to be a tough, no-nonsense manager. That is the explicit role, regardless of the individual's true personality.

If the person playing the Mr. Hyde is really caring, humanistic, and concerned for people, the very act of playing the role can be costly to the individual. This was the case in the situation of L. Robert Patton, who joined Consumer Products Corporation as President.

Bob Patton was a lawyer who had been counsel for George Holtz, owner and CEO of Consumer Products Corporation (CPC), for almost a decade. George Holtz was a brilliant entrepreneur. His firm was successful, and he was a generous person who rewarded his people quite well. Moreover, he was a laissez-faire manager, who believed people should be given a great deal of autonomy to do their "own thing."

Unfortunately, this autonomy had become license, and many people were taking advantage of the situation and George's generous nature. Among George's managerial limitations were his desire to avoid conflict and his need to be liked—characteristics of the Salesperson Syndrome.

George found it difficult to change this side of his personality, and so he hired Bob Patton to come in and clean up the problem. Bob's explicit role was to wear the "black hat." He was to play the role of Mr. Hyde, and he did it well.

Bob Patton thoroughly intimidated people. He issued orders, and if they were not followed, heads rolled. Inefficiency and waste had become a way of life at CPC, and it took Bob Patton more than two years to clean up. Some people resisted and fought back. While Patton lost some battles, he ultimately won the war. However, Bob Patton paid a personal price for all this turmoil.

He considered himself a good Christian and, contrary to prevailing opinion, did not enjoy firing people. He had a job to do, and he did it. His true Dr. Jekyll nature was suppressed while Mr. Hyde was needed. He felt he had to hide his Dr. Jekyll nature or people would take advantage of it, as they had with George Holtz.

In brief, this was a case in which the role of Mr. Hyde was by design, and it cost Bob Patton internal peace of mind to play it to the hilt. Perhaps Bob should not have assumed this role, but he did.

There are many Bob Pattons in business. For them, the role of Mr. Hyde is that of a hired gun. As they play this role, they need to remember their true nature and manage their self-esteem. Hopefully, the period of role playing will be brief, for it can cost this type of Dr. Jekyll/Mr. Hyde a great deal of personal distress.

How to Overcome the
Dr. Jekyll and Mr. Hyde Syndrome

The basic problem for individuals who suffer from the Dr. Jekyll and Mr. Hyde Syndrome is how to resolve the conflict between their need to be liked and their need for control and self-esteem. They need to learn how to satisfy all three needs through the managerial role.

First, individuals who suffer from this syndrome need to learn that they do not have to exercise ultimate control over their subordinates in order to be successful. They *do* have to motivate and direct subordinates' actions so that they are consistent with organizational goals, but in doing so, they can give subordinates freedom to make certain decisions about how they perform their jobs. In allowing subordinates to make certain decisions themselves, these managers need to learn to accept the fact that the delegated tasks will probably not be completed exactly as they would have completed them and that subordinates may bend an organization's rules to meet their particular needs. When either of these events occurs and the manager thinks some correction is necessary, he or she must be able to provide feedback in such a manner that subordinates do not feel they are being abused. Basically, a Dr. Jekyll/Mr. Hyde needs to learn how to provide constructive feedback.

The second thing sufferers of the Dr. Jekyll and Mr. Hyde Syndrome need to learn is that they can satisfy their need to be liked in their role as managers. In fact, there are many individuals who are successful leaders simply because their subordinates love and respect them. These individuals, known as charismatic leaders, are successful because they recognize and attempt to satisfy the needs of their subordinates. While few people can manage solely through this type of leadership, recognition of subordinates' needs is an important strategy for playing the Inner Game of Management effectively. Further, when subordinates believe that their manager really cares about their needs, they will tend to like the manager, and therefore the manager's own need to be liked will be satisfied.

What action steps can a Dr. Jekyll/Mr. Hyde take to overcome this syndrome? The first thing these individuals should do is to practice showing the Dr. Jekyll side of their personality to their subordinates. For a variety of reasons, a Dr. Jekyll/Mr. Hyde fears, or is at least uncomfortable with, showing this side to others. The person should experiment with revealing this side and then assess people's reactions. Some people fear that their nice side will be seen as weakness and, therefore, overcompensate with the Mr. Hyde side. The practice of gradually revealing the Dr. Jekyll side can help overcome these concerns.

A Dr. Jekyll/Mr. Hyde also must learn how to "bend the rules." An action step here is to discuss a particular problem involving a violation of a rule with a trusted associate to gain a different perspective on what is reasonable in the situation.

A third strategy is to modify the "John Dillinger theory of management," which states that you can get people to cooperate with a gun. The revised theory is that you can get more cooperation with a smile and a gun than with a gun alone. In other words, the Dr. Jekyll/Mr. Hyde should begin to become more approachable.

The final lesson for sufferers of the Dr. Jekyll and Mr. Hyde Syndrome to learn is that since their own effectiveness as managers rests on the ability and willingness of their subordinates to achieve organizational objectives, they must be careful to temper their need for control with their need to be liked. They must try to satisfy both in the performance of their managerial role, for it is in this way that they will increase their ability to play the Inner Game of Management effectively.

Chapter 8
The Hamlet Syndrome

The classic personification of indecision in Western literature is Shakespeare's Hamlet. In this play, Hamlet recites a soliloquy that begins: "To be or not to be; that is the question . . ." In this speech, Hamlet describes the frustration that he feels because he cannot decide what course of action to take and yet knows that action is needed. His uncle has murdered his father, the king; has wed his mother; and has assumed the throne, which is rightly Hamlet's. Hamlet feels compelled to avenge his father's death, but does not want to act until he has completely analyzed the situation in which he finds himself, and is certain of the facts.

Hamlet's analysis begins with an attempt to determine whether his uncle really murdered his father. The information that leads him to suspect that the crime has been committed is provided by a ghost, whose existence, Hamlet believes, could be a product of his own imagination. Hamlet, therefore, concocts an elaborate scheme designed to determine whether or not the ghost's account of the murder is accurate. Rather than confront his uncle (the king) with the information he has received from the ghost, Hamlet hires an acting troupe to present a play in which the performers reenact the circumstances surrounding his father's murder. During the "play within a play," Hamlet monitors the expressions of both his uncle and his mother in order to assess whether they reveal the truth of the ghost's accusations.

On the basis of his own assessment of his uncle's and his mother's reactions, backed by the observation of his friend, Horatio, Hamlet decides that a crime has been committed and must be avenged.

Having established that a murder has indeed taken place, Hamlet must

116

now decide how and when to carry out his revenge. Unfortunately, he continues to be nearly paralyzed by indecision. Even when presented with the opportunity to slay his uncle with little risk to himself, he finds himself unable to act. Finding his uncle in prayer, Hamlet initially decides to take his uncle's life and thus have his revenge. Within a few seconds, however, he begins to question whether killing his uncle while he is in prayer represents sufficient revenge. Hamlet convinces himself that it is better to wait until he finds his uncle engaged in what he calls "slovenly acts" so that there will be no time to repent and escape certain eternal damnation.

As the play unfolds, it appears that the king suspects that Hamlet is plotting against him. While Hamlet is engaged in planning his attack, the king acts to rid himself of Hamlet forever. The king sends Hamlet on a mission to England with a letter containing his death warrant. Fortunately, Hamlet is able to foil the plot against his life and returns to England, only to find that he now has another enemy in Laertes, the son of the Lord Chamberlain.

Laertes wants to avenge his own father's murder, which Hamlet committed as the Lord Chamberlain was spying on him. After telling Laertes that it was his madness that drove him to kill the Lord Chamberlain and begging his forgiveness, Hamlet agrees to meet him in a fencing match. Still plotting his uncle's death, Hamlet begins the fencing match, never suspecting that Laertes and the king have already planned his death. Laertes's sword, which has been dipped in lethal poison, strikes Hamlet, and he begins to die after witnessing his mother's death from a poison-laced drink intended for him. At this point, Hamlet must kill his uncle, because there will be no other opportunities for him to do so. He strikes his uncle with Laertes's poison-tipped sword, and his uncle dies. The tragic Hamlet was finally able to act and get his revenge, but he had to be forced into action by his own impending death.

The Hamlet Syndrome in Management

It is important that individuals who are promoted to managerial roles learn how to make decisions effectively and efficiently. Unfortunately, many individuals are, like Shakespeare's Hamlet, paralyzed by some form of indecision. They cannot decide what course of action to take or when to take it, so they do nothing at all until they are forced to. Sometimes, as was true of Shakespeare's Hamlet, their inability to make a decision and carry it out eventually leads to their organizational demise.

For individuals who suffer from what we call the Hamlet Syndrome, decision making represents a threat to both their self-esteem and their need to be liked. They fear that if they make the wrong decision, they will be seen as inadequate. If they make a decision that not everyone likes (which is true of many decisions), then others will resent them. As a result of these fears, these individuals prefer to defer decision-making responsibility to either their subordinates or superiors or to simply do nothing at all, hoping that the dilemma represented by the decision-making situation will simply resolve itself. Eventually, as was the case with Hamlet, they may be forced to act, but the delay their indecisiveness has brought about may cause their actions to be inappropriate or ineffective.

Variations on the Hamlet Theme

We believe that there are three basic methods Hamlets use to avoid making decisions. The first is the Information Seeker. These Hamlets believe that if only they could collect enough information, then they would be able to make a rational and effective decision. In other words, these individuals suffer from "paralysis through analysis." These individuals, when confronted with a decision, will invest a great deal of energy into finding out all they can about the various alternatives before making a decision. While this is an appropriate strategy and certainly one that can be very effective in many situations, Hamlets tend to carry it to an extreme. They continue to collect information until a "higher authority" presses them to make a decision. If no such pressure exists, they may postpone the decision indefinitely until, eventually, the decision is made for them.

A second strategy that Hamlets use is that of the Buck Passer. Individuals who use this strategy deny that they have responsibility for decision making. Sometimes, they find support for this abdication of authority in the lack of clearly defined roles and responsibilities. These individuals can simply say, "It's not my job." Others who adopt this strategy "plead ignorance" to avoid having to make decisions. They may say, and may truly believe, "I thought *you* were going to do it." Still others appeal to their superiors for direction and complain that it is their supervisors' problem that things aren't getting done, because they have not provided enough direction. Whatever method these Hamlets use to avoid responsibility, such avoidance often frustrates the individual's superiors and subordinates. Tasks are not completed and problems remain unresolved, because the Hamlet is constantly trying to defer decision-making responsibility to someone else. Again, the effectiveness of decisions that are made is decreased.

The third strategy that Hamlets use—and perhaps the worst for their own well-being—is that of the Agonizer. These individuals are paralyzed by an intense fear that the decisions they make will, somehow, hurt them, their company, or other employees. Like the Information Seeker, they always fear that they don't have enough information, but they do not seek more information. They do not avoid responsibility (like the Buck Passer), but instead feel overly responsible for the decisions they have to make. Like the Shakespearean Hamlet, these individuals suffer a great deal, because they know that they need to act but do not know what to do. They don't delegate, and they don't plan. They spend much of their time worrying about the decisions they have to make, and their fear of making the wrong decision is so great that they do not make decisions until they absolutely have to. These individuals hope that, somehow, things will take care of themselves. Unfortunately, they never do, and these Hamlets may soon find that the effectiveness of their work group has decreased and that they are about to be fired.

Whatever strategy the Hamlet adopts to avoid making decisions, it will eventually lead to a dysfunctional work group. Subordinates are looking to the manager for direction, and if he or she cannot or will not make a decision, subordinates may begin doing nothing at all or doing whatever they want to do. The manager, by avoiding decision making, has given up control of the work group and in so doing may be injuring the effectiveness and productivity of the organization as a whole. The Hamlet's superiors may begin to wonder whether they have promoted a true leader, and if this individual is constantly seeking their advice before making a decision, the answer to their question will be a flat "No"—and the manager will be out of a job.

The following case studies illustrate the problems people encounter when they employ the Information Seeker, Buck Passer, or Agonizer strategies. The final section of this chapter describes how these problems can be overcome.

Chadwick Ishikawa:
The Information-Seeking Hamlet

Chadwick Ishikawa had always been well respected for his analytical ability. He prided himself in being able to find the right answers, if given enough time and resources. Lately, however, his tendency to gather as much information as possible before making a decision seemed to be getting him into trouble. His boss, who happened to be the president of the company, was beginning to complain that Chad was not making decisions fast enough. Chad could not understand how anyone would want him to make decisions any faster, because without adequate information these decisions could be incorrect, and that would reflect badly on him and, perhaps, on the entire company.

Chad's Early Years

Chadwick Ishikawa was the son of an engineer who loved to tinker around the house. From an early age, Chad began to follow in his father's footsteps; he always had a variety of projects to which he was devoting his time. His parents and teachers often commented on how meticulous Chad was in whatever he did. It seemed to take him forever to complete anything, but when he finally finished, whatever he was working on was nearly perfect.

In school, Chad earned high marks in math and science as a result of his ability to solve complex problems through seeking the information needed. He decided, therefore, that he would pursue a career in the sciences as a way to use the skills he possessed. He received numerous scholarship offers and decided to enter UCLA, which had a good reputation for its chemistry program.

Chad excelled in the chemistry program at UCLA, receiving some of the highest marks in his class. This did not come easily for him, however. He worked very hard and spent much of his time in the library researching whatever problems he had been assigned so that he would be sure not to miss any aspect of a problem. He wanted to know everything so that he would not look foolish.

Chad Becomes a Research Chemist

After graduation, Chad went to work for a relatively large bio-engineering firm, BioTech, as a research chemist. His job involved working on complex problems that were assigned to him by his team leader. Chad found the work rewarding and discovered that what he had always been skilled at (finding the right answers after thorough research of the questions) was highly valued by the company. He liked the fact that he could work independently to solve problems and that others in his group shared his enthusiasm for quality research.

Things ran pretty smoothly for Chad during his eight years with the company. He received numerous raises and was promoted to team leader during his fifth year on the job. He continued to excel in his area, but was beginning to wonder whether he should try something different at another company. Chad thought a great deal about whether to leave the company and even compiled a list of the pros and cons of remaining or leaving. He had begun to look into other opportunities, but hadn't yet found out everything he needed to know about the companies he was considering when a "golden opportunity" presented itself.

During Chad's seventh year with BioTech, he was asked by one of its former employees to join a relatively new company as a member of the research and development team. This company was only five years old, yet was making great strides in new-product development. It had established itself as a firm to be reckoned with. Chad had read a lot about the exploits of its founder and president, as well as the success the company had enjoyed since its founding. The company wanted to hire him, and Chad saw this as his chance to leave BioTech without having to go through any further job search. He decided to accept the position, which carried with it more responsibility as well as increased salary and prestige.

Chad Becomes a Member of NuChem Products

Chad entered NuChem Products as a member of the research and development team, a job very similar to that which he had had at BioTech prior to his promotion. At NuChem, however, things moved along much more rapidly than they did at BioTech. To Chad, it seemed that everyone wanted the answers faster than was reasonably possible. He often felt that the company was taking too great a risk on some projects, because he and his team members had not had time to thoroughly research the problems. Most of the time, however, the company's strategy seemed to pay off: the products were usually readily accepted by its customers.

Chad was a well-respected member of the team, known for his thoroughness. Whenever he was given a problem, management knew that he would devote ample time to finding the right answer. He also seemed to work well as a member of a team.

Chad Becomes a Vice President

As the company continued to grow as a result of its continued success at product development, its president soon found that he needed more senior managers. At this time, Chad had been with the company nearly three years, and the president felt that it was time for Chad to move up. He promoted Chad to Vice President of Production, a position in which Chad would be in charge of all research and product development. It was at this point that Chad's thorough research techniques began to get him into trouble.

Chad's new position required him to make a great many decisions regarding the acceptability and applicability of new products. He was to report directly to the president on the progress of the research and development teams and to make recommendations for product acceptance. His technical knowledge seemed to make him the perfect candidate for such a role. His desire to have all the information before making a decision, however, severely hampered his ability to make these decisions quickly enough to meet the company's and the president's needs.

Often, team leaders would send reports to Chad for his approval of their projects, and Chad would simply return them with a comment, "Insufficient Discussion of Product and its Application." In fact, this became nearly a standard practice. Team leaders began to expect that every report would be returned at least once. This frustrated the team leaders, because they had to spend what they believed to be too much time writing, rather than actually producing and refining the product.

Team leaders were not the only ones who were frustrated. Chad was frustrated because he could not understand why his subordinates wouldn't do it right the first time. Further, he had to spend a great deal of time poring over each report in order to assess its thoroughness, and there just never seemed to be enough information so that he could strongly recommend that the product be pursued.

While Chad believed that he was doing a more-than-adequate job, the president began to wonder what was going on. It seemed that Chad could never meet his deadlines and always said that it was because he needed just "one more piece of critical information." The president tried to convince him that in a growing firm in a highly competitive field, it was better to "go with a product" that seemed reasonable than to "mess around with the details." He emphasized that if the company waited too long, one of its competitors would "beat NuChem to the punch."

Chad simply could not understand this. He feared that if he didn't have accurate and complete information on the products, he might be responsible for costing the company a lot of money. This, he feared, would ruin his career, so he continued to operate in much the same fashion as he had done before, ignoring the president's pleas for more rapid decisions on product lines.

The president kept trying to push Chad into what he called a "rapid-decision-making mode." He even tried imposing deadlines on product-idea submissions, but Chad always had an excuse for not meeting deadlines. One day, Chad's reluctance to commit himself to a product did cost the company money, and it was at this point that Chad realized what an impact his good intentions had had on his company's success.

One team at NuChem had been working feverishly on a new industrial resin for nearly a year under Chad's supervision. It had recently had a break-through which appeared to solve all the problems it had encountered in the past. The team truly believed that the resin had been tested enough and was ready for market. When Chad read the report, however, he had a number of questions and disagreed with the conclusion that it was "ready to go." He told the group to run some more tests and said that he would take it to the president after that. The team members reluctantly went back to work, but during the next month, while they were rerunning a series of tests at Chad's request, another firm came out with a similar product that greatly reduced the market share for NuChem's product.

When the president heard that the company had been beaten to market by competitors, he was incensed. He could not understand what was going on in research and development, so he decided that it was time to talk to the team leaders. He called in the team responsible for the product and began, "I don't understand what's happening down there on the floor. How could Dozier beat us when we've been so close for so long?"

The team leader said, "Well, Chad believed that we weren't ready. He told us that he wanted more tests run before he would be able to recommend that we go with the resin. We were just doing as we were told, but I'll tell you this: we sure didn't like it. We had a great product nearly three months ago."

The team leader's comments only solidified what the president had believed for some time: Chad could not operate as a manager in a fast-paced work environment. He just worked too slowly, and while that was appropriate for some firms, in the aggressive atmosphere that the president was trying to create, it could be disastrous. He decided to have a talk with Chad.

When the president decided to talk with Chad, Chad knew that it had something to do with the Dozier fiasco. He felt confident that he could make a case for why he had delayed the production of the product, so he entered the president's office in a fairly confident mood.

The president began, "Chad, it seems that we have a problem in research and development. We aren't getting products out fast enough anymore. Is there some reason for this?"

Chad replied: "I think we're doing a good job, given the status of most reports I receive from the teams. It seems to me that the teams are just not doing a good enough job testing the materials before they submit their reports. I want to be sure that the product is a good one before I waste your time with it. So, I often have them run a few more tests just to be sure."

The president was trying to contain his anger at this point. He and Chad had had this conversation several times over the past two and a half years since Chad's promotion, apparently with little effect. He said, "Chad, I know you're just trying to do a good job for the company, but as I've told you over and over again, we're in a fast-paced industry where, if we don't get new products out the door quickly, we lose—and lose big. During the last week, in fact, our inability to get the product out cost us, in my estimate, at least several million dollars. Now, do you know who I blame for this?"

Chad knew now that he was about to be hit over the head with a big one and that his only defense was that he truly believed his actions were in the best interest of the company. He replied: "O.K., O.K., I get the point. I only delayed the decision on the product because I didn't want us to market anything less than a quality resin. I really believed that I didn't have enough information to ensure that the product would be a good one. I guess I really blew it."

The president said that he wanted Chad to think seriously about whether or not he could adjust his style so that it would fit in with the goals of the company. If he felt that he could not, the president said, he would help Chad secure a similar position at a more established firm where his style would more closely match the way the firm operated.

How Chad Ishikawa's Inner Game Playing Created Problems

Chad Ishikawa was successful in his profession because he possessed the ability to patiently seek out all the information he needed before committing himself to a course of action. This was a valuable skill when he occupied the role of doer and team leader, because others assigned the projects to him and imposed external deadlines. He did not have to assume responsibility for many of the decisions affecting him.

Once Chad became a member of senior management in a fast-growing firm, his way of solving problems was no longer appropriate. His position now involved making rapid decisions, often without time to gather all the information he preferred to have. Chad could not accept this situation and continued to operate much as he had done in the past. He greatly feared that, without adequate information, he would make an inappropriate decision and be blamed for it, which would deal quite a blow to his self-esteem. Chad felt threatened and thus continued to operate as he had in the past.

Chad retained control of decisions (by asking team leaders to get him more information, even when they thought he had enough), yet seldom made a decision until the president blatantly asked him for one. Other Hamlets attempt to defer decision-making responsibility to others, as we will take note in the case of Rachelle Garcia, the Buck Passer, who is the subject of our next case.

Rachelle Garcia: The Buck-Passing Hamlet

Rachelle Garcia was the type of person who, to the outside world, always seemed to know what she wanted and how to get it. Inside, however, Rachelle was often wracked with indecision. It seemed that life was always presenting her with a series of critical choices and that she could just never make up her mind. She constantly felt that she should take a more proactive attitude toward her life, but since she could often not make up her mind about what she wanted to do, she just let things happen or let someone else make the decision for her.

Rachelle's life goal had been to be an engineer, since she believed that this occupation provided her the opportunity to combine her mathematical and creative skills in solving problems. She worried, however, that she might not succeed, because she believed herself to be somewhat ordinary in terms of her intelligence and she knew that it would be tough to be a good engineer. In college, she dedicated herself to learning all she could about her chosen field so that she would be well qualified. Her willingness to give more than 100 percent to produce excellent work earned Rachelle numerous academic awards at the Berkeley campus of the University of California, from which she graduated. At graduation, Rachelle was considered one of the top young engineers and, as a result, was offered attractive jobs by some of the industry's better firms.

Rachelle did not know what type of firm she wanted to work for and agonized over the decision until a friend of hers told her that he was going to work for Aerospace Corp. She had always respected Lenny's opinion, so she decided to go with Aerospace. She soon found that this firm had a "friendly" atmosphere in which everyone was known and referred to by his or her first name, which made Rachelle feel that she had made the right choice. The thing that impressed her the most, however, was that the manager in charge of the unit to which Rachelle was to be assigned, Alan Barrett, provided a great deal of direction and advice to his employees. This was important to Rachelle, because it relieved her of having to make a lot of decisions regarding her work. She could just do what she was told to do, and since she was a talented engineer, she believed she would be a success.

Working at Aerospace Corp. was fascinating and challenging to Rachelle. She liked the members of her work group, and they liked her. Her fellow employees saw her as both bright and personable, although somewhat shy. Many members of her work group turned to her for advice on projects, because they knew they could get the right answers in language they could understand. Al Barrett saw Rachelle as fundamentally sound technically. She was not only able to accurately apply her knowledge to solving those problems *assigned* to her, but was also able to effectively help others solve their problems. It was for these reasons that after Al Barrett was promoted to Group Engineering Director, he recommended that Rachelle Garcia be promoted to succeed him. His recommendation was accepted, and he was pleased.

Rachelle Becomes a Manager

Rachelle was very pleased with her promotion, since it meant recognition and increased responsibilities as well as increased compensation. She worried, however, that she might not be able to handle some aspects of her new job. Al said that he felt Rachelle would be a good department manager because she got along well with people and, most important, she got results. Rachelle knew that results were important to the firm and hoped that, somehow, in her new position she would be able to make a significant contribution to the firm's productivity through helping others achieve their goals.

In her new job, Rachelle acted as a friendly adviser to those she supervised. She was acquainted with all of her subordinates, since she had worked with them over the years. They were all good workers in her eyes, so she never felt the need to discipline them. They seemed to know what needed to be done and did it without much supervision. Consequently, Rachelle could continue working much as she had always done, except that now she was responsible for providing reports on the department's progress to both the group itself and senior management.

Rachelle decided that the best way to gather the information needed to make these reports was to continue Al Barrett's practice of having weekly meetings in order to set and monitor group goals and generate new ideas. At these meetings, Rachelle placed a great deal of emphasis on her subordinates' participation in decisions affecting their work, and, for the most part, each member set his or her own goals within the framework of the group's ultimate goals. This was an effective way to manage the group, since it was fairly well integrated, having worked together for several years. Further, through such a practice, Rachelle did not have to make all the decisions, and she could ensure that people were working on those aspects of the project that appealed to them the most. She didn't have to force people to do things they didn't want to do.

The team continued working well together under Rachelle's leadership (as it had under its previous leader) for about a year and a half, but then things began to go wrong. It all began when one of the senior members of the team, Francine Hughes, left the company. Francine had traditionally had the informal role of report writer for the group. She enjoyed writing the reports, was good at it, and always seemed to get them to Rachelle's supervisor, Al Barrett, well ahead of schedule. The team valued Francine because practically everyone else, including Rachelle, hated report writing. With Francine's departure, however, Rachelle needed to find someone else to take on her role. She asked Harry Larson, another senior engineer, to write the reports. Even though Harry really didn't want the job, he felt compelled to help Rachelle out and, therefore, accepted the position.

Rachelle assumed that her problem was solved, but unfortunately, her troubles were just beginning. Since Harry disliked writing the reports, he never seemed to get to them, or when he did, he did such a poor job that they usually had to be rewritten. Al began to notice that the quality of the reports was declining and that they were also not getting in on time. He mentioned this to Rachelle, and Rachelle assured him that it would just take some time—that Harry just wasn't "in the swing of things yet." She said that she would talk with Harry and assured Al that the problem would be taken care of.

Unfortunately, Harry's report writing was not Rachelle's only problem. Al was becoming increasingly concerned about the apparent drop in creativity and initiative that Rachelle's group was exhibiting. When Al was team leader, it seemed that his group (which was now Rachelle's group) was at the forefront in the company. It always seemed to be generating new ideas for projects and did not wait until it was assigned a project. This group trait was no longer as prevalent with Rachelle at the helm, and Al began to wonder why.

Rachelle believed that she was operating in the same fashion as Al before her and just assumed that if Al wanted something specific done, he would tell her to do it. In the absence of such direction, Rachelle just continued allowing group members to do whatever they wanted to do. They were producing, and she knew that that was what the company valued. What Rachelle apparently did not know, or what she refused to believe, was that Al was beginning to get some flak from upstairs about the creativity drop in Rachelle's group. Finally, during Rachelle's second year as a team leader, Al decided to talk to her about her performance.

Al began by telling Rachelle that, while he was fairly pleased with her performance, there were some very definite problems that had to be resolved. First, there was the issue of late and unacceptable progress reports. Rachelle said that she had talked to Harry about the problems and that Harry would solve them. Al said, "Look, Rachelle, I know that you've given this job to Harry, but he clearly is not working out. The bottom line is that the progress reports are ultimately your responsibility. When they are incomplete or poor, it reflects on your performance and not just Harry's. If he's not doing his job, you need to find someone else to handle it or take over the responsibility yourself."

Rachelle was somewhat irritated by Al's insinuation that she wasn't as good a manager as she thought she was. She said, "Well, Al, I'm sorry. I wish you'd told me about this sooner, because when I didn't hear any more from you about the reports, I assumed that the problem had taken care of itself."

Al replied, "Rachelle, I think that's one of the problems you need to resolve if you're going to go anywhere in management. You assume that things are taking care of themselves, and instead, what's happening is that a lot of problems just keep springing up and getting worse. You need to take more responsibility for what's happening in your area. And that reminds me: I've been concerned that members of your group are doing only what they are assigned. That's fine, but they also should be trying to generate new projects."

Rachelle could not believe this. She was doing exactly what Al told her to do, and now Al wanted her to stimulate more creativity. She said, "Al, I've done everything that's required of me by my job. My team works well together and we get results, which is what I'm assigned to do. If you wanted me to do something else, you should have told me."

Al began to wonder if Rachelle was ever going to get the gist of his message. He was afraid that the situation might be hopeless, but decided to try one more time. "Rachelle," he said, "I know you have what it takes to be a good manager. I just want you to take more responsibility for your group. Try to make some decisions on your own without having me tell you what to do—don't be afraid to be a leader, because that's what the company wants you to be. For the most part, you're doing fine, but if this situation is not resolved, I fear that you may be reassigned."

How Rachelle Garcia's Inner Game Playing Created Problems

Rachelle Garcia performed very well in situations in which she was under someone else's direction, as when she was a "doer." When Rachelle became a manager, however, and had to take over the responsibility for directing her own and others' actions, things began to fall apart for her. She did not want to take responsibility for the decisions affecting others or, for that matter, for the performance of tasks that needed to be done by her group, so she deferred the responsibility to either her subordinates or her superior. This was her way of protecting her self-esteem: if others made decisions, then she could never be blamed for a mistake.

Rachelle was a classic Buck Passer: she allowed others to make decisions for her and found ways to blame them whenever a decision was wrong or a task was not completed satisfactorily. She was able to, in her mind, avoid all responsibility, and consequently was not a true leader. Allowing her subordinates to make their own decisions was an effective strategy for a time; but as Al pointed out, Rachelle also had to try to stimulate new ideas and to take command at times so that the group could continue to produce as it had in the past.

In the next case, you will see how another Hamlet was able to assume the responsibilities of a manager, but how his tendency to worry excessively about the decisions he had to make resulted in another set of problems for him.

Larry Friedman: The Agonizer Hamlet

Throughout his early school years, Larry Friedman was considered a very bright student who had a creative mind. He was the middle child in a family of high achievers.

Larry's father, Marvin Friedman, set the highest standards for himself and his employees. He was a demanding task master, and this carried over to his children. He believed that to be successful, you had to be the best at what you did. He was the kind of parent who would question his son about why he got a B when Larry got four A's and one B in a semester at school. Although Marv Friedman loved his children, he rarely praised them. Their excellence was what he expected. However, he was inwardly quite proud of their achievements.

Marv Friedman was also a man who had little tolerance for mistakes. Although he would rarely lose his temper, he would give someone a cold stare of disapproval, and that was usually enough. His own children found that they much preferred the work involved in getting good grades to having to explain why they had not achieved their potential.

The positive side of this upbringing was that Larry developed an appetite for achievement and excellence. The negative side was that he was so uncomfortable with failure that he sought perfection in everything he did. This meant that he tended to agonize about relatively unimportant details.

Larry attended the University of Illinois and majored in computer science. Shortly after graduation, he joined a large consulting firm headquartered in Chicago. Since he had a background in systems hardware as well as software, he proved to be of great value to the firm. After two years, Larry was promoted to Senior Consultant. He had some project-level supervisory responsibilities, but because he was working in a consulting firm, he was still involved in much of the technical work.

Larry Becomes a Manager

His firm continued to experience rapid growth, and Larry was promoted to manager. A manager's responsibilities involved the supervision of several ongoing projects simultaneously. Although there was still a great deal of technical work, the manager was responsible for project planning, coordination, and control. The work was very fast-paced. Larry soon found himself bombarded with requests and decisions to be made.

Larry was an orderly, systematic person. He liked the challenge of resolving technical problems, but found that the pressure of having to worry about "billable hours" was not compatible with his work style as a manager. He liked to think about things, ponder them, and consider all the ramifications. He did not like to do things "quick and dirty."

Larry left the consulting firm and joined the computer staff of one of its clients, where he became Manager of MIS Operations. He felt that this would reduce the pressure to produce billable hours rather than a good product. However, Larry encountered a new kind of pressure. His new firm was a rapidly growing direct-mail marketing company, with ever increasing demands for new computer applications.

The line managers at Mail Marketing Corp. seemed always to wait until the last moment before requesting their applications. They did not seem to appreciate the complexities of delivering what they were requesting. He had other problems to face in his new job as well. Specifically, Larry had inherited a department in which people did not have well-defined jobs; there were few systems and procedures; and many of the staff members were of questionable competence. Larry felt that he knew what needed to be done and set about designing an orderly plan to do it.

In his typical style, Larry wanted to do everything "the right way." He considered all his organizational moves from every angle. He agonized about how to place his people in roles and about which ones had to go. He personally reviewed all new systems and procedures. He was making progress, but very slowly.

Unfortunately, the organization could not wait for Larry to resolve the problems at his pace. He began to get the reputation of a procrastinator. Decisions were too slow in coming out of his office. Requests for systems and new applications were met with delays. A joke began to circulate around the company concerning MIS: "If you want to get a program from the MIS group, you had better go out and learn to program yourself. You will get it faster that way." Moreover, Larry began to be referred to as "the electronic snail." He and his staff had lost credibility.

How Larry Friedman's Inner Game Playing
Created Problems

Even though Larry Friedman was bright, well motivated, and technically creative, he was a classic example of the Agonizer variation of the Hamlet Syndrome. He was a perfectionist and was unable to adapt to a fast-paced organization in which cost-effectiveness rather than perfection was the bottom line.

His problem was caused by an underlying need to be correct and not make mistakes. It was his need for perfection, which was the basis of his self-esteem, that hurt him as a manager. It motivated Larry to agonize about everything, and the very process of trying to be perfect was his undoing.

In the next section, we will describe the steps people like Larry, Rachelle, and Chad can take to overcome the Hamlet Syndrome.

How to Overcome the Hamlet Syndrome

In this chapter, you have seen three strategies that individuals who suffer from the Hamlet Syndrome use to avoid the responsibility associated with decision making. They are the strategies of the Information Seeker, the Buck Passer, and the Agonizer. In avoiding responsibility, Hamlets subconsciously believe that they can protect their self-esteem needs and their need to be liked. However, as we have seen in this chapter, avoiding such responsibility can lead to problems for the manager and perhaps to failure.

In order to overcome or avoid this syndrome, then, individuals need to develop different strategies for satisfying their self-esteem needs and their need to be liked—strategies that do not interfere with decision making. For each variation of the Hamlet Syndrome, this involves slightly different things.

The Information Seeker must learn to be a risk taker: to make decisions in the absence of what he or she believes to be adequate information. It is a good practice to seek information before making decisions, but too much time spent on information seeking can make the decision ineffective. A strategy for these Hamlets to use in overcoming this problem is to set a time limit for gathering all information relevant to a particular decision. When that limit is reached, the decision must be made, no matter how uncomfortable it may be to make it. Some decisions will be wrong, but the individual must realize that this usually does not mean ultimate disaster. As we saw in the Chadwick Ishikawa case, waiting too long to make a decision can be just as disastrous.

Buck Passers need to learn to accept the decision-making responsibility of managers. Like all other Hamlets, they need to learn that it is a manager's responsibility to make decisions for the group and that no one else, neither subordinates nor supervisors, can share this burden. Mistakes will be made, but blaming others for them does not reduce the ultimate responsibility that managers are given by the organizations that employ them. One way to begin doing this is for these Hamlets to ask their supervisors what exactly they have decision-making responsibility for. Then, they should begin practicing making timely decisions along these lines. Buck Passer supervisors can help them in this process by providing them with evaluations of the extent to which they have been successful at meeting their responsibilities.

Agonizers need to learn to act on their beliefs about what the right course of action is. As was true of Larry Friedman, when Agonizers worry too much about the decisions they have to make, they will be seen as procrastinators and will lose the respect of their subordinates, peers, and superiors, because they never make a decision without being pressured into it. If they do not change, they will ultimately fail as managers. These Hamlets need to practice making timely decisions. This can be accomplished by prioritizing decisions and setting realistic deadlines for each decision. Then, the Hamlet should evaluate the feelings associated with making the decision by the deadline. These individuals will usually find that it is more comfortable to make decisions than to spend time agonizing over them.

Whatever strategy Hamlets use to avoid decision-making responsibility, the most valuable lesson they can learn is that it is all right to make mistakes. In fact, as we saw in the case of the Shakespearean Hamlet, it is often better to act when given the chance (no matter how unsure one is of one's decision) than to wait until someone else, at a critical juncture, forces one into action.

Chapter 9
The Salesperson Syndrome

In Arthur Miller's play *Death of a Salesman*,[1] the principal character, Willy Loman, says, "Be liked and you will never want." This, in fact, is the guiding tenet of Willy's life. This belief is so strong that he remarks to his brother, Ben, in a flashback: "It's not what you do, Ben . . . It's who you know and the smile on your face. It's contacts."[2] Willy believes that if only he can act in such a fashion that everyone will want to be his friend, then he will be a success as a salesman. He believes that it is through pleasing others that one can ascend to great heights.

Willy desperately wants to succeed in his life. He wants to show the world that he is somebody. In his own mind, he has succeeded in this quest, because, as he tells his sons: "And they know me, boys, they know me up and down New England. The finest people. And when I bring you fellas up, there'll be open sesame for all of us, 'cause one thing, boys: I have friends."[3] Unfortunately, others do not treat Willy as a success, and this frustrates him.

In an attempt to reduce this frustration, Willy adopts two strategies. The first strategy involves openly expressing his frustration to his wife and his best friend, Charley. The second strategy, and the one Willy uses most throughout the play, is to create a fantasy world for himself in which he *is* a success and

[1] Arthur Miller, *Death of a Salesman* (New York: Viking Press, 1949).
[2] Ibid., p. 86.
[3] Ibid., p. 31.

anyone who denies that he is a success must be mistaken. The use of this latter strategy is best exemplified in the scene where Willy approaches his boss (a much younger man) to ask that he be assigned to the home office so he will not have to travel. When, to Willy's surprise, his boss says that he is letting Willy go, Willy refuses to believe what he hears. Willy believes that his boss has made a tragic mistake, because everyone likes Willy Loman. He tries to appeal to his boss's sense of rationality by highlighting his success, but Willy's sales figures do not support his claim and he is terminated.

It is at this point, when openly confronted with his failure, that Willy's life begins to fall apart as he is forced to see that even in terms of what he considers "success"—people liking him—he has failed. He has been forced out of his career by his boss, and even his family treats him like a failure. Further, it seems as if no one even knows him anymore. For Willy, this is the end, and he decides that the only way he can escape his sense of failure is through suicide. The cause of Willy's death is explained by his best friend, Charley, at his funeral: "He's [a salesman:] a man way out there in the blue riding on a smile and a shoeshine. And when they start not smiling back—that's an earthquake."[4] When the world quit smiling back, it was indeed the end of Willy Loman—it was the death of a salesman.

The Salesperson Game That Managers Play

Individuals who believe, like Willy Loman, that the best way to succeed in business is to be liked suffer from what we call the Salesperson Syndrome. They may, in fact, succeed as salespeople, because they seem to have a natural ability to be liked. The fact is that they expend a great deal of energy, like Willy Loman, to ensure that they *are* liked. Usually they are quite successful at the strategies they adopt.

The fact that Salespeople are well liked and are often skilled at the technical side of whatever they do contributes to their success in the doer's role. As a reward, they are eventually promoted to management positions. Upon promotion, most people who suffer from the Salesperson Syndrome believe they can continue to operate in the same fashion as they did in the doer's role. They believe that if they just treat everyone in a caring fashion, they can't help but be successful. Unfortunately, their tendency to "love and care for everybody" can get out of control. They may devote so much time to caring for subordinates' needs that they neglect their other responsibilities

[4] Ibid., p. 138.

as managers. The technical side of management (the Outer Game) may be ignored. In other words, Salespeople suffer from exactly the opposite problem of the one Dr. Jekylls/Mr. Hydes suffer from: they overemphasize rather than underemphasize the human side of management. They are good interpersonally, but are poor administrators.

Salespeople also have a reputation for being "pushovers"; that is, they can be manipulated. This is because Salespeople have a difficult time telling their subordinates what they can and cannot do. They believe that if they force individuals to perform tasks against their will or refuse subordinates' requests too often, then they will be disliked. They therefore tend to use a laissez-faire style of management, allowing their subordinates to do whatever they want.

While Salespeople fear being disliked, they may also realize that they are being taken advantage of by their subordinates. This may cause Salespeople a great deal of anxiety, but they tend to hide it, either because they do not know how to express it or because their fear of rejection overpowers any attempt at such expression. Whenever the frustration builds to an intense level, Salespeople may find avenues for its expression in situations other than work: for instance, they may begin to take out their frustrations on their families.

Aside from causing personal frustration for the manager, the manager's inability to provide direction may also begin to affect the work group's performance. A problem with a laissez-faire style is that unless subordinates are highly motivated and highly skilled, they may not perform the tasks required of them or may not complete them satisfactorily. Whenever that happens, Salespeople tend to simply ignore the situation and hope that, somehow, the task will be completed successfully. This is because Salespeople find it difficult, if not impossible, to provide negative feedback to their subordinates. They fear that such feedback may not only cause subordinates to dislike them but also disrupt the harmony of the work group, which Salespeople believe to be important to its success.

The major problem with the Salesperson's management strategy, in fact, is that they cannot accept the fact that conflict exists. They attempt to cover it up with statements like: "Just give it time and it will work itself out," or "It really isn't that bad." Unfortunately, by ignoring conflict, Salespeople may actually contribute to its increase. Tension may increase throughout the work group or organization because subordinates are afraid to express, or discouraged from expressing, their dissatisfaction with the technical or interpersonal sides of their jobs. Morale may decrease, and the effectiveness of the group or organization may begin to decline. Soon, the Salesperson may find himself or herself out of a job.

Salespeople rarely recognize that they are having problems until it is too late. This is because these individuals believe that they are successful as long as everyone is "getting along." They believe that if the group is operating in a harmonious fashion, the technical aspects of the job will take care of themselves and any problems will eventually be worked out. When Salespeople are confronted with the reality of the situation, they cannot believe that they have failed and, like Willy Loman, may simply leave the organization (commit organizational suicide).

You will see in the following cases how two people, Dwight Washington and Karen Jones, failed as managers because they could not learn how to manage their need to be liked in ways that did not interfere with the requirements of their role.

Dwight Washington: A Salesperson Who Became President

Dwight Washington always seemed to get what he wanted: he had a terrific job, a wonderful wife, and lots of friends. Everyone seemed to like "Ike," as he was known to his friends. He was the kind of guy who'd go out of his way to help people. People knew they could count on Dwight, and he knew that he could count on people being there for him when he needed them. Sometimes, however, Dwight feared that he was too "soft" with people—that he gave them too much freedom to do as they pleased. Recently, he had begun to feel that at least some of the problems his company was having were a direct result of being *too* kind, but he wasn't sure he could or wanted to change that part of his personality.

Dwight's Early Years

Dwight had grown up with the reputation of being something of a "nerd." He was always one of the smartest kids in the class and felt somewhat self-conscious about this. He believed that if he acted "too smart," others wouldn't like him—and he desperately wanted to be liked. He had learned, therefore, at an early age that if he wanted to "fit in," he had to give others what they wanted. If they wanted his help on their school work, that's what he gave them. He even recalled, in later years, how he had knowingly let his classmates cheat. If he found that some people were looking at his paper during an exam, he just let them copy his answers. He didn't care. It was one way that he could be accepted by the other kids.

After graduation from high school, Dwight applied for and received numerous scholarships and was accepted at a small private West Coast university. He planned to study engineering, because he liked mathematics and saw a lot of opportunities in that field. He also wanted, however, to learn all he could about computers, because he believed computers were the field of the future.

Dwight found college to be easier than he had expected. He also discovered that, as was true in high school, he was able to make friends easily if he just gave others what they wanted. His classmates looked to him for help in solving their own problems, and he gladly provided it to them. Sometimes he felt that he was being taken advantage of, yet he could never bring himself to say no when asked for a favor.

As graduation drew near and Dwight began to interview for jobs, he decided that he would be most satisfied with a position in a small firm where he would have a lot of opportunities to use the skills he had learned in college. He decided to go to work for Gamma Industries, a small and growing manufacturer of computer hardware products. At the time Dwight entered the firm, the company was about to open a small software division.

Dwight Joins Gamma Industries

Dwight found the work at Gamma Industries to be both challenging and fascinating. It seemed as if practically every month, the company was involved in some new-product development, and Dwight enjoyed the creativity and freedom that his work afforded him. He worked as a member of a six-person team headed by Calvin Phillips, a 28-year-old computer whiz who, after about four years with one of the major computer manufacturers, had decided that he wanted to work in a smaller company and had joined Gamma as a team leader.

As had been true in high school and college, Dwight again found himself occupying the role of technical expert on many of the group's projects. Calvin was very willing to let Dwight have this role, because it gave him uninterrupted time to work alone on ideas for new products and to accomplish all the other tasks the company required of him in his role as manager.

At Gamma Industries, it was also true that everyone liked Dwight. People found him pleasant to work with and very knowledgeable about the technical side of the business. Dwight never seemed to complain about anything and was usually the first to volunteer to stay after hours to work on, or help someone else complete, a project. He was truly a"joy" for the organization to have. Dwight found his work satisfying, and he liked the fact that everyone seemed to be his "friend."

Dwight Becomes a Manager

During Dwight's fourth year at Gamma Industries, Calvin decided to leave the organization to pursue other interests, and the president of the company decided to promote Dwight to the role of group leader. His co-workers were ecstatic about the choice. They knew that Dwight would be a pleasure to work under and looked forward to enjoying continued success as members of "his group."

Dwight found that, in his new role, he could continue operating much as he had before. The only difference now was that he was burdened with more administrative work. He could still, however, continue to be the technical expert and was still on a friendly basis with his former co-workers, now turned subordinates. The president of the company, who by this time had become a close friend of Dwight's, recognized his ability in the industry and feared that he might some day leave to start his own firm. Unfortunately for Gamma Industries, but fortunately for Dwight, the president was right.

Dwight Becomes His Own Boss

Shortly after Calvin's departure and his own promotion, Dwight began to realize that there was a great deal of money to be made in the computer industry, so he began planning and saving for the day when he could start his own company. Dwight saw his opportunity at the beginning of his eighth year with Gamma when Calvin, with whom he had remained in close contact, called to suggest that they go into business together. Calvin said, "I've got this great idea for a product, and I even have some people willing to invest in it. All I need from you is a small investment and your guarantee that you will run the company and leave me alone to work on whatever projects I choose. In other words, I will be your *very* silent partner."

Dwight could not believe what he was hearing. This was the break he had been hoping for. He jumped at the offer, and within six months, Calvin and Dwight had started their new company. At first, things were very difficult. Dwight had to hire all the employees, which initially amounted to only five; he had to go out and sell their product (which was actually very easy for him, because people just naturally liked him); and he had to manage the business while Calvin continued to "crank out" new ideas. Fortunately, his hard work and dedication and Calvin's genius paid off. During the company's eighth year, business began to boom as customers placed an ever-increasing demand on the company for its products.

By this time, the company had grown to nearly 100 employees and had sales of $13 million. Dwight was still running the entire show, but things seemed to be falling apart for him. The "charismatic" leadership that had served him so well in the past was beginning to fail him, and he wasn't sure why. People still seemed to like him and to like working for the company, but there appeared to be an underlying tension that he could not place his finger on. Even Dwight himself began to feel that if something wasn't done, he would explode.

Dwight Falls Victim to the Salesperson Syndrome

As the company had grown, Dwight had continued to manage in much the same manner as before. He acted toward others in a friendly way and did not like having to reprimand employees for not doing their jobs. In fact, he often decided that it was better to ignore problems than to make a big deal about them. Dwight believed that they would eventually "work themselves out" and that there was no need to get everyone upset.

Dwight firmly believed that as long as all employees knew their jobs, they would perform them to the best of their ability. In fact, he was described by his employees as "someone who likes to give people leeway and expects people to perform their jobs." He saw his role as that of attracting new business and of helping the organization run smoothly. Dwight was very successful in meeting the former responsibility, but in the latter area he was beginning to fail miserably.

On the surface, the problem was that people no longer understood their jobs or what the definition of success was in the organization. They therefore began to define both their jobs and success in whatever terms met their individual needs. This, of course, led to problems as responsibilities began to overlap and certain tasks remained undone because no one would claim responsibility for them. The company, in essence, was becoming increasingly inefficient.

The problems leading to these inefficiencies were not being resolved, because people in the company had come to believe that if they wanted to remain with the organization, they should avoid conflict. This belief developed over time as a result of Dwight's management style. As the firm grew, Dwight's tendency to be a "nice guy" had become an accepted part of the company's culture. Further, individuals believed that they would never be fired, no matter what they did or did not do, because that would produce conflict, and there was a mandate against conflict.

Conflict avoidance was played out in the organization everywhere from Executive Meetings to one-on-one sessions between supervisors and subordinates. Problems were not openly discussed among people, and resolutions were often not reached. Dwight could feel the underlying tension that this situation produced and, at times, could see it vented when discussions of even trivial matters erupted into heated debates between department heads. Sometimes he felt that he should take a stand and try to resolve the problems, but he simply did not know how. Instead, he would let his own anxiety reach such a high level that he found himself yelling at his children for no apparent reason.

Other individuals also perceived that there were problems and attempted to resolve them by going directly to Dwight. In fact, it was believed that most problems could "get fixed" only if Dwight took care of them. Unfortunately, Dwight was at the base of the organization's problems, since he, himself, could not face conflict. Therefore, many interpersonal and other problems remained unresolved, morale began to suffer, and the company began to experience problems in the distribution and sale of its products. Dwight felt that he was under an increasing amount of pressure and decided that the best way to alleviate it was to stay out of the office as much as possible.

It was at this point, during Dwight's tenth year as president, that Calvin began to notice the changes in the company and in Dwight. He felt that the "silent partner" could remain silent no longer. Something had to be done, so he went to Dwight to have a chat. "It's come to my attention," Calvin began, "that a lot of people are very unhappy here these days. Do you know why?"

"I've been trying to figure that out for some time," Dwight replied. "But frankly, I'm stumped. Everyone seems to be so pleasant whenever I talk to them in a group, but as soon as I'm back in my office, they're all in here complaining about something. I believe that some of our product managers are simply incompetent and are causing the problems, but I keep hoping they'll wise up. They're frustrating the hell out of me, but I don't know what to do about it."

Calvin said, "I think you know exactly what needs to be done: they need to be fired. I just think you can't bring yourself to do it. I believe, in fact, that there are a lot of incompetent people out there who are here only because our philosophy has always been to let people do whatever they want to do in the service of the company. In the past, this has produced some terrific products and ideas, but I think it's no longer an appropriate strategy. I also get the feeling that there are a lot of good ideas as well as constructive criticism about this organization that we never hear because people think we don't want to hear it. I've actually heard some people say that they believe if they complain, they will get canned."

At this point, Dwight was really confused. "I don't understand how, in creating an atmosphere of friendship, I let things get so out of hand. I realize, now, that part of the problem lies with me and the style of management I've always tried to use. I've always given people the benefit of the doubt and hoped that things would work out. I see that this can't work in a company this size and that it's time to do some house cleaning. I'm sorry that it went this far. I only hope that I can be strong enough to get rid of the deadwood. I really don't want people to dislike me or the company, but I guess some people are going to have to be hurt if the company is to survive."

How Dwight's Inner Game Playing Created Problems

Dwight Washington had an intense need to be liked and, as a result, had developed a strategy for increasing the probability that people would accept him. Basically, this involved giving people whatever they wanted. This strategy apparently worked, since he gained a reputation for being a "nice guy" both in school and on the job. Further, Dwight's interpersonal ability, combined with his technical expertise, helped him succeed as an engineer and helped him in developing his own business.

When Dwight became a manager and even the president of his own company, he could continue to operate much as he had done before, because employees were apparently highly motivated to perform tasks in the service of the organization. Dwight was able to supervise, through direct interaction, all his subordinates, thus ensuring that they would work for the good of the organization. As his company grew, however, such direct supervision was no longer possible, and the policies and practices Dwight wanted to promote became increasingly unclear to his employees.

Dwight's tendency to create situations in which people would like him (by giving them what they wanted and trying to avoid conflict) became an accepted part of his company's culture. As the company grew, however, this philosophy became inappropriate. As more and more employees joined the firm, each attempting to satisfy his or her individual needs, the amount of conflict increased. Dwight could no longer work to resolve all the conflicts, because he could no longer have direct interaction with all his employees. Consequently, a great many problems went unresolved. Further, Dwight's own seemingly benign beliefs that "everyone should like everyone" and that harmony should prevail in the organization became transformed into the belief that conflict should be avoided at all costs. As is typical in growing firms, the culture of the firm reflected the owner/president's personality.

The major problems that Dwight and his firm were experiencing, then, were a direct result of his tendency to avoid conflict. His firm was becoming inefficient because people were afraid to openly discuss their problems, and without such discussion, many critical problems remained unresolved. Everyone appeared to be getting along, which Dwight believed to be indicative of a "successful organization," but under the surface a volcano was forming.

Dwight was experiencing "mini volcanic explosions" in his personal life, but he could not make himself believe that his company was having similar problems. This is fairly typical of Salespeople: as long as everyone appears to be happy, they brush their personal frustration off as "personal problems" and continue to operate as they have before.

Fortunately for Dwight, Calvin realized what was happening and was able to convince Dwight that it was time for a change. Calvin attempted to show Dwight that the major reason for the problems at the firm was that employees believed it was appropriate to avoid directly confronting others with problems. With this realization, Dwight could begin working to overcome the problems he was experiencing. We shall provide some suggestions for overcoming this in the final section of this chapter, but first we will present another case study of someone who failed as a manager because she could not overcome her tendency to play the Inner Game by the rules of the Salesperson Syndrome.

Karen Jones: A Victim of the Salesperson Syndrome

It had been nearly five years since Karen Jones had entered the real-estate profession as a sales associate at Ivory Realty. From the beginning, residential real estate had seemed the ideal profession for Karen, since it allowed her to make a comfortable living while giving her the feeling that she was doing something good for people. She had always liked working with people, and she found in real estate the opportunity to develop close relationships with both her peers and her customers.

Not only did Karen like her job, but she was fairly good at it. Her peers respected her sales ability, and some of them were envious of the network of satisfied customers she had developed—a network that seemed to increase steadily as time went on. Customers often remarked that they liked doing business with Karen because she acted as if she really cared. She did not force them to make a decision but helped them define their "ideal" home and then waited until she could find it for them.

Fellow sales associates also described her as "very helpful and caring." She would often, when asked a question, drop everything and come to the aid of a co-worker. Everyone knew that he or she could turn to Karen for help, and Karen liked the fact that people asked her.

Karen Becomes a Manager

The firm saw in Karen the potential to become a manager. She had always been an effective salesperson, and the firm believed the qualities which helped make Karen successful in this role would also contribute to her success as a branch manager. So, after five years of service, Karen Jones became a branch manager.

At first, Karen seemed to have no difficulties with her new position. She continued to operate in much the same manner as she had when she was a senior sales associate. She allowed her subordinates a great deal of autonomy but was available to answer questions about the technical side of the business or to "just talk." She gave all sales associates her home telephone number, and they were encouraged to contact her at home whenever they had a question or problem.

Karen liked the "people side" of her new job but found the administrative side to be very difficult to handle. For example, she had a budget, but she did not monitor it closely. Karen thought, "Top management will take care of that part of my branch's operations. I need to be more concerned with the morale of my office and people's productivity." Her philosophy was, "If I love my employees and treat them well—show them that I care—then they will be productive, and the rest of my responsibilities will take care of themselves."

Unfortunately for Karen, the other side of her branch operations did not "take care of itself." At a time in which many of the other branch offices at Ivory were prosperous, Karen's branch was losing money. This distressed the president of the company, so he called Karen into the main office to ask her what the problem was. Karen responded that she knew her branch was having financial problems, but that many of her sales associates were new; they did not have the experience that those in other branches had. She said, "We just need more time."

The president said that he was implementing a management development program which would help Karen and other branch managers be better at their jobs. Karen was enthusiastic about learning new skills, since she was continually searching for ways to improve herself. She was looking forward to the training sessions.

The management development program stressed the need for branch managers to be concerned with budgeting, planning, and decision making, as well as managing people. Exercises and group discussions were used in order to give the branch managers practice in how to "do it." During the course of the program, managers were encouraged to begin applying what they had learned and report back to the group about any problems they were having.

From this training, Karen gained a better understanding of the need to manage the budget and set and meet goals. She went back to her branch with every intention of applying what she had learned, but somehow, she never quite found the time to implement the programs which the trainer had suggested. She designed a budget and a strategic plan and worked with sales associates to create goals. The problem was, she could just never bring herself to follow up on these goals, once they were established. "People know what they're supposed to do," she thought. "There's no reason for me to criticize them for not meeting their goals. They'll do better next time." The problem with Karen's strategy was that because she never criticized them, her subordinates never knew exactly how well or how poorly they were performing. Karen always acted as if everything was all right, no matter what happened.

Karen could always find an explanation for her branch's failure to meet its budget: "The market was bad all over the area, but it was worse for my branch," or, "My sales associates are not yet trained." The fact was, however, that Karen monitored neither the expenses of her branch nor the productivity of her sales force. She assumed that the budget would "take care of itself" if she "kept her people happy."

Karen Commits Organizational Suicide

After several months of continued poor performance, Karen was again summoned to the president's office. He explained that her management of the branch was not working. Karen replied, "I've done everything I can to make my branch a good place to work. I can't understand why you are pushing me to operate in another way when my sales associates are happy the way things are. I just can't bring myself to reprimand people for poor performance. Besides, they know when they're not doing well. I'll just keep working with them until they improve."

The president recognized Karen's dedication to the company. He was also acutely aware of her success as a sales associate and her subsequent failure in performing the duties of a manager. It was clear that after two years of management experience as well as additional training in the skills necessary to be successful as a manager, Karen had been unable to make the transition to a manager's role.

After a lengthy discussion, the president and Karen agreed that Karen should resign from her position as manager. The president offered Karen the opportunity to remain with the company as a sales associate, but Karen refused. She ended her career as a manager with Ivory Realty by saying, "Maybe my problem has been that it all happened too fast. I've had some personal problems during the past year which may have contributed to my failure. Perhaps this 'break' from work will allow me to solve them."

How Karen Jones's Inner Game Playing Resulted in Her Failure

Karen Jones, like Willy Loman, believed that her success was contingent on having people like her. She apparently had developed some very successful strategies for accomplishing this goal, since her customers and her co-workers often commented that she was friendly and that she seemed to really "care." Fortunately for Karen, her winning personality was an asset when she was a salesperson, but once she became a manager, it became quite a liability.

When Karen was first promoted to the position of manager, she did not attempt to make the transition to her new role. She believed that if she continued to "love everybody" and to create an atmosphere of friendship and caring, she would continue to be a success. In fact, she believed that the people side of her job was so important that she could just ignore the technical side of the manager's role. This is a fairly typical problem encountered by Salespeople. They have always been successful simply because they were able to get people to like them, but now their role forces them to do things that will make people dislike them. They continue to believe that if everyone is happy (at least outwardly), their work group will be a success. As we have seen in the case of Karen Jones, nothing could be farther from the truth.

Karen, like many salespeople, truly believed that the technical problems would work themselves out. She didn't even realize, in fact, that the problems her branch was experiencing were a direct result of her inability to adjust to the requirements of her role. To Karen's credit, however, once the president showed her that she was having problems, she did take steps aimed at learning about the technical side of her job. While she learned the techniques needed to be successful as a manager, however, she was still unable to succeed, because her Inner Game playing was inconsistent with the requirements of her new role. Karen's need to be liked interfered with her ability to play the Inner Game effectively.

When it was clear to the president that Karen was not going to change, he confronted her with her own failure. Much like Willy Loman, Karen was unable to believe that she had failed, because such a reality was inconsistent with her definition of success. Everyone liked her, so she had to be a success. Even in the end, Karen didn't realize what the real problem was, so she blamed her failure on inexperience and "personal problems." She could not see the true cause of her failure.

Not all Salespeople suffer from such blindness. Some, as we saw in the case of Dwight Washington, are forced to see that they have a problem, before it is too late. Then, they can begin working to overcome it.

Overcoming the Salesperson Syndrome

The major thing that Salespeople need to learn is how to perform the technical side of their managerial roles without letting their need to be liked interfere with it. They have to learn that their jobs as managers may involve asking subordinates to do things that they do not want to do. They may find it difficult to accept this responsibility, but it must be accepted if they are to be successful managers.

One of the most unpleasant tasks for managers is telling people to do something they do not want to do. This produces a great deal of conflict, which Salespeople believe should be avoided. However, if they are to be successful, they must learn to face the conflict and to find ways of encouraging a resistant subordinate to complete an assigned task. They should be firm whenever they delegate a task. They can provide assistance, but they should not do the task for the subordinate.

If the task delegated is not completed or is not completed satisfactorily, the Salesperson needs to learn how to express his or her dissatisfaction. This involves learning how to provide negative feedback and constructive criticism which will help the subordinate better his or her performance. One way to practice providing feedback is to perform a simulated performance appraisal with a close friend and act out the role to be played. This will make the individual more comfortable in an actual situation.

Providing feedback may be difficult, at first, since no one likes to be criticized. Salespeople may fear that their subordinates will no longer like them if they provide such feedback. These managers need to realize, however, that in the absence of such feedback, people cannot improve. Further, if subordinates are given only positive feedback, they may begin to question whether or not they are really performing as well as the manager says they are. In other words, they may begin to discount the feedback they are given and begin to do whatever they want to do, since they are never criticized. This can lead to inefficiencies in the work group and ultimately to the manager's failure if it goes unchecked.

Salespeople also need to learn how to say no to people in different types of situations. When asked to do something they do not feel they should do, they need to practice simply saying no. Having done so, they should analyze how they feel and try to understand the reasons underlying the feelings. It is also important to assess the reaction of the other person. In most instances, Salespeople will find that saying no will cost very little.

Basically, Salespeople need to learn how to confront conflict in any situation: giving feedback to a subordinate, resolving interpersonal problems among a group of subordinates, or resolving a conflict by saying no to a subordinate's request. As in the case of Dwight Washington, this can be a very important lesson for senior executives to learn since they have a substantial influence on their company's culture. They need to learn that if there are problems in the organization, they should be brought out in the open. Since Salespeople are skilled at creating a friendly atmosphere, they may find that they are able to foster an atmosphere of trust in which individuals feel free to discuss interpersonal and technical problems. This is an important step in resolving conflicts, and reducing the likelihood that tension will become so high that it will cause irreparable damage to interpersonal relationships within the work group or the organization.

Chapter 10

The Entrepreneur Syndrome

During the past few years there has been a widespread increase in entrepreneurship throughout the economy. A wide variety of people have established
new ventures ranging from catering businesses to high-technology electronics
firms. As a result of this trend, many new businesses have emerged. Companies such as Domino's Pizza, Mrs. Field's Cookies, Apple Computer, and
Federal Express, to name just a few, now employ thousands of people and
are economic powerhouses.

Unlike IBM, General Motors, ARCO, and other large, well-established
companies, many of these newly emerged entrepreneurships are still run on
a day-to-day basis by their original founders, who are very much entrepreneurs, rather than by professional managers who have climbed up through
the ranks.

There are many myths surrounding the founders of both successful and
unsuccessful entrepreneurial companies. These include stories about Steve
Jobs of Apple Computers, Fred Smith of Federal Express, and Adam Osborne
of Osborne Computer. The stories range from accounts of heroic feats against
all odds to tales of personal foibles and tragic mistakes.

There is one truth in all these myths about entrepreneurs: they really
are a very different breed from their Fortune 500 counterpart. Rather than
possessing an MBA from a prestigious university, and the well-honed political
skills to navigate the corporate maze of an existing business, the typical entre

preneur is someone who had an idea and the personal tenacity to convert it into a new business.

Although the term "entrepreneurship" is colloquially used in a wide variety of meanings, by definition an entrepreneur is someone who creates a new business venture. This is a very different phenomenon from working within an existing business and requires a different person.

In one sense, the phrase "the typical entrepreneur" is almost a contradiction in terms, for entrepreneurs come in all shapes and sizes: they may be male or female; be young or old; belong to any race or religion; and hold any political belief. Whatever background entrepreneurs have, however, the successful ones do tend to have one thing in common: they are people who "live" their businesses.

The business is the virtually all-consuming passion of the entrepreneur. He or she thinks of the business constantly, not only while working, but also while eating, driving, and dressing; while attending the theater; perhaps even while dreaming. For them, the business is an extension of themselves. It is their "baby," whether the entrepreneur is male or female.

Symptoms of the Entrepreneur Syndrome

For successful entrepreneurs, the business is the vehicle for the satisfaction of some deep-seated personal needs. Since it is their creation and a manifestation of their personal efforts, a great deal of self-esteem is justifiably derived from its growth and success. Accordingly, the larger the business grows and the more profitable it becomes, the greater is the self-esteem of the entrepreneur.

Many successful entrepreneurs are highly intelligent, regardless of whether they had formal university or business-school training. Although there are exceptions, they also tend to be people who are colloquially characterized as Type A personalities: competitive, preoccupied with time, always in a hurry, impatient for results, and with a tendency to become bored easily.[1] Given these personality traits, it is understandable that business often becomes a complex "game" to the entrepreneur. As one entrepreneur stated, "My business is like a game of Monopoly with real chips."

Unfortunately, as is true in many areas, the very traits that are a person's strengths can eventually become limitations. In the case of the entrepreneur,

[1] Hans Selye identifies and describes the Type A personality in *The Stress of Life* (New York: McGraw-Hill, 1976).

the very things that made him or her successful at the earliest stages of developing the firm can lead to problems at later stages. Thus, some basic traits of the entrepreneur, when carried to the excess, become symptoms of the Entrepreneur Syndrome.

The most typical of these traits/symptoms are:

1. The tendency to seek control over all aspects of the firm's operation, from the largest matter to the very smallest detail.
2. The tendency to personalize the firm to the extent that no one else has any real authority to make decisions or receive any recognition for its success (a self-esteem issue).
3. The tendency to constantly focus on the business to the exclusion of everything else, and to expect that everybody else will do the same (a self-esteem issue).
4. The tendency to make decisions and change directions so rapidly that others see these movements as contradictory ("shooting from the hip").

The Need for Control

A major dimension of successful entrepreneurs is that they have strong opinions about the way things should be done. Their views may concern things ranging from very large decisions to minutiae. They are concerned about how the ashtrays are laid out in the conference room, what color the wall paper should be, whether a lightbulb has been replaced quickly enough, whether the right vendors of new typewriter ribbons have been chosen, and how the new supply room should be laid out. The typical successful entrepreneur will ask, remind, or nag (depending on your perspective) employees about a seemingly trivial matter (to the latter), until it is resolved to the entrepreneur's satisfaction.

The Need for Esteem

The entrepreneur's esteem needs are satisfied by the firm in a variety of ways. First of all, the act of personalizing everything about the firm is a powerful source of self-esteem. The entrepreneurial manager tends to think in terms of "my firm," "my money," and "my people." There is both justifiable pride in what the person has created and an undeniable amount of narcissism. The net effect, however, is a powerful motivator for the entrepreneur.

There is another dimension of the entrepreneur's esteem needs that manifests itself through the process of building the company. Regardless of the size of the company—whether it has $1 million, $10 million, $100 million, or $1 billion in annual revenues—the classic entrepreneur wants to increase the firm's size. If the firm has $1 million, the entrepreneur wants it to double to $2 million. If it is $10 million, the entrepreneur wants it to grow to $25 or even $100 million. Actual size is largely irrelevant. What matters is the process of taking the firm to the next plateau, whatever that is.

In this sense, size is another dimension of the "scorecard" the entrepreneur keeps in his or her head as an indication of how well things are going. The larger the company, the more has been achieved.

The Entrepreneur's Energy, Adrenalin, and Pace

Most entrepreneurs are high-energy people. To some extent, they get high on their own adrenalin. They like a fast pace. The movement and activity which swirl around them give them a feeling of importance. To them, the pace also increases the meaningfulness of the game. It is analogous to the pace of "lightning chess," which imposes a time limit on chess moves, as opposed to the slow, contemplative pace of traditional chess.

The entrepreneur's energy and pace get translated into his or her decision-making style. Decisions tend to be made very rapidly, frequently without detailed study and analysis, which the entrepreneur thinks of as a meaningless "academic" exercise. Some entrepreneurs tie rapid decision making to their image of themselves as executives. They think of themselves as decisive because they are able to commit large sums of money with the same degree of analysis as they would apply to the task of choosing from a dinner menu.

One entrepreneur, whose story was presented in Chapter 6, had developed this practice into an art form and was therefore nicknamed the "thirty-second decision maker" by his staff. He made decisions with lightning speed. This was true both for his initial decisions and for the two or three decisions that amended or reversed the original decision during the course of a day or week. Not surprisingly, this manager came to be viewed as indecisive, even though he thought of himself as extremely decisive. Moreover, subordinates often played a waiting game to see what the real decision would ultimately turn out to be.

When a person becomes a victim of the Entrepreneur Syndrome, it can cause significant problems both for the individual and the organization, as we shall see in the following case study.

Mark Richardson: Entrepreneur

Mark Richardson was a classic entrepreneur. He was above average in intelligence, extremely energetic, quick to perceive new opportunities, and willing to take advantage of the business possibilities presented to him. Mark was a natural salesman. He was charming and articulate and created a sense of competence and trust among the people he met.

Mark began his career with Metropolitan Mutual Insurance Company. He was soon one of the company's highest producers and was constantly at the top of the sales leaders. He was successful not only because he was intelligent, but because he worked long hours and drove himself to succeed.

In a sense, sales was a means to an end for Mark Richardson. Whenever he made a sale of insurance to someone, he was, in essence, selling himself. To make the sale, the client had to have confidence in Mark's judgment; therefore, his success was very personal.

After five years with Metropolitan, Mark decided to leave and start his own company. It was a decision he reached with a mixture of enthusiasm and trepidation. On the one hand, Mark was attracted by the idea of being in control of his own destiny and liked the potentially greater financial rewards of running his own company. On the other hand, he was well aware of the risks involved. He also had the classic salesman's fear that it might all vanish.

Although Mark initially began his firm as an independent insurance broker, he quickly perceived a market for insurance-based "products" for executive compensation and benefits programs and began to move in that direction. After 18 months, he changed the name of his firm to reflect this different orientation. It was now called Execucomp Corporation.

As a result of Mark's skills in personal selling as well as his accurate perception of a business niche, his firm grew rapidly. Initially, he hired a variety of support personnel to assist with the day-to-day operation of the firm. Even with the additional support, however, Mark found himself stretched increasingly thin as the company continued its rapid growth. He simply did not have time to take advantage of all the selling opportunities presented to him by referrals from existing clients and extensions of his existing clients' business. Similarly, he did not have time to supervise his office staff adequately.

Mark found himself constantly on the run. Since he was a high-energy individual, he was able to meet the rigorous demands of constant travel. He had to work 12 to 16 hours a day, six to seven days a week, to keep up with the growth of his business. His wife sometimes complained about his schedule, but there were rewards for the whole family. Mark's income rose substantially, and when they did have time for vacations, they were able to afford some of the most interesting places in the world. They could also afford to have a very comfortable home in a prestigious area and send their children to good private schools.

After about six years of this, the growth of the business continued beyond even Mark's considerable energies, and he found that he needed to add still more staff. This time, however, he realized that the business required more than mere helpers; it also required other salespeople to take advantage of all the market opportunities. Further, it required someone to organize and manage the office staff and run the business on a day-to-day basis, while he continued to do the marketing.

Since the business was highly profitable and continued to generate more than Mark needed to draw out for his personal needs, he had the financial resources to invest in building his company. He recruited two "heavy hitters" who had track records as big producers from other insurance companies and hired a former administrator from an insurance company as his Executive Vice President. The former were supposed to develop their own practice in the firm while simultaneously helping to serve Mark's clients, while the latter's job was to put in the systems needed by the rapidly growing firm and also to manage it on a day-to-day basis.

Unfortunately, while the plan was good in concept, it did not work out as expected. Mark was stronger both in terms of sales skills and technical abilities than either of his heavy hitters, but he did not have sufficient time to train them. He decided to travel with first one and then the other to show them how he operated, thinking that he could introduce them to his clients and then gradually turn over the relationship to one of them while he went about developing new business. He found, however, that because the clients viewed him as the star, they were unwilling to work with either of his new men. Mark now had additional overhead and had to work even harder to keep everything going.

Mark had mixed feelings about this result. He was obviously disappointed that his new salespeople were not working out well. However, he could not help feeling proud that his clients preferred to work with him. After all, he was much stronger, both technically and in sales ability, than either of his staff. He had a nagging doubt about whether he had hired the right people.

The new Executive Vice President was also a disappointment. Mark had his own way of doing things, and he hated what he termed "unnecessary paperwork and bureaucracy." His new EVP, Reed Collins, seemed to fail to grasp that Execucomp Corp. was not the size of Prudential Insurance or Northwestern Mutual Life. Mark found that he had to ignore or go around the new organizational structure and systems that Reed had put in place. He also found that Reed seemed to lose interest in his job after a few months, as he started taking long lunches and leaving early. For Mark, who worked all the time, this was particularly galling. Although Mark was irritated by it, he said and did nothing, because he frankly was too busy to take the time to deal with the problem. Business was simply too good to worry about the administrative side of his company.

Although he did not confront the overall problem directly, Mark did take some action. Whenever he saw something he did not like, he either talked about it with Reed or whoever else was involved and made a request for change. When Reed developed a plan for a new telephone system, Mark had to get involved to change it to what he preferred. When there was a need to reconfigure the office space, Mark went over every detail and made the final decisions. He found he even had to review decisions about stationery: how much to order, the design, and the like.

There were all sorts of little things about the functioning of the offices that Mark did not like. People tended to use the most expensive express mail carrier rather than a perfectly good alternative that was less costly. Things seemed to take too long to get done or corrected. For example, when a picture in the conference room fell off the wall and was damaged because of a faulty nail, it sat on the floor for more than six weeks before it was even brought in to be fixed. When Mark asked about the picture, he was told that everyone was too busy with client work. Mark, however, was a strong believer that his office had to look first-rate for clients, and this picture marred the overall look of the room. He was, therefore, irritated that nothing was done for so long. He also took it as an indication that there must be other untreated problems which were unseen but potentially more serious. As he stated: "If I can't rely on my office staff to get a lousy picture taken care of, then what else is out of control that I don't know about?"

Mark had mixed feelings about how things were working out in his firm. Sales continued to go well, but the organization had not developed as he had hoped. Although he had hired so-called heavy hitters, people who commanded high salaries, they were not performing as he had expected. He wondered whether he had hired the wrong people or whether he, himself, had done something to make them ineffective after they had joined his company. In either case, something had clearly gone wrong.

How Mark Richardson's Inner Game Playing Created Problems

Without being aware of it, Mark Richardson was encountering a variety of problems in dealing with the Inner Game of Management. He was a victim of the Entrepreneur Syndrome. Mark was having difficulty managing his need for self-esteem so that it did not interfere with the development of his staff, and he also had trouble managing his need for control. Together, these problems led to the failure of Mark's plan to develop and professionalize his organization to cope with its rapid growth.

Mark's Need for Self-Esteem. Unconsciously, Mark Richardson was competing with his own sales staff. He had conflicting goals. Although at one level he wanted to turn over existing clients to his new salespeople, Brad Phillips and Howard Bernstein, at another level he was secretly pleased when his clients balked at this plan. It flattered his sense of self-esteem. He was still more valued than these two heavy hitters he had hired.

Unfortunately, while this result led to a short-term feeling of superiority, it did nothing in the longer term to resolve the problem of being stretched too thin. Mark neither recognized this problem nor did he take any steps to resolve it.

To deal with this problem, Mark Richardson would have had to recognize that he was failing to manage his own esteem needs in a manner appropriate to his new role. Unconsciously, although Mark had the title of President of Execucomp, he was still viewing himself as a salesman. And as a salesman, who for many years had competed to be the best, he understandably still strove to be the highest producer and took pride in the result. It was understandable—but still, it was self-defeating.

Whether he realized it or not, Mark's new role in his firm was that of a player-coach rather than simply a player. He had to learn to train Brad and Howard so as to make them more effective, and he had to "train" his clients to wean them from himself, if he was to be effective in his new role. As a prerequisite to doing this, Mark had to want to do it, and in order to want to do it, he would have had to reconceptualize his role.

Mark was facing a different kind of problem in managing Reed Collins, but it was a problem that was also traceable to difficulties in mastering the Inner Game of Management. Specifically, Mark was having difficulty with respect to both his need for control and his desire to be liked.

Mark's Need for Control. For several years, Mark Richardson had managed his business exactly the way he wanted to, without interference from anybody and without having to justify anything to anyone else. Now, with the addition of Reed, he found it difficult to give up the degree of control he had gotten used to exercising. When he first joined the company, Reed did things his own way—but unfortunately, from Mark's viewpoint, it usually was not the way Mark wanted things to be done.

Although Mark had told Reed that he wanted him to join the firm and take over the day-to-day management, he found that what he really wanted was someone to whom he could delegate specific problems and who would do things the way Mark would have done them if he had had the time. Consequently, whenever Reed made decisions which Mark did not like, he simply had the decision changed to suit his preferences.

Mark Richardson did not anticipate or recognize the consequences of these actions. One effect was that he almost totally eliminated Reed's influence in his organization. Recognizing that anything which Reed did could be overruled by Mark, anyone who objected to a decision made by Reed, however trivial, just went to Mark Richardson and complained. Frequently, Mark took action on the complaint by countermanding Reed's policies and practices. The net effect of this process was to turn Reed into a "managerial eunuch," someone with a titular position in the organization but without any real power in the day-to-day running of the firm.

Reed himself did not handle the situation very well. He was being well paid—in fact, he was receiving a salary significantly greater than what he could hope to earn elsewhere. Therefore, he was not motivated to bite the hand that fed him. His private view, expressed to no one, was that if Mark Richardson was stupid enough to pay him a handsome salary to be a high-priced messenger boy, then that was his problem. Until he found something as good, he would bide his time.

Mark's Need to Be Liked. Another aspect of the Inner Game problems that Mark Richardson was encountering concerned his unwillingness to confront Reed with his disappointment. Inwardly, Mark was angry with Reed, but he did not like conflict. He wanted people to like and respect him, so he tended to avoid criticizing people. He would ask them to do things or change things, but he avoided direct personal or professional criticism. In brief, he was unable to manage his own need to be liked in such a way that it didn't interfere with his ability to manage the firm.

After this situation had gone on for more than a year, Mark was sufficiently distressed to hire a consultant to evaluate the firm's operations and structure. The consultant was asked to assess whether the company was organized adequately and whether the required roles were being performed effectively. After a series of interviews, the consultant concluded that the EVP was not performing adequately in his role, and that the reason for this was the way he was being asked to operate. Mark used this report as an instrument to request that the EVP resign.

Reed did resign, and Mark hired an executive search firm to find a replacement. Initially he was enthusiastic about Carl Framson, the new EVP, but within six months the same pattern had reemerged at Execucomp. Framson, too, became a managerial eunuch.

Mark decided that it was just too much to expect that he could hire anyone as good as himself. After all, if they were really any good, they would probably own their own business rather than work for him.

Although Mark continued to operate his own firm on a reasonably profitable basis, the company never grew and realized its potential. He continued to operate in his old way, never realizing that he had failed to master the Inner Game of Management or that he was a classic victim of the Entrepreneur Syndrome.

Overcoming the Entrepreneur Syndrome: The Case of Dan Sandel

Dan Sandel was born in Israel and came to the United States in 1961. He received his BS degree from UCLA in 1968, followed by an MBA from USC.

For a number of years, Dan worked for Will Ross. He left Will Ross in 1975 to found his own company, Devon Industries.

Devon Industries was founded, as Sandel stated, to "solve nurses' problems." This means that the company focused on the design and manufacture of products which are used by nurses in hospitals.

Sandel was a classic entrepreneur and a classic entrepreneurial success. In the early days of the firm's development, he was involved in all aspects of the company's operation.

Dan's managerial style was also the classic entrepreneurial style, and he was, in fact, a victim of the Entrepreneur Syndrome. As Sandel himself stated, "I was behaving very much like a camel, sticking my nose into everything." He was also described as the "twenty-second decision maker" by one of his employees, who stated: "Dan makes decisions very quickly, too quickly. He takes about 20 seconds to make a decision, and he thinks that even *that* is too long."

Like other entrepreneurs, Dan Sandel saw Devon Industries as an extension of himself. He was concerned about all aspects of the company's functioning. Sandel was a workaholic, and because of his need to feel in control over everything, he was constantly talking to people either face-to-face or by telephone.

Unlike many other entrepreneurs, Sandel decided to do something about the problems of the Entrepreneur Syndrome. The stimulus was a seminar dealing with the subject of "making the transition from entrepreneurship to professional management." After attending the seminar, he hired the professor who had presented it as a consultant to assist him and his organization.

From their discussions, it became clear that Dan had to change certain things about the way he was managing his company. First, he had to change his role from a "one-man band" to the orchestra leader who recruits and selects people and makes sure they are all playing in harmony. Sandel committed himself to hire strong people and to turn over authority to them.

He turned over the sales function to one of his regional managers, whom he appointed as National Sales Manager. He also went outside and recruited a strong controller, who was asked to develop the accounting and financial systems required to help the firm grow to the next plateau. He recruited a professional personnel manager and established a management development program for the senior managers in the firm. He also began to invest in training for all his supervisory employees. In other words, he began to build a strong organization.

He initiated a planning process to get the input of his managers in planning the future direction of the company. He also began to get less involved in the manufacturing function and allowed his VP of Manufacturing to make his own decisions.

His own role began to change as he found himself with less to do. He still had the urge to interfere in whatever others were doing, but he began to interfere to a lesser extent. People began to see a change in his behavior, though it was probably not as fast as they would have liked it to happen. Nevertheless, Dan Sandel was in the process of giving up increasing amounts of authority and control to others. He was beginning to listen more to other people.

The organization was running with less and less day-to-day participation by Dan Sandel. This was a difficult thing for someone as hyperactive as Dan to accept, and it should not be inferred that he did it 100 percent. There was grumbling that Sandel interfered too much, but everyone agreed that change had occurred.

It was fortunate both for Dan Sandel and for Devon Industries that change had occurred. For about one year after the beginning of the change, at age 48, Dan Sandel unexpectedly had open heart surgery. He was hospitalized and later went through a lengthy rehabilitation period.

During this time, Devon Industries continued to operate effectively and grow. This was possible because Dan Sandel had been sufficiently foresighted and strong to take steps to overcome the Entrepreneur Syndrome.

Overcoming the Entrepreneur Syndrome

As you may recognize, the Entrepreneur Syndrome is related to another Inner Game syndrome, the Doer Syndrome, which was described in Chapter 2. The two syndromes have the same underlying causes and produce some similarities in their symptoms.

One major difference is in the role of the victim. Victims of the Doer Syndrome tend to hold managerial positions in other people's firms, while victims of the Entrepreneur Syndrome have founded their own enterprises. However, the most significant difference is that while the Doer wants to control his or her own work, the Entrepreneur wants to control *everything* that happens in his or her company.

Since Entrepreneurs wish to control everything in the company, they typically have an insatiable desire for information. Nothing that happens in their company is too small or too trivial for their attention. Victims of this syndrome can drive their subordinates mad with their incessant desire to control everything.

As with other syndromes, the first step in overcoming the Entrepreneur Syndrome is to recognize the need for change. The victim must recognize that he or she is pursuing an impossible strategy—it is not feasible to control everything all the time.

The victim of the Entrepreneur Syndrome must make several specific changes. First, he or she must begin to give credit to the efforts and contributions of other people in building the organization. The company must go from being "my firm" to "our firm." This means that the Entrepreneur cannot take all credit for what happens.

Second, the Entrepreneur must overcome the need for total control of everything. He or she must delegate real authority to other strong people. This means that the Entrepreneur *will* lose some degree of direct control over things. It also requires that the Entrepreneur begin to trust other people and get used to the idea that there *will be* some waste and inefficiency in the organization. People must be permitted to make their own decisions. There will be some mistakes, and things will be done differently from the way the Entrepreneur would have done them—but this has to be accepted, or the organization will experience a version of the Pygmy Syndrome, with all strong people leaving. Strong employees will not tolerate being treated as puppets or pygmies. The organizational consequence of this syndrome is, therefore, stunted growth.

Chapter 11

The DOE (Daughter of the Entrepreneur) Syndrome

Meredith Cohen was an intelligent, personable, attractive, young woman. By the age of 23, Meredith, or "Merry" as she had been called since childhood, was a vice president for Sommerset Publications. The company was a magazine publisher with several properties in a variety of areas, including sports, women's issues, health, and gardening. The firm also had a small book-publishing subsidiary that specialized in relatively small-quantity custom and vanity books.

Sommerset was a privately held, family-owned business, with annual revenues of approximately $75 million. The firm had been founded by Meredith's father, Ben Cohen, and had been in business for more than 30 years.

Ben Cohen had come to the United States in 1937 at the age of 18. He had been educated at the City University of New York as an accountant and had begun his career with a small publishing house in New York City. Since he was intelligent and hardworking, the owners gradually decided to give him a wider range of assignments. Ben learned the business quickly.

In 1946, Ben perceived that demographics and tastes were changing, so he tried to interest the owners of his company in launching a magazine subsidiary. The owners were comfortable with their life and company and refused. Reluctantly, Ben decided to leave and start his own company, which he called Sommerset Publications.

The company's name was somewhat grander than its resources, but Ben was successful in launching a specialized gardening magazine geared to the interests of relatively affluent suburban homeowners. The magazine was called *Organic Gardening* and was geared to people's increasing awareness of environmental and health-related issues. Ben Cohen parlayed the success of this magazine into other successful properties, and within ten years, Sommerset Publications was a relatively prestigious niche publisher. Ben Cohen had become another American immigrant success story.

Meredith Cohen: MBA and DOE

Ben and his wife Edith had three children. Their son, Carl, became a lawyer, and their daughter Francine became a high-school teacher. It was their youngest child, Meredith, who showed the most interest in and aptitude for the family business. Meredith attended Princeton University and received her BA in history. She then attended Columbia University, where she received her MBA.

During her high-school and college years, Meredith worked part-time and summers at Sommerset. She held a variety of jobs ranging from a clerk-typist to assistant-level jobs in "rights and permissions" and in circulation. Since she was "Mr. Cohen's daughter," Meredith was welcomed by whatever department she wished to work in. While she was getting her MBA, she held a variety of jobs in the editorial and advertising departments.

When Meredith was a teenager—and even while she was in college, before receiving any formal training in business—she had observed many things at Sommerset that she thought did not make sense. When she made comments and suggestions to people, however, they tended to patronize her and ultimately ignore her ideas. The implicit message was clear: "Be a good girl, don't bother us, and we'll all get along fine."

Even her father, Ben, tended to patronize her. He thought it was cute that she made suggestions, but his classic response was: "That's a good idea. Let me think about it." Nothing ever seemed to change, and Meredith felt as if her ideas had disappeared into a black hole.

During her MBA program at Columbia, Meredith used Sommerset as a case study for a term project required by one of her instructors. This was the first time she'd tried to put all the pieces together. Her conclusions simultaneously made her excited about the possibilities for developing the company and anxious about its problems, for Sommerset had been experiencing difficulties for the past few years, as new entrepreneurial companies entered the field while larger companies with greater resources also aimed at the company's niches.

When Meredith tried to talk to her father about her conclusions, she found his reaction frustrating and bewildering. Ben was proud that she had received a grade of A on the paper, and he told almost everyone in the company, as well as some visitors to Sommerset, about it. He referred to her as "my brilliant daughter," but he refused to acknowledge the validity of anything she said in the paper as a basis for changing the company. He was polite but brushed off her analysis as "too academic."

Meredith felt "schizophrenic," as she put it to her closest friend. She was getting stroked for being a good, intelligent daughter; but she was being ignored as a meaningful contributor to the family business.

The situation experienced by Meredith was made more complex by other personal and family considerations. Meredith had been dating a man by the name of Donald Robbins. Don Robbins was a graduate of Harvard College and Yale Law School, now employed by one of the most prestigious New York law firms. He was talented and charming, and his future seemed assured. He wanted to marry Meredith, and this was known by Ben and Edith Cohen, who also wanted Meredith to settle down. Subtle hints about grandchildren were made at family gatherings.

Meredith was torn between what she perceived as two opposing life styles. As attractive as the thought of marriage to Don Robbins was, it also posed some difficulties. She perceived that theirs would have to be a relatively traditional marriage if it were to be successful. Don's career would have to come first. At one level this was a very comfortable idea. It was the model with which she had grown up. However, Meredith was a very achievement-oriented person. She wondered whether she would not be happier in the long run with a career of her own, and married to someone who would be supportive of that. However, whenever she even hinted about this to her family, the response was that she "must be crazy" to even think of giving up someone like Don Robbins.

Problems at Work

Meredith's problems at Sommerset involved not only her family. She began to encounter a variety of problems with other people at the company as well.

When Meredith was growing up, people tended to accommodate her as Mr. Cohen's girl. Now, even though she had her MBA, she seemed not to be taken seriously, and even seemed resented.

She even began to hear "MBA" jokes and found people somewhat distant. Problems increased after Meredith was promoted to circulation manager for one of the company's magazines. This happened after one of the company's relatively long-term employees left. There was some grapevine grumbling about "what it takes to be promoted at Sommerset."

In her new position, Meredith found it necessary to coordinate with all other parts of the company. However, she found that people either treated her with that same patronizing manner or seemed almost to fear her because she was "a Cohen." She tried to address the issue with her father, but he just told her not to worry about it; things would be fine over the course of time, he said.

Even more distressing, Meredith found that her role as a manager was bringing her into conflict with her father from time to time. She found that his ideas about how a company ought to be run were quite different from hers. When she tried to discipline people in her department, she was surprised that they "used the back door" to her father and got him to overrule her. She felt that her position was being undermined and that she could do nothing about it.

Meredith found, to her horror, that the way to get her father to do something was to ask as she would as a child: "Please, Daddy, why can't we . . ." Ben Cohen could refuse his daughter almost nothing. But when she wore her MBA hat and tried to convince him of the need for changes in the business, she was either patronized or rebuffed.

Over time, Meredith found it easier to cajole her father into making decisions by playing the role of his daughter than to get his agreement by playing the role of a manager. What's more, Meredith found that the same strategy worked almost equally well with the other executives in the firm—the women as well as the men. People seemed to find her less threatening when she behaved like Ben Cohen's daughter than when she acted in the role of a manager.

Meredith developed a variety of "girlish" habits in dealing with people in the company. Her voice became softer, and she was even a bit flirtatious. Her dress changed: she went from blue and grey suits to dresses.

Occasionally, Meredith would reassert herself as a manager, but this tended to lead to conflict with her father as well as others. Finally, Meredith Cohen, who had earned her BA from Princeton and her MBA from Columbia, retreated to her cajoling strategy and became a victim of the DOE Syndrome.

*How Meredith Cohen's Inner Game Playing
Created Problems*

The basic Inner Game problem facing Meredith Cohen involved the management of her own self-esteem. In brief, Meredith was facing a conflict between two roles she valued greatly. One role was that of a professional manager at Sommerset Magazine; the other was that of "the good daughter." Meredith found that both her family and the other workers at Sommerset viewed her primarily in the role of "Ben Cohen's daughter" rather than as a capable manager.

Her dilemma was that Meredith derived a great deal of her self-esteem from being a "good daughter," and this led her to adopt an organizational role of a DOE rather than a manager. Although this was less threatening to people, and even though Meredith found it an expedient way to get things done, she was developing habits and a mindset that would not make her an effective manager in the longer run. Her influence at Sommerset was based not on her own capabilities but on the reflected power of her father, Ben Cohen, and even after his inevitable retirement, she would still be viewed as a "little girl."

The DOE Game That Managers Play

The DOE Syndrome is a problem faced by women. The term DOE in this syndrome has a dual connotation. It simultaneously stands for doe, which is an adult female deer, and also serves as an acronym for "daughter of an entrepreneur."

The DOE Syndrome refers to the conflict faced by some women in business who are trying to simultaneously fulfill two roles: the role of the manager and the role of the daughter. When faced with a conflict between these roles, some women choose to fulfill the role of the "good daughter" at the expense of being an effective manager, and thus they become victims of the DOE Syndrome.

Women who are caught in the DOE Syndrome behave in a somewhat childlike manner. They tend to be nice and nonassertive and not very effective as managers. Although the term refers to an adult deer, in this context it is intended to connote someone who behaves like "Bambi," a baby deer. The baby deer is not threatening. It is attractive and childlike and requires nurturing. Women who suffer from the DOE Syndrome often seem a lot more passive than they would like to be.

Variations on the DOE Theme

The underlying problem of a victim of the DOE Syndrome is a conflict between two roles: a personal or family role and a professional role. There are other versions of the DOE Syndrome. For example, there is the WOE Syndrome, which refers to the business problems facing the wife of an entrepreneur. There is also a masculine version of this syndrome, the SOE Syndrome, which can afflict the young son of an entrepreneur.

The problems faced by people in these situations lead to intense personal and interpersonal conflict, and such conflicts are not always resolved successfully, even if the individual does not fall victim to the DOE Syndrome per se, as in the next case.

Overcoming the DOE Syndrome: The Gina Lacommare Case

The day Gina Lacommare graduated from San Francisco State University with a bachelor's degree in business administration, she was hired by her father to work full-time as top manager in his clothing manufacturing firm. It was a small company, specializing in hand-tailored wool coats.

Joe Lacommare had immigrated from Italy 25 years before and had started Lacommare's Coats with a tailor, two cutters, his wife as part-time bookkeeper, and himself as the only employees. He found his niche in the coat market by specializing in wool coats. The business expanded. Within a few years, he moved into a mid-size warehouse, in what was then the major industrial sector of the city.

For 15 years, the business grew steadily. Although most coat factories were automated, Mr. Lacommare took pride in his exclusive, but moderately priced, hand-sewn coats. He employed more than ten tailors and seamstresses and numerous cutters. He even opened a small shop in front of the warehouse. The same pride Mr. Lacommare took in his workmanship he took in the personal service he provided. His customers drank tea and coffee with cake as they waited to be measured and fitted by the tailor. Mr. Lacommare was highly visible, chatting frequently with customers, helping with fittings, or giving advice on a certain cut. As the reputation of Lacommare's Coats grew, the revenues from the warehouse store, as well as from factory orders, increased.

Recently, however, the business had begun to decline as a result of the fierce competition from large companies making similar, less expensive tailored coats. Since the factory-made coats could be purchased for a much lower price than Lacommare's coats, Mr. Lacommare lost much of his mid-income clientele. He was pushed into the exclusive coat market, with a whole different set of competitors that he had never dealt with and did not really understand. The area in which the warehouse was located also posed a problem. It had changed from the center of industry into a crime-ridden outskirt that discouraged his now wealthier clientele. Mr. Lacommare had never seen the use for a large sales force, since he had been dealing with the same companies for many years. The sales force of Lacommare's Coats consisted of an inefficient, rather incompetent salesman who had been with the company for 15 years. This was the status of the business when Gina Lacommare came to work for her father.

Mr. Lacommare was fiercely possessive of the business and wanted it to stay in the family through one of his sons-in-law (he had three daughters and no son). His two older daughters were married, but their husbands showed no interest in the coat business. On the other hand, although all his children had worked in the office at one time or another, only Gina, the youngest, showed any long-term interest in the firm. She had worked steadily part-time since high school. She started by sweeping scraps, checking stock, and cataloging orders, and then moved to the upper office where she helped with accounts payable, accounts receivable, and shipping. By the time she graduated from college, Gina had worked in almost every aspect of the business. Gina planned on being the one to take over the business when her father retired and never even considered looking for another job upon graduation. Mr. Lacommare, wanting the business to continue and seeing no immediate hope of a son-in-law to fill his place, encouraged Gina's interest and agreed to hire her full-time. It was then that the problems began.

While working part-time, Gina had seen flaws and inefficiencies in the way her father was running the company. She recognized the downhill trend and thought of ways to improve the situation. She made suggestions to her father at the time, but Mr. Lacommare always resisted, and Gina eventually stopped suggesting. When she did occasionally venture a suggestion, Mr. Lacommare listened patiently and then reminded Gina that she was too young to completely grasp the situation. In addition, he always stressed his many years of experience in the business. He promised, however, that if and when Gina joined the business full-time, she would definitely have more to say.

Another stumbling block to having her suggestions taken seriously was Gina's work relationship with her father. Throughout high school and college, although she was paid, Gina did not view her part-time position as work but as help to the family business. Therefore, she dealt with Mr. Lacommare never as her employer but always as her father. For all issues, including salary, vacations, work responsibilities, and raises, Gina and Joe Lacommare made their decisions more on the basis of their father/daughter relationship than on the basis of what was best for the business. Mr. Lacommare rarely denied Gina's requests, even if they were an inconvenience to him, because "after all, she was his little girl." By the same token, Gina was conscientious and responsible and tried to do the best for her father; but if there was a problem, it was dealt with on a personal level between her and her father, bypassing any supervisors in between. Mr. Lacommare also saw no problem with their relationship, because at the time he still hoped that it would be Gina's future husband who would take over some day and that Gina would not have to work.

Gina was not unaware of her father's plans when she accepted the full-time job, but decided to show him gradually what excellent work she could do. She believed that as she proved herself, he would slowly ease more and more responsibility onto her. By the day of her graduation, Gina had a working knowledge of the business and at least a theoretical knowledge of how to expand and improve Lacommare's Coats. After graduation, Gina joined Lacommare's Coats as Vice President.

Gina Becomes Vice President

In title, the position Mr. Lacommare gave Gina was one of high responsibility—an ideal place from which to implement some of the changes she had planned. Practically, however, Gina's responsibilities remained very similar to those she had while she worked part-time. Her ideas were still rejected by her father. At first Gina accepted this, thinking the situation was a temporary introduction period, but after three months, nothing had changed. The workers and other supervisors did not treat her any differently and often bypassed her to ask her father questions that she could—and, in her position, should—have answered. Her father did not discourage this practice, and although he had never double-checked her work when she was working part-time, suddenly he was rechecking everything.

During the fourth month after joining Lacommare on a full-time basis, Gina got up the courage to set a special planning meeting with her father. She told him what problems she saw in the company and what she thought were the reasons for the relative decline of Lacommare's Coats. In this list she included incompetent salesmen, her father's reluctance to fire incompetent salesmen, the lack of a marketing plan to compete within their new market, and various other problems that resulted from the lack of a cohesive long-term growth strategy. She then carefully described her suggestions for solving these problems. She talked about creating a sales department; at least moving their shop, if not the whole company, into a better area in order to increase their customer base and reduce theft; and, to facilitate growth, introducing a line of new clothing, such as men's and women's tailored suits and clothing. She outlined a few other changes and requested that her position be made clear to the workers, so that they would stop going to her father for every decision.

Mr. Lacommare listened silently. He then agreed to clarify Gina's position with the staff and called the meeting to a close. Gina did not leave, but tried again, backing up her ideas with painstakingly prepared financial reports and estimates, showing both the profit decline of the company and the potential growth. Mr. Lacommare still resisted, refusing to make any changes and clinging stubbornly to the idea of producing only the wool coats which brought him his initial success. He again reiterated that he had been in the business for many years and knew what he was doing. He dismissed the downward trend as a temporary lull, repeated that he liked the business the way it was, that it had been successful all along, and that he saw no reason to change it now. When Gina persisted, her father became angry, and the argument ended with Mr. Lacommare telling Gina, "That was no way to talk to your father!"

Another issue had added to the problems between father and daughter. Gina's attitude about working at Lacommare's Coats had changed since her part-time days. She took her job seriously and no longer just viewed herself as the daughter in the family business. She saw herself as a competent manager trying to keep things running smoothly. At work, she now treated her father mainly as a boss, whereas Joe Lacommare still acted like a father toward Gina. They had many miscommunications, because they dealt with each other on different levels, each not understanding the other.

Gina Lacommare stayed with her father's business for ten months. The problems they encountered in their working relationship during the first few months did not go away, and actually expanded. Unfortunately, those were the only things expanding, as the profits continued to fall. Gina still had very little say, since all control and decisions were in the hands of her father, the original entrepreneur. The more Gina pushed for change, the more her father resisted.

Finally, to the sadness of both, Gina left Lacommare's Coats to work as a mid-level manager at a larger company. She simply could not handle being the daughter of an entrepreneur, instead of a manager in her own right.

Overcoming the DOE Syndrome

The DOE Syndrome presents a special problem because it involves the behavior of more people than just the victim. In this syndrome, the victim, such as Meredith Cohen or Gina Lacommare, is encouraged to adopt a certain behavior pattern because it fits the needs of others, especially her parents.

The dilemma facing the potential victim of the DOE Syndrome involves a conflict between two different forces, both of which affect her sense of self-esteem. The individual literally must make a choice between her need for self-esteem as a manager and her need for self-esteem from being a "good daughter."

The only alternative that will permit a potential victim of the DOE Syndrome to simultaneously satisfy both sets of needs involves changes in the behavior of others. For example, her parent must begin to see her as a professional at work rather than as a child.

The strategic objective of the potential DOE is to change the perceptions and behavior of the parent. The DOE must recognize what is going on in the mind of the parent and patiently deal with it. She must also recognize that merely demonstrating to the parent that the DOE is a capable professional is not always sufficient, as shown in the case of Gina Lacommare; rather, the DOE must deal with the psychological needs of the parent.

It is quite typical for the entrepreneur in this case to be a victim of the Godfather Syndrome, described in Chapter 4, and most likely the parent will be a Caretaker Godfather. If the DOE is to avoid the syndrome and still remain in the organization, the entrepreneur must learn to treat his or her child differently. Unfortunately, it is not very likely that this will occur without some family conflict. It has been our experience that the entrepreneur is more likely to listen to an independent third party than to the DOE herself. If the emerging syndrome is noticed by a board of directors or an independent adviser, perhaps these outsiders can confront the entrepreneur and motivate him or her to change. The DOE can also try to arrange for a third party to intervene in her behalf.

The same underlying problem presents itself in the case of the wife or son of the entrepreneur, and the same strategy needs to be followed. The key is to get the entrepreneur to recognize what is happening and to try to motivate that person to make the transition from treating someone as a family member to treating him or her as a professional.

Part Three
Important Inner Game Issues for Organizations

Chapter 12

Improving Your Mastery of the Inner Game of Management

Some fortunate people have the natural ability to do the things required by the Inner Game of Management. This simply means that through education, family culture, and personal experience, these people have learned how to play the Inner Game effectively. These relatively few fortunate individuals can be termed "Inner Game naturals."

There are always some people who seem to have a greater innate ability to play any game. Mickey Mantle, the great center fielder of the New York Yankees, was a natural in baseball. Pete Rose, who now holds the record for the greatest number of base hits, was not a natural. He was not blessed with the innate ability of a Mantle. While Mantle achieved greatness through his natural ability, Pete Rose did it the old-fashioned way through motivation and hard work. As the career of Pete Rose indicates, it is possible to learn how to play most games reasonably well even if you are not a natural. Rose is now a player/coach and on his way to learning the game of management, just as he once learned to play the game of baseball. As part of this process, he will have to develop a coach's psychology—that is, learn how to master the Inner Game of Management.

Becoming an Inner Game Master

The first step in beginning to master the Inner Game of Management is simply to become aware that there is a game to be played. This means you should become aware of the need to consciously manage your self-esteem, your need for control, and your need to be liked, as described in Chapter 1.

Once you have become aware of the need to manage these Inner Game variables, the next step is to assess the extent to which your management of each of these aspects needs to be improved. People will differ in this respect.

To help you determine in what areas you need to improve your Inner Game, the next section examines the 11 most common symptoms of ineffective Inner Game playing. These 11 symptoms are found in varying combinations and to varying extents in each of the ten syndromes. Thus some symptoms are common to more than one syndrome.

Next, we provide a method of scoring the extent to which you are suffering from these symptoms. Then, we describe a three-step approach for improving the effectiveness of your Inner Game. Finally, we present a case study of someone who is in the process of mastering the Inner Game of Management, to illustrate how this can be done.

The 11 Most Common Symptoms of Ineffective Inner Game Playing

As people are promoted into managerial roles, they can begin to experience a variety of symptoms indicative of a failure to master the Inner Game of Management. These symptoms, if not "cured," can eventually result in failure or, at the very least, can cause people to play a game other than that of an "Inner Game Master." The 11 most common symptoms of an inability to master the Inner Game are as follows:

1. Tendency to emphasize performance rather than supervisory activities.
2. Inability to deal with the ambiguous nature of the managerial role.
3. Inability or unwillingness to make decisions in a timely fashion.
4. Feeling in competition with subordinates for the position of technical "guru."
5. Tendency to hire people who are technically or interpersonally less skilled than oneself.
6. Desire to be recognized by others as a powerful person.
7. Inability or unwillingness to delegate tasks to subordinates.

8. Inability or unwillingness to delegate decision-making responsibility to subordinates.
9. Need to be evaluated on one's personal performance rather than on the performance of subordinates.
10. Tendency to avoid rather than deal with conflict.
11. Inability or unwillingness to praise subordinates.

The purpose of this section is to describe and illustrate each of these symptoms as they relate to the key components of the Inner Game.

Emphasizing Performance Rather Than Supervisory Activities

One of the most common and most easily recognized symptoms of a failure to master the Inner Game of Management is a tendency to emphasize performance activities rather than supervisory activities. Most, if not all, managers are promoted to their positions from performing roles and are, therefore, accustomed to "doing a job" rather than supervising one.

Managers who experience this symptom feel confident as performers but not as supervisors. Hence, to protect themselves from feelings of inadequacy (to protect their self-esteem), they tend to avoid supervisory activities and emphasize performance activities. For example, a person promoted from the position of an engineer to the position of Engineering Project Manager may like to do engineering work rather than perform the new job requirements, and many people simply "recreate" their old jobs by becoming "hands-on managers." This means that the manager does not have time for such tasks as planning (deciding what to do, when to do it, who should do it, and so on), conducting meetings, and organizing the work of others. When these tasks are ignored, work-group productivity may decrease, and subordinates may become dissatisfied with their jobs, since their manager is not spending enough time providing them with the direction they need.

Time, then, is one of the most basic but critical managerial resources. Decisions are made constantly about what to do with an individual's time: how to spend it, what the priorities ought to be, and the like. If an individual does not conceptualize his or her role properly, time may be misused. Too much attention may be devoted to the things that the person wants to do rather than the things he or she must do to be effective as a manager. As we saw in Chapter 2, Bob Miller was spending too much of his time as a salesman rather than as a sales manager, because he liked to sell rather than to manage. Thus this symptom is typical of the Doer Syndrome, discussed earlier in Chapter 2.

Inability to Deal with the Ambiguous Nature of One's Role

A second symptom of ineffective Inner Game playing is an inability or unwillingness to deal with the ambiguity which is inherent in the managerial role. When a person is promoted to a management position, that individual may realize that he or she has become "the boss," but few people understand what the boss does. This causes people a certain amount of discomfort and uneasiness, since they do not understand how to satisfy their achievement need (a self-esteem need) in this role; that is, they don't know how to be "good" managers. Consequently, there is a tendency to retreat to using performance skills, since they have so far served these individuals well. These skills, however, do not help them accomplish the tasks required by the new role and can ultimately result in their failure. This is another symptom of the Doer Syndrome.

Inability or Unwillingness to Make Decisions

People who feel uncomfortable with the ambiguity of their role as managers and whose self-esteem is threatened by the possibility that they will "do something wrong" because they do not know what is right, may become indecisive. This is another symptom of ineffective Inner Game playing. Some individuals who suffer from this symptom postpone decisions until they absolutely have to be made, while others may defer decisions to either superiors or subordinates in order to avoid responsibility. The first alternative is a symptom of the Superperson Syndrome (discussed in Chapter 3), while the second is indicative of the Ugly Duckling Syndrome, as discussed in Chapter 3. Those individuals who suffer from chronic indecisiveness are victims of the Hamlet Syndrome, which was discussed in Chapter 8. People who play this game cannot decide what to do because they don't have a clear understanding of their role, so they either do nothing at all or delay the decision for so long that it is no longer appropriate to the situation. Subordinates recognize this and either follow the manager's lead and do nothing at all or take matters into their own hands, which eventually results in chaos throughout the manager's work group.

Competing with Subordinates

A fourth symptom of ineffective Inner Game playing is feeling that one is competing with subordinates for the position of technical guru. Many, if not most managers, are promoted to their positions as a result of possessing great technical capabilities in some area. It is a fact in our society that one way to recognize excellent technical performance is through promotion to a management position. Therefore, it is often the case that those whose new job is to supervise others are looked to, at least initially, as technical experts or gurus.

Managers who are "experts" derive a great deal of self-esteem from being seen as technically superior by their subordinates. It feels good to be acknowledged as "the best" in one's work group. Unfortunately, the situation in which they are the technical experts may not last for long, because as people develop and new people are brought in, it is common for managers to find themselves supervising people with superior technical skills. The managers may come to feel inadequate, because they truly believe that their success as managers is linked to the ability to be the best technically. Given this belief, the manager may believe it important to seek the knowledge that will restore him or her to the position of technical expert instead of trying to learn the skills necessary to make him or her a managerial success. This symptom is characteristic of the Pygmy Syndrome, described in Chapter 6, as well as the Doer Syndrome, described in Chapter 2.

Tendency to Hire Weak People

Another symptom of ineffective Inner Game playing that is used to protect one's self-esteem is to hire people who are technically or interpersonally less skilled than oneself. Managers who suffer from this symptom have low self-esteem. They attempt to increase their feelings of self-worth by ensuring that they will be the technically most competent (through hiring less skilled subordinates) or by hiring people with weaknesses that they can exploit. Managers who exploit others' weaknesses do so because they want to hide their own weaknesses behind a facade of power. This is a distinguishing characteristic of the Pygmy Syndrome, which was described in Chapter 6. It is also associated with the Napoleon Syndrome, discussed in Chapter 5.

When a manager hires only weak people, his or her work group may suffer from low creativity, low morale, and low productivity. If the manager is successful at recruiting only people with skill levels lower than his or her own, the chances for innovation are minimized. If the manager is unsuccessful and recruits individuals who represent a challenge to his or her technical expertise and/or authority, the entire work group will be placed in a conflict situation as the manager attempts to prove that he or she is the most skilled. If the manager tends to openly exploit others' weaknesses, subordinates will either spend a great deal of time trying to make the manager happy so as to avoid abuse or simply stay out of his or her way.

Desire to Be Recognized As a Powerful Person

Another symptom of ineffective Inner Game playing is the need to be recognized as a powerful person. People who suffer from this symptom have relatively low self-esteem and high needs for control.

Some individuals who suffer from this symptom surround themselves with weak people, because they believe that weak people will not challenge their authority. Hence, they are protecting themselves from being "overthrown." Other individuals who suffer from the need to be recognized as powerful surround themselves with strong people, because they believe that they will be seen as powerful simply because they associate with powerful others.

In either case, it is very important to people who suffer from this symptom that others overtly acknowledge and respect their power. Those subordinates who refuse to do so suffer adverse consequences (such as being publicly humiliated or even fired), while those who are respectful of these managers' power are rewarded. This symptom is found associated with several syndromes, including the Godfather, Napoleon, and Pygmy Syndromes.

Inability or Unwillingness to Delegate Tasks

Ineffective delegation of tasks is a symptom of ineffective Inner Game playing that results from high control needs. Managers who suffer from this symptom, like the Doers described in Chapter 2, tend to either do everything themselves or delegate tasks by telling subordinates exactly what needs to be done and how to do it. These individuals waste a great deal of the time they should be devoting to administrative activities performing tasks their subordinates should be handling. They never seem to get as much done as they would like to have done, yet they believe they are doing the best they can. Managers who suffer from the Superperson Syndrome, described in Chapter 3, also exhibit this symptom.

The performance of their work group may suffer because subordinates may come to believe that their managers do not trust them, since the assignments they are given are trivial and do not allow them to use all their skills. So, while the manager is busy doing everything, the subordinates are slowly suffering a decrease in morale and performance. Performance of the entire group suffers, and the manager may eventually fail.

Inability or Unwillingness to Delegate Decision Making

While some managers with high control needs suffer from an inability to delegate tasks, others suffer from an inability to delegate authority. These individuals believe that in order to ensure that the right decisions are made, they must retain ultimate control over all decisions. Managers who suffer from this symptom of ineffective Inner Game playing are characterized as over-bearing by their subordinates. Their subordinates usually are either afraid of them or are constantly plotting their downfall. A favorite statement made by these managers is: "Check with me before you do anything." In some cases, these individuals operate under the guise that they are actually giving subordinates a certain amount of input into decisions, but this usually means that they allow their subordinates enough rope so that when appropriate, they can either "pull in the reins" (stop the decision-making process before it is complete) or use the rope to beat their subordinates (when a decision made is not "the right one").

This symptom occurs in several syndromes, but perhaps most frequently in the Entrepreneur Syndrome, discussed in Chapter 10. It can also be found associated with the Hamlet Syndrome, described in Chapter 8.

Obviously, the inability to give a certain amount of decision-making responsibility to subordinates tends to overburden the manager. He or she spends a great deal of time "checking up on subordinates" or, if subordinates are fearful of him or her, telling subordinates about the appropriateness of the decisions made for them. This results in an inadequate amount of time being spent on other critical requirements of the managerial role. It also produces a decrease in morale among subordinates, which can lead to decreasing productivity and eventual failure of the manager.

Need to Be Evaluated on One's Own Performance

This symptom is related to a need to derive one's self-esteem from direct results and an unwillingness to give up control to subordinates. The manager suffering from this symptom believes that personal performance is what counts and that to be evaluated on subordinates' performance is both risky and unrewarding. Being evaluated on subordinates' performance is risky in the sense that you cannot be certain that subordinates' results will be positive. By contrast, if one maintains control over the results and performs everything oneself, then there is a better guarantee that performance will satisfy self-esteem needs. This thinking is characteristic of the Doer Syndrome.

Tendency to Avoid Rather Than Deal with Conflict

This symptom of ineffective Inner Game playing results from a desire to be liked at the expense of performing the requirements of the manager's role. An individual who suffers from this symptom is so intent on being liked by his or her subordinates that whenever a potential threat to the tranquillity of the work group occurs, he or she ignores it. If a subordinate does not want to do a certain task, the manager who suffers from conflict avoidance may ask the subordinate to do it, but if the request is refused, the manager may simply do the task himself or herself. The manager does not criticize subordinates, since this, too, might be disruptive.

Unfortunately, ignoring conflict will eventually backfire. An undercurrent of hostility will develop, and if the manager continues to act as if nothing were wrong, subordinates may simply leave the firm or walk over the manager. An inability to deal with conflict is typical of the Salesperson Syndrome, discussed in Chapter 9. Moreover, a version of this symptom is associated with the DOE Syndrome, when the individual is unable to confront her parents concerning the role conflict she faces.

Providing Insufficient Praise

This symptom is inversely related to the need to be liked and is also usually an indication that the manager is suffering from low self-esteem. In this case, the manager believes that he or she is worthless and therefore not capable of either being liked or providing praise to others. This symptom is characterized by the statement: "Subordinates know when they are doing a good job, since I do not criticize them. I do not need to praise them, because I don't care whether or not they like me as long as they are doing their job." The symptom is associated with the Malevolent Godfather, the Napoleon, and the Dr. Jekyll and Mr. Hyde Syndromes.

The result of such a philosophy is that subordinates may suffer from morale problems, since they really may not know that they are doing a good job. They may believe that they simply "got away" with something this time and may begin to question their adequacy to fill certain positions. A manager who adopts the attitude that subordinates do not need praise may soon find that he or she has no subordinates to manage.

Measuring the Effectiveness
of Your Inner Game Playing

To assist you in assessing the extent to which you (or one of your subordinates) suffer from the symptoms we discussed, we have developed the ques-

Table 12-1. How to interpret scores from the Inner Game Mastery
Questionnaire.

Score Range	Color	Interpretation
14–19	Green	Everything is O.K.
20–29	Yellow	Some things to watch.
30–39	Orange	Some areas require attention.
40–49	Red	Some very significant problems exist.
50–70	Purple	High potential for managerial failure.

tionnaire shown in Figure 12-1 (on the following pages). This instrument consists of 14 questions that identify various aspects of the symptoms of ineffective Inner Game playing.

The questionnaire is based on a five-point scale, with descriptors ranging from "to a very great extent" to "to a very slight extent." By placing check marks in the appropriate columns, respondents indicate the extent to which they believe they are experiencing each of the symptoms.

Scoring the Questionnaire

Once the questionnaire has been completed, the number of check marks in each column is totaled and recorded on line W. Each item on line W is then multiplied by the weight of that column (this weight is shown in line X). The weighted total for each column is then recorded on line Y. For example, Figure 12-1 shows that the respondent entered three check marks in column B. Accordingly, we multiply 3 (line W) by the weight of 4 (line X) and record the result, 12, on line Y, column B. The final step is to add the numbers on line Y. That total represents the extent to which the person is able to successfully play the Inner Game of Management. The score can range from 14, which is the most favorable, to 70, which is the most unfavorable.

Interpreting the Scores

To help you determine the meaning of the scores, we have developed a simple color-coding scheme that represents the degree of seriousness of the symptoms. The scores derived from the questionnaire may be interpreted as shown in Table 12-1.

(text continued on p. 185)

Figure 12-1. The Inner Game Mastery Questionnaire.

Question	A Very great extent	B Great extent	C Some extent	D Slight extent	E Very slight extent
1. I tend to spend more time on performance/doer activities than on supervisory activities.	X				
2. I feel uncomfortable because my managerial responsibilities are ambiguous or ill-defined.		X			
3. I tend to make decisions only when I am forced to.		X			
4. I prefer to check with my superiors before making decisions.					X
5. At some level, I feel that I am competing with my subordinates for the position of technical expert.		X			
6. I tend to hire people who are less skilled than I am.					X
7. I tend to hire people with weaknesses I can exploit.					X

Figure 12-1, continued.

Question	A Very great extent	B Great extent	C Some extent	D Slight extent	E Very slight extent
8. I like to be seen as someone with power over others.				X	
9. I frequently do not delegate tasks to subordinates, because I'm not sure they'll accomplish the tasks correctly.			X		
10. I believe my subordinates should check with me before making "significant" decisions.			X		
11. I tend to evaluate myself on my own performance rather than on the performance of the people I supervise.			X		
12. I tend to avoid criticizing my staff to avoid conflict.					X
13. I don't like to set goals for others and ask them to do things they don't want to do.					X

Figure 12-1, continued.

	A Very great extent	B Great extent	C Some extent	D Slight extent	E Very slight extent
Question					
14. I do not feel the need to praise my subordinates—as long as I don't criticize, they know they are doing a good job.	_____	_____	_____	X	_____

SCORING

		A	B	C	D	E
W	Add the total number of re-sponses in each column and record numbers here	1	3	3	2	5
X	Multiply the num-ber on line "W" by the number on line "X" and re-cord on line "Y".	5	4	3	2	1
Y	Result of line W times line X.	5	12	9	4	5
Z	Add up the num-bers on line Y, columns A–E, and place the total on this line.	35				

A Green Score. A green score suggests that you have a good mastery of the Inner Game of Management. Provided you have developed the skills to play the Outer Game of management effectively, it suggests that your chances of failing as a manager are minimal.

A Yellow Score. A yellow score suggests that you are able to play the Inner Game of Management effectively on most levels, but that there are certain areas in which you could improve. This is analogous to a patient who is told that his or her blood pressure is on the high side, but within the normal range. To lower the blood pressure, the patient might restrict salt intake or take up an exercise program. Similarly, to improve your ability to play the Inner Game of Management, you might concentrate on the particular area of difficulty indicated by the questionnaire and try to overcome any symptoms indicated.

An Orange Score. This score indicates that you have some problems that are preventing you from playing the Inner Game of Management as effectively as you should. There are certain areas that deserve your attention—areas in which you may need to make a change if you are to be effective in the managerial role. The problems may not be too serious yet, but they require corrective action before they become serious.

A Red Score. A score which falls in this range indicates that you may be severely handicapping your ability to be an effective manager because you are extremely ineffective at playing the Inner Game of Management. You may already be experiencing difficulties and may not understand why. The results of this questionnaire may give you a clue on where to look for the source of your problems.

A Purple Score. This score indicates a very serious situation. The person who has such a score is on the brink of career failure. Action should be taken immediately to overcome whatever problems the person may be suffering from.

The score on the questionnaire gives a preliminary indication of the extent to which you are able to play the Inner Game of Management. If your overall score exceeds 29, a more in-depth analysis to identify the problems and develop recommendations for future action is probably required. Scores that exceed this number indicate that you probably have not yet learned to play the Inner Game of Management effectively. The seriousness of your problems may not be evident to you currently. But, as you move up the organizational hierarchy, your inability to play the Inner Game of Management can be fatal.

Becoming an Inner Game Master:
Three Action Steps

The process of playing the Inner Game of Management effectively cannot be reduced to a simple formula. Organizational life is too complex for that. However, from our research, as well as development work with hundreds of managers during the past decade, we have identified three basic action steps that managers can take to improve their ability to play the Inner Game:

1. Perform a self-assessment of your ability to play the Inner Game of Management.
2. Formulate a plan to reduce symptoms of Inner Game problems.
3. Implement the plan you have designed and practice performing as a "Master" of the Inner Game.

Each of these steps is discussed below.

Action Step 1: Self-Assessment

Once you have recognized that the Inner Game exists, the first action step for improving your ability to play the Inner Game of Management is to recognize what your current ability is. This involves understanding the dimensions of the Inner Game of Management and being able to critically evaluate your ability on each dimension. To do this, you should complete the "Inner Game Mastery Questionnaire" (see Figure 12-1).

No matter how painful such an assessment may be, it is important that you be honest with yourself. If you do not accept your weaknesses, you will be unable to improve your ability to play the Inner Game. However, don't get overwhelmed with guilt and feelings of inadequacy. As we stated at the beginning of this chapter, few people are Inner Game naturals. Nearly all of us, then, have at least some area of our game plan in which we can make improvements.

Action Step 2: Formulate a Plan for Self-Improvement

Once you have completed a self-assessment, you should develop a plan that will help you improve your ability to play the Inner Game. To be successful at this process, you should begin by selecting a particular area on which you wish to concentrate and then design a plan for that area. Here are some examples of plans for self-improvement, given various symptoms of poor Inner Game playing:

Discomfort with Role Definition. If you discover that one of your symptoms is that you are uncomfortable with your management role because you don't understand what constitutes success in this role, there are several steps you might take to overcome these feelings. First, try to recognize that most people who enter new positions do not clearly understand their roles and are not "excellent managers." It takes time, sometimes a year or two, before people can completely understand their role.

Next, write down what you believe you are expected to accomplish in your role. It is important that you clearly understand what you will be evaluated on. Ask your supervisor to explain the performance-evaluation criteria for someone in your position. On the basis of these criteria and with the help of your supervisor, set some performance goals that you can realistically achieve in a specified time period. These goals will provide you the direction you need to be successful.

Inability to Make Timely Decisions. If you tend to procrastinate over decisions or tasks because you fear that you might make a mistake, try setting deadlines for when decisions must be made or tasks must be accomplished. Make a list of decisions, prioritize them, and list realistic deadlines for the accomplishment of each. Design a work plan that allows you to meet your goals within the time allocated.

Tendency Not to Delegate Tasks or Decision-Making Responsibility. If you tend not to delegate tasks (or decisions) to subordinates because you fear that they will not accomplish them (or make decisions) in a manner that meets your standards, pick a particular task or decision that you normally would not delegate and ask a subordinate or a group of subordinates to do it for you. Once you've delegated, try not to intervene unless your subordinates ask for your help. See what happens. Meanwhile, analyze your own feelings and think about what will happen if your subordinates fail to live up to your standards. Chances are, they will perform the task adequately, even if it is not exactly as you would have done it. If it isn't done well enough the first time, remember that your role is to motivate others to achieve organizational goals, not to do all the work yourself. Try the same exercise again.

Tendency to Emphasize Performance Tasks Rather Than Supervisory Activities. If you tend to spend a lot of time on performance activities, try to organize your time so that you spend increasingly more time on administrative activities. Use an hourly log to plan your day so that it consists mostly of meetings, writing reports, and advising subordinates rather than actually "doing the work."

Feeling in Competition with Subordinates. If you feel threatened because one of your subordinates has greater technical knowledge than you do, your objective might be to overcome these feelings of inadequacy. First, you must recognize that when this person comes to you with the solution to a technical problem, he or she is not trying to humiliate you. Rather, your subordinate is legitimately looking to you for praise. He or she assumes that you will be proud. Therefore, one goal for you to have in working to overcome your feelings of inadequacy might be: "To offer legitimate praise to technical stars whenever they solve a problem."

Action Step 3: Implement and Evaluate Your Plan

Once you've picked a particular area in which you want to improve your ability to play the Inner Game of Management and you have designed a plan you think you can live with, begin implementing it. Keep a list of your goals and evaluate your progress on each. You may want to keep a written record of your feelings and the extent to which you achieved your goals. This will help you clearly see the progress you are making and identify other areas for improvement.

During this personal development period, you will need to be patient. It takes time to change behavior patterns and their accompanying feelings and to become comfortable with the changes. It may be very difficult, but you will find that with a little work and thought, you can learn to overcome your problems and begin playing the Inner Game of Management effectively. The most important point is for you to recognize that you are having some problems, to identify the sources of these problems, and to take steps to overcome the problems.

We conclude this chapter with a case study of how one individual, Betsy Knapp, successfully completed the three steps we described. This case study will illustrate the actual process of becoming an Inner Game Master.

Mastering the Inner Game: The Betsy Knapp Case

Betsy Knapp's given name is Elizabeth Wood Knapp, but she uses the nickname Betsy professionally. She currently serves as President and CEO of her own company, Wood, Knapp & Co. Inc., and is a member of various professional business associations, including the "Committee of 200," an organization for women entrepreneurs and top executives. In very real terms, Betsy Knapp has achieved a great deal of managerial success, but over the course of her career, she also had to overcome a number of Inner Game problems.

This case will trace her career from co-founder of her own software company, to senior executive of a major publishing firm, Knapp Communications Corporation, to CEO of her own firm, which develops products for the electronic media (video, TV, computers, and so on). In this case, we emphasize the origin of her professional career and the steps Betsy took during her tenure as a senior executive at Knapp Communications to overcome her Inner Game problems and make the successful transition to a senior management role.

Background

As a result of post-college work experience, Betsy developed a keen interest in business applications of computers. Three years after college, Betsy decided that she could put her knowledge of computer technology to work in her own business. So, in 1968, Betsy and an associate founded Telmar Communications Corp. The company was positioned in the advertising industry, between the research companies and their clients. Its primary business was to electronically deliver information on media and market research and simultaneously analyze it. Betsy's initial title was Vice President. Along with her associate, who served as President, she was in charge of marketing and selling. One of the other employees at Telmar served as the technical guru, and the other was in charge of technical media information.

Since the firm was successful in identifying a market and a relevant set of services, the business grew, which brought a variety of changes in personnel and responsibilities. Betsy grew tired of marketing and selling and of training new users in the company's services, so she moved into the technical side of the firm, where she became technical director.

In her new position, she became deeply involved in the programming and systems design of Telmar's products. Such technical involvement is common among "senior executives" in entrepreneurial firms. In fact, Betsy became so intrigued by this side of the business that she installed a computer terminal in her apartment so that she could work nights and weekends.

Betsy had graduated from Wellesley College with a degree in economics and minors in math and music. She had no formal college training in management or technical subjects. Her first exposure to computers occurred while she was working after college at the MIT Sloan School of Management, where she taught herself to write computer programs and followed the master's degree readings in marketing and management. Subsequently, she began to devour computer manuals and learned from discussions with talented programmers who worked for Telmar.

She developed her technical and managerial skills on the job. "In a small start-up company you must wear many hats. You are constantly switching between doer and manager as the organization grows."

As her managerial skills improved, she expressed her desire to be President and COO of the firm and was appointed to that position. Betsy understood that she did not have all the skills required for the job, but she was enthusiastic and eager to take on the new level of responsibility. During the period from 1968 to 1978, the company grew to over 50 employees and 300 clients and established offices in four U.S. cities plus Canada.

In 1979, Betsy made a major change in her professional and personal life when she met and married Bud Knapp. Bud is the owner and founder of Knapp Communications Corporation, publisher of *Architectural Digest, Bon Appetit,* and *Home.* It also includes a subsidiary company, The Knapp Press, which publishes books. Betsy and Bud met in 1978, when Bud's California-based company became one of Telmar's clients. Upon her marriage, Betsy left Telmar and moved to California, where she spent her first year looking into new business opportunities.

Toward the end of that year, she was approached by the Senior Vice President of Operations at Knapp Communications Corporation (KCC) to come and work as a consultant in the information systems area. The company had experienced tremendous growth in revenues, but little increase in sophistication of computer technology. KCC had grown from about $5 million in 1975 to nearly $50 million at the time Betsy entered the firm. Betsy's consulting assignment was to untangle some nagging computer and organizational problems in the information systems area. Her assignment lasted a few months, during which time several people at KCC realized that the company needed someone with solid technical and managerial experience to take over and develop the information systems area. Betsy was hired as Director of Information Systems with a staff of about 15 people in 1980 and was promoted to Senior Vice President, Information Systems and Electronic Media, in 1981.

Her responsibilities as Senior Vice President encompassed all of the computer activity for the company, including data processing, word processing, and electronic type setting. She was also responsible for magazine fulfillment. KCC's computer capability underwent a major restructuring after 1981. Hardware and software changes and the introduction of new technology caused some turnover in the information systems department while new positions were created at all levels.

Sensing a change in media markets and an opportunity to get back into line management, Betsy asked for permission to take over a third area of responsibility—Electronic Media. This involved the conceptualization, design, and creation of electronic products based upon KCC's printed products. Her total staff was about 55 people.

During the period from 1981 to 1984, Betsy's involvement and responsibilities became extremely complex at KCC. She was involved not only in information systems and electronic media but also in the overall management of the company. As a member of the board of directors and as Corporate Secretary, she became a participant in a broad spectrum of planning and business issues. Finally, in 1984, she became responsible for four additional areas: human resources, administration, corporate communications, and rights and permissions.

Her involvement at KCC on all these levels put a great many demands on her time. She was also forced to shift gears frequently from a senior manager's role in running the human resources and administration, to an entrepreneurial role in developing the electronic-media area and the new corporate-communications function, to a diplomat role as a board member of KCC as a whole.

Action Step 1: Self-Assessment

It was clear to Betsy that as a result of her tendency and perceived need to play all these different roles, there were too many demands on her time. She has said of this experience: "I felt like I was wearing too many hats and was being pulled apart." Even though she held the title of Senior Vice President, she was not always thinking and acting like a senior executive. Sometimes she was a doer, sometimes she was an entrepreneur, and sometimes she was a manager. She needed to decide what her role as a senior manager should be and to find ways of becoming comfortable in this role.

Managing the Need for Self-Esteem. Although she had been promoted to Senior Vice President, Betsy had not yet made the transition in her source of self-esteem from her technical MIS role to the broader role of a senior executive. The critical Inner Game issue that faced Betsy involved the choice between the technical role of the MIS guru and specialist and the more ambiguous and ill-defined role of the senior-level executive. Betsy had been comfortable in her role in MIS. She had mastered systems.

From an Inner Game perspective, she had achieved a considerable amount of her self-esteem through her skills and mastery of the technical aspects of information systems. Moreover, she enjoyed "playing with computers." The challenge she faced was to learn to like her new role and responsibilities, and to redefine her source of self-esteem from the technical and managerial aspects of her role to the more abstract role of a senior-level leader. As she stated: "My identity was pretty much wrapped up in the technical side of MIS. It was not wrapped up in human resources, administration, and other areas for which I was now responsible."

Betsy spent a considerable amount of time pondering the nature of her future role in the company. She talked with a number of people, including her husband, Bud Knapp, and a consultant who tried to help her understand the transitional issues she was facing. Specifically, she spent a lot of time assessing whether she really wanted to make the transition from an MIS manager to a senior executive with broader responsibilities. It meant giving up something which she did well and on which she based a great deal of her self-esteem.

Managing the Need for Control. For a person facing the transition to a managerial role, it is essential to learn how to manage the need for control. In her transition to a senior-executive role, Betsy Knapp faced some problems with her need for control. As she states: "As a technical MIS professional, you are directly in control of the result. As a senior manager, you really have to give up the idea that you did it. You have got to let the people who are managing those areas have the authority to do their jobs."

Giving people such authority is often very difficult, and Betsy realized it would not be easy. She enjoyed being involved in the day-to-day operations of her area, but began to realize that she could no longer attempt to directly control results because it was putting too many demands on her time.

Managing the Need To Be Liked. Another aspect of the Inner Game of Management that must be dealt with is the need to be liked. A doer can afford the luxury of being liked; but a manager is not there to win a popularity contest. There are many times when the manager has to challenge or criticize people.

This is difficult for most people, because they fear rejection. Betsy was no exception. She wanted to manage her area with as little conflict as possible, but she began to realize that avoiding conflict also caused problems.

Action Step 2: Formulate a Plan for Self-Improvement

During 1984, Betsy Knapp made the commitment to change. She decided to give up her old role as operational manager of the information systems area and concentrate her energies on new ventures in electronic media and her role as a senior executive with diplomat responsibilities. She made this decision because, as she said: "I just didn't feel good about what I was doing." She said she felt she had problems and she wanted to solve them. She had developed an intellectual fascination with, and a professional and emotional stake in, managerial transition.

Managing the Need for Self-Esteem. Once Betsy made the decision to change, she needed to find ways of redefining her source of self-esteem. She needed to accept her new responsibilities and change the way she spent her time. As she stated: "I had to learn to like my new responsibilities. I really didn't know what they involved. I jumped in cold to administration and human resources." The process of learning to like her new responsibilities was going to take some time, but it was essential in helping her learn to play the Inner Game effectively. She had to learn how to juggle her time among the six areas of responsibilities, rather than concentrate it in the areas in which she felt more comfortable.

She also had to learn to like meetings, an important part of her new role. She said of this: "I had difficulty accepting the idea that my job was going to meetings." However, she knew that this was a part of her role, and accepting it was an important step toward becoming an efficient and effective manager.

Unlike many managers, Betsy Knapp did not feel threatened by strong people. She had no problem hiring other strong managers to work for her. As she stated: "I have always tried to hire the strongest people possible. I prefer working with people who are bright and seek to surround myself with people who have complementary skills."

Managing the Need for Control. A manager's need for control affects a wide variety of things. It affects the decision-making authority and nature of the tasks the manager delegates to subordinates. Betsy said of her experience with delegation: "I had to learn to rely on other people and not do it myself." She accomplished this through a lot of practice at simply giving tasks and authority to others and waiting for results rather than jumping in.

A manager's need for control also affects the amount of information he or she needs to "feel in control." As Betsy Knapp stated: "I had to learn how much information I really needed to give me adequate control. If you hire good people, they will not sit still for you to continually control them through requesting every detail of their operations."

Betsy said that learning to ask the "right question" was important in this regard. The right question for someone in her position, she said, focuses on macro-issues such as "Did the job get done?" rather than day-to-day concerns like "How will you correct the errors in the last program?"

Managing the Need To Be Liked. Betsy found management of this need to be a personal challenge. She states: "I had to challenge the people who were working for me so I could motivate them to think differently. Sometimes, I found myself saying: 'You have to confront the hard questions, you must see yourself as the leader, you must visualize the goal you want to achieve.' "

She began a conscious effort to face conflict and to provide criticism where necessary. Although it was difficult, she could see its value in increasing others' performance.

Action Step 3: Implement and Evaluate the Plan

Betsy Knapp made significant progress toward making the transition to her diplomat role as Senior Vice President at Knapp, and now she is in the process of another transition to President of her own firm. She said of her experience in the new firm: "In my new company, I am attempting to pull together all facets of what I've learned about management—from a doer to a diplomat. My primary focus now is as a diplomat—I have a very talented staff, delegate as much as I can while maintaining an atmosphere of communication and collaboration about the direction of the business. I still seek help from others; I must maintain perspective about myself; I push myself and my staff to learn as much as we can, and my goal is to build a major company in its field."

Unfortunately, many managers are unwilling to take the risk of moving from their comfort zone and making the transition to a new management role, as Betsy has done. They will accept a new role in title, but will continue to think and act as they did in their former jobs. This, in turn, increases the risk of failing in their new roles, because they are not performing the responsibilities that they must in order to be successful.

Many people are victims of the Inner Game syndromes without recognizing it. To overcome these syndromes, they must be willing, as Betsy Knapp was, to give up doing what they know well. They must learn to manage their need for self-esteem, their need for control, and their need to be liked so that they can make the successful transition to the new role in their organization. In this way, as Betsy Knapp did, people can learn to play the Inner Game of Management effectively.

Chapter 13

Inner Game Effectiveness Through Management Development

Throughout this book we have described the problems faced by individuals who do not play the Inner Game of Management effectively. We have seen how a wide variety of people have encountered career difficulty and even failure because they could not master the Inner Game of Management.

Individuals who suffer from the symptoms of ineffective Inner Game playing are not the only victims; the organizations that employ these managers can suffer a great deal as well. There are very substantial costs to organizations that are run by managers unable to play the Inner Game effectively. These costs can range from low profitability to organizational unrest and even bankruptcy.

Organizations have a responsibility to recognize that managers may suffer from the various syndromes of poor Inner Game playing. They need to take action steps to help people overcome these problems as much as feasible. This is not only in the interest of the company's employees but also in the firm's interest.

The Role of Management Development

One of the most powerful tools an organization has to help people deal with the problems and challenges of the Inner Game of Management is management development. A well-conceived and well-executed management development program can play a very significant role in helping to overcome Inner Game problems. This chapter examines how management development may be used in this way.

It should be noted at the outset that, at least at present, there are relatively few examples of organizations that have established management development programs to deal explicitly with the kinds of issues described in this book. The examples with which we are familiar are those companies for which we have worked as management development advisers. It should also be noted that the nature of the management development effort required is different, at least to some degree, from the typical management development program. This is, of course, attributable to the different nature of the things we are trying to change.

Our experience in working with managers with Inner Game problems leads us to believe that a successful program for dealing with these issues must consist of four key parts:

1. Assessment of the extent to which individuals and the organization as a whole exhibit symptoms of the various Inner Game problems.
2. Development of a set of individualized and group-based management development courses.
3. Explicit management of the corporate culture to promote values that will help people become Inner Game Masters rather than victims of the various syndromes.
4. Assessment of the extent to which people have made progress in mastering the Inner Game of Management.

Each of these aspects of the program will be described in turn over the next pages.

Assessment of Inner Game Problems

The first step in helping people master the Inner Game is to make an assessment of the extent to which they exhibit the characteristic symptoms. There are two methods of accomplishing this assessment, which may be used either singly or in combination.

The first method is to develop or use a previously developed instrument for assessment, such as the Inner Game Mastery Questionnaire presented in Chapter 12 (see Figure 12-1). This instrument can be administered to individuals or the organization's management team as a whole. The scores can be compared with the norms or standard scores, shown in Table 12-1. Moreover, the organization can develop its own database to identify its "baseline" scores prior to training and development of its people.

The second method of performing an assessment is to have a trained interviewer meet with people who are well acquainted with the person under assessment. This may include the individual's subordinates, peers, and manager. The interviews focus on the individual's behavior as a manager and attempt to identify critical incidents that typify that behavior. The data obtained from these interviews must then be analyzed to identify present or potential Inner Game problems.

The interview should cover such topics as the way the manager spends his or her time (which is an indication of the possibility of the Doer Syndrome); the extent to which the manager hires and retains strong people (which relates to the Pygmy Syndrome); whether the manager feels the need to be in control of all details (associated with several different syndromes); and how difficult the manager finds it to reach decisions or deal with conflict.

The most effective way to gain a complete picture of the manager's needs is to use a combination of the questionnaire and the interview. The questionnaire will serve as a benchmark to assess future progress, while the interviews permit in-depth probing of particular problem areas.

Designing the Development Program

Once the data from the assessment phase have been obtained, it is possible to design a management development program to help individuals or groups deal with the syndromes identified. An overall management development program of this kind ought to have two basic components: (1) an individual component and (2) a group component.

Ideally, a program dealing with the Inner Game of Management should begin with a group-based training component. This may be a one- or two-day seminar designed to acquaint people with the nature of the problem, the types of syndromes that exist, and the general steps people can take to begin mastering the Inner Game of Management. The overall intent of this phase of the training is to make managers aware of the problem and sensitize them to it.

It must be noted that Inner Game of Management problems are related to deep-seated psychological issues; therefore, there are no "pills" or "quick fixes." People must be made aware of this during the overview phase of development. This phase of development can use several methods, including cases, role plays, films, and management development simulations. These can be based either on preexisting materials or on materials specially designed for the company. At present, not much material of this kind is available. However, as there is a growing awareness of the problems described in this book, we can anticipate that materials will be developed.

As far as feasible, there should also be individualized coaching or counseling. This can range from training managers to focus on some of these Inner Game issues in the performance appraisal of subordinate managers to providing either an in-house adviser or an external consultant to assist people.

As our experience in working with organizations to help them overcome these problems suggests, not everyone can be expected to change. Approximately 10 percent of the people with these problems are unlikely to change at all, even though they may profess to want to change. Another 10 to 15 percent of the people will be able to change merely by being made aware of the problems. They will "self-correct" what they are doing. Most people require a greater degree of management development to help them deal with these issues.

Our experience shows that changes in behavior can occur very quickly, within a matter of weeks, but a period of about two years is required before the changes become permanent. Changing an underlying attitude is even more complex, because it is tied in with notions of self-esteem and personal security. This can be very much a long-term "project." Nevertheless, even though some of the underlying attitudes will change more slowly, people *can* change their behavior as managers.

Managing the Culture to Promote Mastery of the Inner Game

A third component of the overall management development effort should be a program of managing the corporate culture to promote mastery of the Inner Game of Management.

"Corporate culture" refers to the values, beliefs, and norms that govern (explicitly or implicitly) the behavior of people in an organization. The management of corporate culture is ultimately the responsibility of the organization's CEO. Ideally, the CEO ought to be a role model of someone who has mastered the Inner Game of Management. Moreover, the CEO ought to stress the importance of managers' behaving in ways that avoid the various undesirable Inner Game syndromes.

How can this be accomplished? One of the most powerful tools the CEO has is the ability to decide who are the organization's "heroes." The CEO can select managers who best personify the kind of behavior the organization wants to promote. These people should then be given recognition and visibility throughout the firm. In this way, they become managerial role models for people to emulate.

The CEO has a powerful platform from which to create corporate heroes. If, however, the CEO does not make it clear to the organization who the heroes are, then the culture is not being managed and the wrong people may emerge as role models.

What if the CEO is a victim of one or more of the Inner Game syndromes? Unfortunately, it is too often the case that the CEO is not an Inner Game Master. In this case, it is necessary to begin with the CEO and deal with his or her Inner Game problems. If this is done, it can send a powerful signal throughout the organization, because it indicates that even the CEO has made a personal commitment to change.

Reassessment of Development

As we noted, the process of mastering the Inner Game of Management cannot be accomplished overnight. It can take a great deal of time. During this process, however, it is important to monitor the extent to which change is occurring.

One way to measure the progress made is to periodically use the Inner Game Mastery Questionnaire to reassess the extent to which managers are exhibiting symptoms of poor Inner Game playing. Another approach is to do a survey of subordinates to get their perceptions of changes in the behavior of managers. Such surveys must, of course, be confidential in order to encourage people to be candid. Ideally, they are conducted by an independent third party to maintain confidentiality.

Implications for Management Development Programs

Many companies use management development programs. However, most programs focus on the Outer Game of management—the skills and tasks of management—rather than on the aspects of the Inner Game of Management. There are many fine management development programs which are models for teaching managerial skills, but few which have incorporated the concepts developed in this book.

One of the major implications of this for both in-house and external management development programs is the need to explicitly incorporate materials and exercises dealing with the Inner Game of Management. Our research with managers indicates that in 90 percent of cases of "managerial failure," the underlying cause is a failure to master the Inner Game of Management rather than lack of technical managerial skills. People do not know what they are supposed to do as managers. They can recite the litany that a manager is supposed to "plan, organize, lead, and control." They know that an effective manager is supposed to hire strong people and delegate. But many cannot do it.

Unfortunately, most of the people who experience difficulty in their roles as managers simply do not realize why their problems have occurred. Their associates (or former associates) may shrug and say that "so and so was a 'head case' or had an 'ego problem.' " However, little is done to correct or help otherwise talented people with these problems. Perhaps this is because society views Inner Game problems as private issues rather than social problems. Or, more insidiously, perhaps it is because we are cynical about the possibility of people actually changing their behavior.

In either case, the failure of management development programs to address the real underlying causes of managerial "incompetence" and failure is very much akin to the old story about the man searching for his car keys under the street lamp. In the story, a passer-by sees a man searching for something near a street lamp at about 10 P.M. one evening, and asks what the man is trying to find. The man replies: "I've got a problem. I lost my car keys and I won't be able to get home unless I find them." The passer-by says: "Oh, you lost your keys here under the street lamp?" The man says: "No, but the light is better here, so it's easier to look for them here."

This story is always used to illustrate the ridiculousness of trying to solve a problem by offering a "solution" that does not address the problem. The man can look for his keys as long as he wishes under the street lamp, but he cannot hope to find them there. Similarly, management development programs tend to focus exclusively on managerial skills and the Outer Game of management, because that is what we know well. Unfortunately, the real problem is not there. It is in mastering the Inner Game of Management.

In order to assist people in mastering the Inner Game of Management, the content of management development programs will have to be revised. This section outlines the nature of the changes required.

Today, most management development focuses on the skills and tasks of management, which is one essential ingredient of effective management. In the future, however, management development should focus on three related levels in order to develop true masters of the Inner Game: (1) the behavioral level, (2) the attitudinal level, and (3) the skills level.

The Behavioral Level of Management

The behavioral level of management refers to the actual day-to-day actions or behavior exhibited by managers. It has to do with how they spend their time, what they do, and how they interact with people. In short, it is the surface level of management, or what is observable.

People need to learn to behave in ways that are consistent with their managerial roles. For example, Gunther Schmidt, the Executive Chef (cited in Chapter 1), needed to learn to spend his time like an Executive Chef rather than a butcher or technician. Similarly, Bob Miller, the star salesman who had been promoted to Vice President of Sales, needed to begin to act like a manager and recruit and develop his staff rather than continuing to sell products. Others, such as Conrad MacArthur, a victim of the Godfather Syndrome, needed to learn how to deal with people in ways that did not degrade and humiliate them.

The Attitudinal Level of Management

Changes in the surface or behavioral level of management require corresponding changes at the attitudinal level—the concealed inner level. There are three key dimensions of this inner level, which have been the focus of our analysis throughout this book: the individual's self-esteem, need for control, and need for affiliation (need to be liked).

Managing Self-Esteem

People must be taught how to manage two key aspects of their self-esteem. First, they must learn how to manage the *level* of their self-esteem. This refers to the degree to which they feel confident and accept themselves. Victims of the Godfather, Napoleon, or Pygmy Syndromes must learn that they are worthwhile people, and that surrounding themselves with weak people, degrading others, or turning subordinates into managerial eunuchs do not enhance their own significance but actually diminish it.

A variety of management techniques will have to be developed to help people learn these lessons. They may involve such things as role plays and case studies, but the key will be to help people develop skills of self-diagnosis and self-understanding.

Another key aspect of self-esteem that people must learn to manage is the *source* of self-esteem—how they derive their self-esteem. Managers must be taught to analyze how they are deriving their self-esteem, whether it is appropriate to their role, and how it affects their overall managerial effectiveness. Victims of the Doer Syndrome must learn to shift their source of self-esteem from their own performance to that of the people they manage. (We saw, in Chapter 2, how Terry Donahue made this shift.) Godfathers must derive self-esteem from building people rather than protecting or humiliating them.

Managing the Need for Control

People must also be taught how to manage two key aspects of their need for control. The first aspect concerns the *amount of control* they require. Specifically, managers must learn to give up an increasing amount of control as they rise through the organization. This is almost directly contrary to conventional wisdom, which suggests that a manager's power increases as he or she rises in the organizational hierarchy. Power does increase as a person moves up the corporate ladder, but the Inner Game Master will learn to be selective in its use. Victims of the Entrepreneur Syndrome must learn to allow their subordinates freedom of action. They must learn *not* to control everything. They must learn to feel guilty when they seek to control everything rather than when some things are not under their control. Thus, while it is true that an 800-lb gorilla can sleep wherever he wants to sleep, he ought to be quite selective where he chooses to sleep.

Another aspect of the need for control that should be addressed by the management development program is the *kind of control* the manager is comfortable with. Managers must learn to live with indirect control rather than direct, personal control. People who have failed to master the Inner Game are comfortable only with direct personal control. Inner Game Masters are satisfied with knowing that someone (even if not they themselves) is controlling some aspect of performance. In Chapter 10, we saw how Dan Sandel took steps to overcome the Entrepreneur Syndrome and accomplished these things.

Managing the Need To Be Liked

Management development must also help people learn how to manage the need to be liked so that it does not interfere with their effectiveness. First, people need to learn that not everybody will like them and that they do not *need* everyone to like them. Once this attitude is adopted, they must learn how to deal with situations in which they must either say no to people who want something or provide critical feedback.

No one likes to have his or her requests turned down, and few of us like criticism. However, managers must frequently say no or criticize. They must learn that it is not possible to keep all of the people happy all of the time, and that the very act of trying to do so can be unhealthy both for the manager and for the organization.

These lessons are especially relevant for victims of the Salesperson Syndrome. These managers not only require training in conflict management and assertiveness, but they must be made to understand why they feel guilty when they say no or provoke conflict.

The Skills Level of Management

Changes at the behavioral and attitudinal levels of management are prerequisites for changes at the skills level. The managerial skills that are most directly affected by the underlying attitudes and behavior are:

Decision making
Recruiting
Day-to-day leadership and supervision
Personnel development
Time management
Delegation
Planning

All these skills must be taught from an Inner Game perspective rather than merely as technical skills to be mastered. For example, it is almost useless to teach the steps to delegation without dealing with the Inner Game issues of delegation. Similarly, it is fruitless to teach techniques of optimum decision making to a victim of the Hamlet Syndrome who is on an endless search for more information.

Toward a Holistic Approach

In brief, the major implication of our discussion of management development is the need for a holistic approach. As explained initially in Chapter 1, management must be taught by paying attention to the Inner Game as well as the Outer Game. Management development programs that are not designed from this perspective are unlikely to bring individual and organizational success.

The Betsy Knapp case, described in Chapter 12, illustrated how an individual underwent a program designed to help her master the Inner Game of Management. In this context, the word "program" is used broadly to refer to her personal efforts to master the Inner Game, together with the efforts of a consultant to assist her in rethinking her role, behavior, attitudes, and skills.

In the next section, we shall examine how an actual company, Devon Industries, used a combination of group and individual management development programs to help some of the managers become more effective.

An Example of Management Development's Role

To illustrate the role of management development in mastering the Inner Game of Management, we shall examine the example of Devon Industries. This company is owned by Dan Sandel, whose story was presented earlier in Chapter 10.

In September 1984, Sandel attended a seminar dealing with the problems faced by managers as their organizations grow. Sandel, who already had an MBA, recognized that he was facing aspects of the Entrepreneur Syndrome. He also recognized that several of his managers were facing problems associated with the Doer Syndrome, so he invited the consultant who led the seminar to begin a management development program for his company to help people overcome the Doer Syndrome.

Each manager completed a battery of Management Effectiveness Questionnaires, to provide information about the extent to which they were thinking and acting like managers rather than doers. An in-house management development program was then designed for the management group. Sandel himself participated. The program was a two-day management retreat. This program was merely the first phase of the development process. Later, the group-based management development program was combined with a program of individual coaching and counseling for selected managers. This involved a series of meetings between a management development adviser and selected managers.

These meetings focused on several key issues the managers had to resolve in order to overcome the Doer Syndrome. For example, an initial meeting focused on how the individual manager was spending his or her time and whether the way that time was spent was appropriate to his or her role. Where it was not appropriate, the discussion focused on the reasons for the discrepancy and what could be done to change the pattern. Moreover, each manager's subordinates were interviewed to determine the nature of his or her management style and practices. The interviews focused on goal setting, delegation skills, motivation and leadership practices, and the general way the manager interacted with subordinates. Confidential reports were prepared for the manager; the sources of comments were not mentioned by name to preserve the confidentiality of the subordinates. Two senior-level managers participated in this program, and both were able to make significant progress in overcoming the Doer Syndrome.

Sandel recognized the need for changes in his own management style, and he met periodically with the firm's management adviser to consider what changes he ought to make. Like virtually all entrepreneurs, Dan Sandel liked to control everything. Yet he made a conscious effort to hire strong people who would be more likely to challenge him rather than just accept his authority. In one instance, Sandel had decided to hire an individual but was advised not to because the person was not believed to be strong enough to stand up to him. He agreed and sought out another manager, who proved able not only to do the functional job but also to be a forceful player in the company.

There are no miracles in management development, and this case study of the role of management development at Devon Industries should not be read as implying a panacea. There are managers at Devon who still believe that Sandel wants too much information and too much control, but he has made a deliberate attempt to change and overcome the Entrepreneur Syndrome. Management development was a catalyst to his change as well as a source of objective feedback. Similarly, other Devon managers have made significant progress in overcoming the Doer Syndrome as well as certain other syndromes described in this book.

The program began in December 1984, and by September 1986, Devon Industries had grown from approximately $8 million to more than $15 million in annual revenues. It grew profitably and without much of the managerial turmoil that typically accompanies rapid growth. Management development at Devon was certainly a major catalyst in this successful growth.

Outline of an Inner Game
Management Development Program

The concepts and ideas presented in this book are still new, therefore, there is currently no fully developed program of management development dealing with the Inner Game of Management. The purpose of this section is to present a pro-forma outline of such a management development program, entitled "How to Master the Inner Game of Management."

A management development program dealing with this subject should probably be organized in the same manner as this book. The program would have three modules.

Module 1 would introduce and explain the concept of the Inner Game of Management. This module should also provide a brief overview of the ten basic syndromes that occur when people fail to master the Inner Game of Management.

Module 2 should examine each of the ten syndromes in depth. This should include a set of case studies dealing with each syndrome so that the program participants can learn to identify and analyze the symptoms.

Module 3 of the program should deal with the steps people must take to master the Inner Game. This should include an assessment of the extent to which an individual has mastered the Inner Game. It should also include a series of training exercises of the type described at the end of each of the Chapters on the various syndromes. For example, individuals could perform role-play simulations designed to increase their ability to deal with conflict or give negative feedback. Finally, each individual should develop explicit goals for strengthening his or her Inner Game of Management.

It should be noted that what we are trying to do with this type of management development is to help people understand that, as managers, they must play a certain "role" in order to be effective. In a sense, people must learn to be actors and overcome their natural desire to behave in certain ways.

When an actor plays a role, he or she tries to get into the head of the character being played. The manager should strive to do the same thing, and the best tool for this which management development programs can provide is that of role-play simulations.

Although some people are "naturals" in the way they play the Inner Game, most people will require some type of training. People typically fall victim to one or more syndromes, because some part of their psychology is inconsistent with the way effective managers ought to behave. A person does not necessarily have to change inside, as long as he or she learns to play the role of an Inner Game Master. For this to occur, the person needs to understand what an Inner Game Master does and how to do the same things. This, in turn, is the role of management development.

Specific Topics in Inner Game
Management Development Programs

Given the perspective we presented, this section outlines some of the specific topics to be included in a management development program dealing with the mastery of the Inner Game. These topics include:

1. Developing a managerial role concept
2. Time management

  3. Delegation
  4. Giving praise and feedback
  5. Hiring and developing people
  6. Decision making
  7. Managing your self-esteem
  8. Managing your need for control
  9. Managing your need for affiliation
  10. Getting feedback on your progress

Some of these topics are traditionally found in management development programs; however, they should be taught from an Inner Game perspective. Each of these topics should be addressed on three related levels of analysis: (1) attitudes of the Inner Game Master, (2) skills required, and (3) behavioral changes required. The attitudinal level is concerned with how people think. The skills level concerns their ability to perform various tasks. The behavioral level deals with what people do or how they act. It includes such things as how people spend their time and how they interact with others. A brief description of each topic is presented below. Although each component involves all three levels, attitudinal issues are especially important for the first item and the last three.

Developing a Managerial Role Concept

A basic topic for any program aimed at strengthening people's Inner Game of Management is the development of a managerial role concept. At the attitudinal level, the module should focus on issues such as analyzing your current role concept, making a commitment to change your role concept, and accepting that your role has changed. At the skills level, it should focus on the analysis of the kinds of skills (such as delegation, leadership, decision making) required to perform your managerial role effectively. At the behavioral level, it should focus on how time is being, and ought to be, used.

Time Management

Time is a critical management resource, and time use is a reflection of a person's underlying role concept. This module should deal with the attitudes, skills, and behavior required to manage time effectively. It must help people analyze whether their time use corresponds to their role and how they can change their time-use patterns. The ultimate objective is to help managers learn to plan and use their time in ways appropriate to their organizational role.

Delegation

The delegation component of an Inner Game of Management program should focus first on attitudinal change. The specific objective should be to get people to overcome the Doer Syndrome (as exemplified by the belief: "I can do it better and faster") and the attitudes of various other syndromes concerning control over tasks and performance. At the skills level, there should be an emphasis on experimentation with assigning tasks, practice in refraining from second-guessing people and accepting what they do, and an analysis of what different managers should do by themselves and what they should delegate. At the behavioral level, there should be feedback on how each person actually performs in the delegation area and recommendations on what to do.

Giving Praise and Feedback

The objective of this component of the program is to help people learn to feel comfortable in giving praise and constructive feedback. It should focus on the attitudes, skills, and behavior that are required to perform these managerial tasks.

Hiring Strong People and Developing One's Employees

This component of the program should deal with people who tend to hire weak people or fail to develop people. At the attitudinal level, it should focus on making managers comfortable with being surrounded with strong people. At the skills level, it should give people practice in giving up control, helping people grow, and avoiding destructive management practices.

Decision Making

The decision-making component of the program should have as its objective to make people more decisive. To master the Inner Game, people need to learn how to make decisions without complete information. Moreover, many people must learn to evaluate themselves on the basis of decision-making *batting averages* rather than some standards of perfection.

Managing Self-Esteem

This component of the program should give people practice in looking for their own accomplishments. It should include exercises such as making a list of accomplishments. The program should also provide for practice in setting goals at different levels of difficulty. To master the Inner Game, a person must learn to be comfortable with less than perfection.

Managing the Need for Affiliation

To help people learn to manage their need for affiliation, the program must provide practice in giving feedback, asking people to do things, and saying no. Some of these can be achieved in the component on giving praise and feedback, but additional exercises should focus on assertiveness and conflict management.

Managing the Need for Control

The final component of the program must deal with managing the need for control. This component should help people learn how to manage with less direct control and become comfortable with giving up increasing amounts of control.

We have tried in this book to provide some insights into Inner Game playing and strategies for improving that game. Both individuals and management development programs should be able to profit from the approach we described. However, since the recognition of the phenomenon of the Inner Game of Management is so recent, significant future research and development of training techniques will be required before a "packaged" approach is available to help people.

The Role of MBA Programs

Besides corporate management development programs, MBA programs offered by universities can also help people master the Inner Game of Management. The better business schools should be leading the way in developing materials, exercises, and curricula for this area. Unfortunately, this has not happened, and it is doubtful that it will occur, unless there are fundamental changes in values at the leading business schools. The basic barrier is the result of an invisible cultural conflict inside the halls of academia. The B-school is merely a part of the broader university, and although this fact is obvious, its consequences are not. Many managers bemoan the abstract and mathematical nature of today's management education; quite correctly, they ask what its relevance is to them and their problems.

To gain respectability and influence in a university, an academic department must have the approval of its peer departments. Today, there is an undeniable bias toward the quantifiable fields of intellectual inquiry. The modern ideals of the university are mathematics, physics, chemistry, and the like. These are the prestigious fields, because of their perceived precision and intellectual rigor. Other disciplines that have achieved respectability within the university, such as psychology, have had to take the quantitative route. The culture says: "If it's not measurable, it does not exist." This is very much a "street-lamp" mentality and puts the business schools in a bind.

The drive for quantifiability has, to a very great extent, driven out the study of many complex areas that are difficult or impossible to quantify. At the least, it has made them suspect. In brief, the pursuit for quantifiability has put the major business schools in danger of becoming "Graduate Schools of Rigorous Irrelevancies."

Management involves people as individuals and as members of groups, and those people make decisions and take actions to achieve not only profits for the organization but also their own ends. Since people are involved in management, management is not a totally rational and quantifiable process. It is simply not rational to ignore major aspects of management that are critical to either the manager's or the organization's success. Yet, this is precisely what the business schools do: they teach what they *can* teach rather than what needs to be taught.

What management educators need to understand is that a part of the learning process comes from people simply being made aware of a problem. Thus, the very act of "teaching" people that an Inner Game of Management exists and must be mastered will be a significant step toward the solution of the problem. This, of course, requires management educators to recognize that the problem does indeed exist.

A Final Note

In our judgment, the problems described in this book are not merely issues facing individual managers and the organizations that employ them. The issue has broader societal consequences. When individual managers fail at their jobs, for whatever reason, they increase the likelihood of organizational failure; and when organizations fail, they reduce our economic strength. The consequence is a loss of human and other economic resources that is quite significant.

During the past few years, a great deal of inquiry has been focused on the issue of American industrial competitiveness. The primary focus has been on the lack of productivity, the need for reindustrialization, and international barriers to free trade. These things are certainly important factors, but another factor that should not be overlooked is the simple failure of managers to be effective. We believe that a significant reason for that failure is the inability of managers to master the Inner Game of Management.

We hope that this book will help overcome this problem and contribute to individual, corporate, and overall economic effectiveness.

Annotated Bibliography

Chapter 1

Berne, E. *Games People Play*. New York: Grove Press, 1964.

> In this book, which is based on transactional analysis, Berne introduces the term *game* as an interpersonal interaction that has an ulterior motive and some sort of payoff. Berne stresses that the word *game* does not imply fun or enjoyment and that these games can have serious consequences.

Gallwey, W. Timothy. *The Inner Game of Tennis*. New York: Bantam Books, 1974.

> Gallwey contends that excellence is actually achieved on the tennis court by winning the "inner game" against self-doubt, nervousness, and self-condemnation and that this idea is applicable in our lives. The book provides insights into how the various "games" we play on the tennis court closely parallel general experience. Gallwey explores the process of "unlearning" self-conscious bad habits and allowing the unconscious mind to act. This book covers much more territory than the game of tennis; it is a powerful affirmation of human potential.

McClelland, David C. "That Urge to Achieve," originally published in *Think* magazine, published by IBM Corporation, 1966, 82–89; reproduced in *Classics of Organizational Behavior*, Walter E. Natemeyer (ed.), Oak Park, Ill.: Moore Publishing, 1978.

> In this brief article, McClelland states that some people, more than others, are "challenged by opportunity and willing to work hard to achieve." He labels this motivational state as the Need for Achievement, which he contrasts with other motivational states such as Need for Power and Need for Affiliation. Those with a high Need for Achievement set challenging goals for themselves and solicit

feedback on their progress. McClelland claims that Need for Achievement can be taught and cites research showing that those trained to have higher Need for Achievement made more money, were promoted more quickly, and expanded their businesses faster than those who were not trained.

Chapter 2

Badway, M. K. "Why Managers Fail." *Research Management,* May/June 1983, 26–31.

This article explores the reasons for managerial failure among scientists and engineers. Concentrating more on technical skills than on interpersonal and administrative skills is the major reason cited for managerial failure. Bias toward objective measurement and overanalysis in decision making are also named as problems for these managers.

Kanter, R. M. *Men and Women of the Corporation.* New York: Basic Books, 1977, 189–191.

This book addresses the issue of managers who continue as functional specialists rather than act as managers. The author attributes this behavior to the managers' feelings of powerlessness. Reasons for the managers' retreat into technical work are discussed. Among the reasons cited are familiarity, a feeling of power, and a heightening of self-esteem.

Chapter 3

Clance, P. R. *The Impostor Phenomenon: The Fear That Haunts Your Success.* Atlanta: Peachtree Publishers, 1985.

The impostor phenomenon is the name Clance coins for the mask that high achievers wear to hide their feelings of self-doubt and fear. Impostors attribute their success to external forces such as luck and the help of others rather than to their own ability. Self-tests and case studies help readers determine whether they suffer from this phenomenon, as well as provide advice on how to overcome it.

Dowling, C. *The Cinderella Complex: Women's Hidden Fear of Independence.* New York: Summit Books, 1981.

The thesis of this book is that women are raised to be psychologically dependent, which ultimately leads them to subconsciously self-imposed failure where they would have otherwise succeeded. The book gives a relatively complete account of the changing role of women in society.

Kruger, D. W. *Success and the Fear of Success in Women.* New York: Free Press, 1984.

This book discusses sociological, psychological, and developmental aspects related to the success and fear of success in women. The issues of success in the workplace as well as the treatment of women with success phobias are covered. A type of impostor phenomenon is described and explained in terms of psycho-dynamic issues—the main cause for the impostor reaction is seen as the need for perfection coinciding with role repression.

Tresemer, L. W. *Fear of Success.* New York: Plenum Press, 1977.

This book gives a good overview of the phenomena known as the "fear of success" and the "fear of failure." It contains a thorough review of the literature and of measures to calculate the fear of success as well as a discussion of areas for future research. In addition, there is an extensive bibliography.

Chapters 4–6

Adler, A. *The Practice and Theory of Individual Psychology.* London: Rotledge & Kegan Paul, 1920.

This book gives a clear overall presentation of Adler's theories, including his views on power, striving for superiority, life goals, and obstacles to growth. The term *inferiority complex* is coined by Adler to describe the feeling caused by a lack of physical or psychological size or power. Adler explains why the inferiority complex comes about and how it relates to power, self-esteem, and coping methods.

Horney, K. *The Neurotic Personality of Our Time.* New York: Norton, 1937.

Horney examines the characteristics of people who feel that they must control everything in their environment, including the people around them. The reasons behind this controlling behavior, such as low self-esteem, are investigated, and the consequences are discussed.

Kanter, R. M. "How the Top Is Different." In R. M. Kanter and B. A. Stein (eds.), *Life in Organizations: Workplaces as People Experience Them.* New York: Basic Books, 1979.

Through case studies, this article looks at the lives and personalities of top executives. The author discusses the traits that executives require their subordinates to demonstrate—newcomers must be loyal, accept authority, and conform to a prescribed pattern of behavior. Trust is felt to be the most important consideration for some executives, to the point that it overrides merit and achievement. The problem of insulation of the executive as a result of this practice is discussed.

Larned, J. N. "Napoleon: A Prodigy Without Greatness." In *A Study of Greatness in Men.* New York: Houghton Mifflin, 1911.

An insightful historical look at Napoleon is offered, replete with detailed descriptions of his actions, expertly interwoven with the author's view of Napoleon's motivations.

Restak, R. *The Self Seekers.* New York: Doubleday, 1982.

This book describes manipulators—people who get their way by controlling others' responses. The author states that manipulators try to bolster their own weak self-images by bullying others, and that they thrive especially well in a culture that rewards outward image and material success.

Chapter 7

"The Antisocial Executive." *Dun's Business Monthly,* July 1983, 52–54.

The problems of managers who lack interpersonal skills or have undesirable on-the-job behavior to such a degree that it threatens their employment are discussed. The article presents examples of antisocial executives who are abusive to their subordinates and provides some explanations for that behavior. It is suggested that one solution to the problem lies in psychological counseling by firms specially trained to deal with antisocial executives.

Biddle, Bruce J. *Role Theory: Expectations, Identities, and Behaviors.* New York: Academic Press, 1979.

Biddle reviews role theory and research, presenting a conceptual view of how human behavior is affected by the roles we play. The author uses a relatively academic approach to show that role behavior can be caused by instinct, culture, socialization, sanctions or rewards, interaction, or the integration of values. The potential for role conflict is also discussed.

Chapter 8

Bramson, Robert M. *How to Cope with Difficult People.* Garden City, N.Y.: Anchorage Press/Doubleday, 1981.

> This book discusses "indecisive stallers"—managers who cannot make up their minds—and illuminates the reasons behind their stalling. According to Bramson, these types of managers like to please everyone, and if they feel that a decision they need to make will have some adverse effect they will stall, sometimes not making any decision at all. The author provides guidelines for spotting stallers, as well as practical suggestions on how to cope with their indecisiveness.

Delaney, W. A. "Why Are People Indecisive?" *Supervisory Management,* December 1982, 26–30.

> An easy-to-read look at indecisiveness, this article is based on the author's experience as president of a corporation. The problem and repercussions of indecisiveness are discussed, and causes and solutions are presented.

Driver, M. J., and Rowe, A. J. "Decision-Making Styles: A New Approach to Management Decision Making." In C. L. Cooper (ed.), *Behavioral Problems in Organizations.* Englewood Cliffs, N.J.: Prentice-Hall, 1979.

> According to the authors, a manager's decision-making style interacts with social, task, and environmental factors, and personality and politics play a significant, if not an overriding role, in terms of the final managerial decision. A descriptive-differential approach to decision making is recommended, taking into account a manager's decision style, organizational demands, peer pressures, task requirements, and self-definition.

Harrison, E. F. *The Managerial Decision-Making Process.* Boston: Houghton Mifflin, 1975.

> An excellent introduction to the specific subject of management decision making, this book takes an integrated and interdisciplinary approach that fuses both the behavioral sciences and the qualitative disciplines. It offers a balanced view of the many factors involved in making a decision: environment, values, rationality,

and psychology. The book also presents the reader with techniques for decision making, case studies, and a comprehensive bibliography.

Hill, P. H. et. al. *Making Decisions: A Multidisciplinary Introduction.* Reading, Mass.: Addison-Wesley, 1980.

This book examines the managerial decision-making process and its problems. The manager's need for simplicity and consistency is stressed, as are the following managerial personality traits: self-concept, locus of control, and tolerance for ambiguity and risk-taking.

Chapter 9

Caffarella, R. S. "Managing Conflict: An Analytical Tool." *Training and Development Journal,* February 1984 34–38.

Conflict is considered as a constructive managerial tool. It is suggested that conflict can be channeled productively if a complete analysis of the potential conflict situation is made prior to its escalation to unmanageable proportions. A seven-component model is presented for handling conflict situations advantageously.

Goldner, F. H. "Pronoia." *Social Problems,* vol. 30, no. 1 (1982), 82–90.

The author describes the phenomenon of pronoia, the delusion that others think well of one. The reasons for pronoia are outlined, among them the social complexity and ambiguity of society, and the increasing dependence of individuals on the opinions of others for their own feelings of self-worth. Solutions for the problem of pronoia are offered.

Miller, A. *Death of a Salesman.* New York: Viking Press, 1949.

This play is a moving portrait of the life—and death—of a salesman who believed that success could be achieved through being liked rather than through merit or achievement.

Rahim, M. A. "A Measure of Styles of Handling Interpersonal Conflict." *Academy of Management Journal,* vol. 26, 368–376.

This article differentiates styles of handling interpersonal conflict on the basis of two dimensions, concern for self and concern for others. The author describes five different styles of handling conflict: integrating, obliging, compromising, dominating, and avoiding. Scales are developed in order to measure these five styles.

Chapter 10

Blanchard, K., Zigarmi, Patricia, and Zigarmi, Drea. *Leadership and the One Minute Manager: Increasing Effectiveness Through Situational Leadership.* New York: Morrow, 1985.

> Written in an easy-to-read, story-telling fashion, this book discusses the problem of entrepreneurs who feel compelled to be active in each part of their organization, no matter how minute the issue. Leadership styles are discussed, and the use of situational leadership is offered as a solution to these overinvolved entrepreneurs.

Kets de Vries, Manfred F. R., and Miller, Danny. *The Neurotic Organization.* San Francisco: Jossey-Bass, 1984.

> The subject of this book is how the neuroses of top leadership in an organization can cause an entire organization to begin acting neurotically or irrationally. The authors include many interesting examples of different organizational neuroses and their effects on individuals in the organization as well as on the overall success of the organization. Diagnosis and change techniques are presented for the reader.

Manz, C. C., and Gioia, D. A. "The Interrelationship of Power and Control." *Human Relations,* vol. 36 (1983), 459–476.

> The authors of this study claim that the issues of power and control are interdependent, and not independent, as is usually found in the literature. They apply their theory of interdependency to the organizational work situation and discuss its effects and ramifications on organizational resources.

Selye, H. *Stress of Life.* New York: McGraw-Hill, 1976.

> Selye offers a thorough medical and psychological discussion about stress: its origins, symptoms, causes, and cures. He describes the highly stressed, fast-paced personality more recently called Type A. Stress is not presented as intrinsically bad, and its positive as well as negative points are brought out in this book.

Chapter 11

Dyer, W. Gibb., Jr. *Cultural Change in Family Firms: Anticipating and Managing Business and Family Transitions.* San Francisco: Jossey-Bass, 1986.

> Readers will learn how family-owned businesses must cultivate an effective culture to manage transition and growth. Using a wealth of examples culled from researching over 40 family-owned firms, the author discusses the evolution of culture in family firms, describes key problems that may occur at each stage of the firm's development, and makes suggestions for managing the growth/change process.

Naylor, J. C., Pritchard, R. D., and Ilgen, D. R. "Roles and Role Behaviors." In *A Theory of Behavior in Organizations.* New York: Academic Press, 1980.

> The authors offer a complex and complete discussion of the importance and impact of roles and role behaviors in the workplace. They define the concept of roles, describe role process in organizational theory, and discuss compliance, ambiguity, conflict, and negotiation as they relate to roles.

Rosenblatt, Paul C. et al. *The Family in Business: Understanding and Dealing with the Challenges Entrepreneurial Families Face.* San Francisco: Jossey-Bass, 1985.

> The results of an in-depth study of a sample of business families in the United States are presented. The authors have prepared an extensive list of tensions and challenges business firms are likely to face and report on the sources of these conflicts. Each chapter includes conceptual tools for dealing with those challenges productively.

Secord, P. F., Blackman, C. W., and Slavitt, D. R. *Understanding Social Life: An Introduction to Social Psychology.* New York: McGraw-Hill, 1976.

> This social psychology text offers an excellent discussion of every aspect of roles, role strain, and role strain resolution.

Chapters 12 and 13

Dalton, Gene, and Thompson, Paul. *Novations: Strategies for Career Management.* Glenview, Ill.: Scott-Foresman, 1986.

The bulk of this work presents ideas for individuals interested in managing their own development in the organization. The authors outline a series of career stages through which individual employees must proceed in order to remain productive and effective, along with ideas and examples for progressing through these stages. The final chapter suggests ways organizations can use formal management development programs to encourage and promote the progress of individual employees.

Flamholtz, Eric G., and Cranston, H. Stephen. "Management Development." In Eric Flamholtz's *How to Make the Transition from an Entrepreneurship to a Professionally Managed Firm.* San Francisco: Jossey-Bass, 1986, 170–183.

This chapter presents a case study of an entrepreneurial firm that uses a formal management development program to successfully make the transition to a professionally managed firm. The case study describes the experience of Knapp Communications Corporation in developing management skills, promoting a new management style, and reinforcing the firm's culture. The functions and impact of training are discussed.

Naylor, J. C., Pritchard, R. D., and Ilgen, D. R. "Roles and Role Behaviors." In *A Theory of Behavior in Organizations.* New York: Academic Press, 1980.

This article discusses the nature of "organizational climate," showing it to be a useful and important concept that has a direct effect on employee behavior.

Index